Multichip Modules and Related Technologies

Electronic Packaging and Interconnection Series
Charles M. Harper, Series Advisor

CLASSON • *Surface Mount Technology for Concurrent Engineering and Manufacturing*

HARPER • *Electronic Packaging and Interconnection Handbook*

HARPER AND MILLER • *Electronic Packaging, Microelectronics, and Interconnection Dictionary*

HARPER AND SAMPSON • *Electronic Materials and Processes Handbook, 2/e*

Related Books of Interest

BOSWELL • *Subcontracting Electronics*

BOSWELL AND WICKAM • *Surface Mount Guidelines for Process Control, Quality, and Reliability*

BYERS • *Printed Circuit Board Design with Microcomputers*

CAPILLO • *Surface Mount Technology*

CHEN • *Computer Engineering Handbook*

COOMBS • *Printed Circuits Handbook, 3/e*

DI GIACOMO • *Digital Bus Handbook*

DI GIACOMO • *VLSI Handbook*

FINK AND CHRISTIANSEN • *Electronics Engineers' Handbook*

GINSBERG • *Printed Circuits Design*

JURAN AND GRYNA • *Juran's Quality Control Handbook*

MANKO • *Solders and Soldering, 3/e*

RAO • *Multilevel Interconnect Technology*

SZE • *VLSI Technology*

VAN ZANT • *Microchip Fabrication*

To order or receive additional information on these or any other McGraw-Hill titles, in the United States please call 1-800-822-8158. In other countries, contact your local McGraw-Hill representative.

BC14BCZ

Multichip Modules and Related Technologies

MCM, TAB, and COB Design

Gerald L. Ginsberg

Donald P. Schnorr

McGraw-Hill, Inc.

New York   San Francisco   Washington, D.C.   Auckland   Bogotá
Caracas   Lisbon   London   Madrid   Mexico City   Milan
Montreal   New Delhi   San Juan   Singapore
Sydney   Tokyo   Toronto

Library of Congress Cataloging-in-Publication Data

Ginsberg, Gerald L.
    Multichip modules and related technologies : MCM, TAB, and COB
    design / Gerald L. Ginsberg, Donald P. Schnorr.
        p.   cm.—(Electronic packaging and interconnection series)
    Includes index.
    ISBN 0-07-023552-X
    1. Electronic packaging.   2. Multichip modules (Microelectronics)—
Design and construction.   I. Schnorr, Donald P.   II. Title.
III. Series.
TK7870.15.G563   1994
621.381′046—dc20   93-46641
                                                                         CIP

1 2 3 4 5 6 7 8 9 0   DOC/DOC   9 0 9 8 7 6 5 4

ISBN 0-07-023552-X

*The sponsoring editor for this book was Stephen S. Chapman, the editing super-
visor was Stephen M. Smith, and the production supervisor was Pamela A.
Pelton. It was set in Palatino by McGraw-Hill's Professional Book Group composition unit.*

Printed and bound by R. R. Donnelley & Sons Company.

This book is printed on acid-free paper.

To Gerald L. Ginsberg, whose idea and vision formed the elements for this book. His thoughtful preparation and constant inspiration made this book possible.

About the Authors

GERALD L. GINSBERG (deceased) was a well-known electronic packaging engineer and industry consultant who was awarded the prestigious IEPS Pioneer in Electronic Packaging Award in 1987. He was the author of *Surface Mount Technology* and McGraw-Hill's *Printed Circuits Design,* and a contributor to McGraw-Hill's *Printed Circuits Handbook* and *Electronic Packaging and Interconnection Handbook.*

DONALD P. SCHNORR is an electronic industry consultant with more than 30 years of experience in electronic packaging and printed wiring at RCA and General Electric. He was the recipient of the prestigious IEPS Pioneer in Electronic Packaging Award in 1987 and the Institute of Printed Wiring's Presidents Award in 1978. He has authored over 30 articles and was a contributor to McGraw-Hill's *Printed Circuits Handbook* and *Electronic Packaging and Interconnection Handbook.*

Contents

Foreword

Electronic packaging, for many years only an afterthought in the design and manufacture of electronic systems, increasingly is being recognized as the critical factor in both cost and performance. As the functional density of devices and systems increases, the role of electronic packaging and interconnection necessarily becomes more important. In spite of the revolutionary advances in semiconductor device technology, these improvements are insignificant when considering the constraining influence of the package in the system—the huge disparity between the performance of the chip and performance outside the package. Multichip module packaging, a vast improvement over present methods of packaging electronic systems, can cast off these constraints, and improve cost and reliability at the system level. With promise to increase system speed, reduce cost, and improve performance, MCM technology has become a force to be reckoned with in future electronic systems.

This book was written to fill a need for information on this new subject. It explains the technology, examines the alternatives, looks at the basics of the three types of multichip modules, examines thermal and interconnection issues, gives multichip module application examples, and will help to formulate packaging systems decisions.

This book will add to the field of knowledge on this subject and should play a part in the continuing rapid advance of electronics technology.

Charles M. Harper
President
Technology Seminars, Inc.

Preface

The success of most electronic equipment depends to a great degree on the ability to use the most advanced packaging technology that is cost-effectively possible. However, the performance of today's electronic equipment is still limited primarily by the interconnections between components and subsystems and not by the high-speed, very large-scale integrated (VLSI) circuits from which the systems are constructed. Current electronic systems use a packaging technology that limits system performance because of interconnection lengths. As the functional density of devices and systems increases, the role of electronic packaging and interconnection necessarily becomes more important. This book is devoted to the most advanced form of electronic packaging, namely, multichip modules (MCM). Basically, a multichip module is a group of highly functional electronic devices interconnected to some substrate by formed fine-line, usually multilayer, circuitry. MCM modules are categorized into three groups: MCM-C, which has fireable materials as part of multilayer substrates; MCM-D, which uses deposited metals and unsupported dielectrics on top of a variety of base materials; and MCM-L, which utilizes clad/plated copper conductors as part of multilayer, reinforced, organic laminated dielectric substrates. Each of these techniques has cost, performance, and reliability tradeoffs, as discussed in this book.

The driving force behind the use of MCM modules is the increased system performance resulting from decreasing the length of wiring needed to provide interconnections between integrated circuit devices (chips). Not only is the "time of flight" reduced, but parasitic capacitance is reduced and system electrical performance is enhanced. While the current volume usage of MCM packages is still relatively low, it is broadly accepted that MCM technology is the packaging and interconnection route to the future, offering decreasing and more competitive costs per interconnection as the technology matures. MCM packages will clearly play a major role in emerging and future electronic products such as HDTV, image processing, voice recognition synthesis, character recognition, multimedia/video processing, artificial intelligence, and other products that can benefit from the improved power and speed potential of MCM packages. This book well describes the technologies and major considerations associated with each of the MCM categories and the related technologies.

This book is designed to provide the reader with a practical knowledge of the subject of multichip modules: types, materials, processes, and applications. It addresses not only the direct MCM categories, but also important considerations associated with the related technologies, as well as alternative approaches. After a clear presentation of the basic electronic packaging driving forces, the ensuing group of chapters deals with the overall considerations for MCM packages, basic elements of MCM packages, the important bare-die termination techniques, and the critical design considerations. Next follows three chapters devoted specifically to MCM-C, MCM-D, and MCM-L technologies. These chapters deal not only with design, but material and process details. The next two chapters cover supplemental interconnection devices and the always critical and applicable thermal design considerations. The final chapter gives a thorough presentation of MCM applications. With this arrangement and coverage, the reader will gain an excellent knowledge not only of the basics of multichip modules, but also of the design, material, and fabrication aspects of MCMs, and, finally, the state of the art for applying them.

This book is intended to serve a multitude of users. It is appropriate as a text for college or graduate study in electrical and mechanical electronic packaging; for design, fabrication, and process engineers dealing with this technology; for managers planning new and alternate technology; and, finally, for marketing and sales personnel who need a practical knowlege of multichip modules and alternate technologies.

Completing a book of this scope and complexity requires the material assistance, skills, and talents of many individuals. Special thanks go to Judith Ginsberg, of Component Data Associates, for material support in research and manuscript preparation, and Jonathan Rosenberg for invaluable assistance in word processing. Technical editing of the manuscript was done with the expert help of Charles A. Harper, of Technology Seminars, Inc. I extend thanks to Lyman S. A. Perry Associates for material assistance and support in preparation of the manuscript. I am further indebted to the McGraw-Hill staff, especially Stephen Chapman and Stephen Smith, for assistance in the editing and production of this book. Finally, I am especially grateful to Dolly Hill Schnorr, for her continuous support and encouragement during the preparation of this book.

Donald P. Schnorr

1

Electronic Packaging Driving Forces[1]

The success of most electronic equipment depends to a great extent on its ability to use the most advanced packaging technology that is cost-effectively possible. However, the performance of today's electronic equipment is still primarily limited by the interconnections between components and subsystems and not by the high-speed, very large scale integrated (VLSI) circuits from which the systems are constructed. Thus, to achieve high performance at a reasonably low cost, it is imperative that the technology used builds on existing design, manufacturing, assembly, and testing expertise.

1.1 Costs

In any electronic system, there is a plethora of interconnection technologies. At each level of interconnection, the driving force is to lower cost and improve performance. The importance of this is shown in Fig. 1.1, which indicates how the cost per connection increases dramatically from on-chip to system-to-system interconnections.

To achieve the desired level of performance as cost-effectively as possible, it is important to

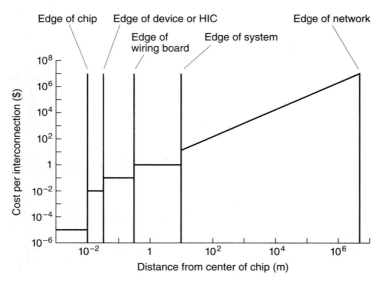

Figure 1.1. Approximate cost of system interconnections.[1]

- *Decrease distance between chips.* Increasing the level of integration enhances the system throughput, thereby improving the level of performance.

- *Reduce the cost per connection.* The successful manufacturers of integrated circuits have shown that this can be achieved most effectively by increasing functional and interconnection density. As the level of integration increases, the connection cost decreases, because more connections are made. The result is increased yield and reduced use of materials and processing.

- *Increase input/output (I/O) per chip.* System output is increased directly.

- *Use off-the-shelf devices.* On-chip customization is prohibitively expensive unless large quantities of devices are used. The passive interconnection of less complex commodity integrated circuits with self-contained functions can help to minimize the duration of the design-test-manufacturing cycle and provide cost-effective complex customized circuitry.

- *Improve thermal management.* Materials with a high thermal conductivity should be used as close to the heat source as possible so as to minimize the need for using more sophisticated heat-transfer mechanisms elsewhere.

- *When applicable, use common technology for electronics.* Future systems may require increased integration among electronic components. Using common technology to package these devices reduces material and processing costs.

1.2 Integrated Circuit Fabrication

Increases in integration level have required increased capital investment to handle more sophisticated integrated circuit processing technologies. The success of most silicon integrated circuit foundries depends critically on leveraging volume production and sales against the high capital cost of plant facilities. Thus the efficiency of a given manufacturing investment is measured in throughput (wafer starts per week) and yield (qualified product per wafer lot).

Some of the driving forces that may call for a reevaluation of the state-of-the-art integrated circuit fabrication line concept include

- *Fabrication time.* Duration time in production of wafers needs to be decreased to optimize integrated circuit design and processing to meet market demands.

- *Customization.* Expansion of the product mix is forcing the use of a traditional clean-room layout and decreasing efficiency of routine and unit processes.

- *Capital requirements.* Increases in the cost of manufacturing plant will stop or hinder development of semiconductor technology before physical limits will unless large changes in material processing and manufacturing methods take place.

- *Complexity of process.* These diverse requirements demand the incorporation of simplified processes.

Integrated circuit device and circuit fabrication has ceased to exist as a sequence of independent unit processes. Tight budgets for critical parameters dominate process design. Thus a mechanical budget defines wafer design, a thermal budget limits the use of high-temperature processing, a particulate/contamination budget defines the performance of the manufacturing facility, and a time budget determines the acceptable throughput in order to sufficiently amortize capital investment.

Accurate computer-aided process design is also required on an advanced fabrication line with a sequence of from 300 to 500 process steps as every bit of available process margin must be squeezed into the facility.

1.3   System Performance[2]

In response to the demands from electronic systems houses for increased speed, semiconductor foundries have continued to provide devices that operate at higher frequencies with increased densities and gate counts (see Fig. 1.2). However, systems and semiconductor companies are realizing that as electronic products are pushed to operate above 50 MHz, the delays from the limitations of conventional packaging and interconnection technologies become the pacing item for system clock speed (see Fig. 1.2).

As integrated circuits accelerate in speed and complexity, the percentage penalty imposed by the package for the device and by the assembly interconnections increases. This occurs because of the penalty imposed on the maximum system frequency by off-chip resistive, inductive, and capacitive loads.

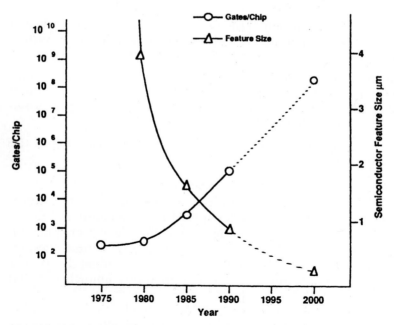

Figure 1.2. Semiconductor device gate technology trends.[3]

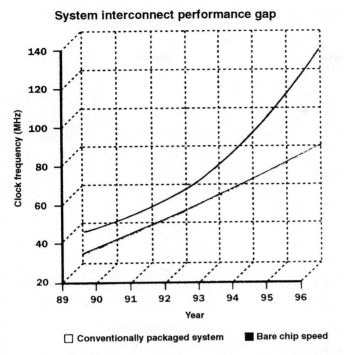

Figure 1.3. Bare-chip and conventional packaging speed trends.[2]

The significance of this penalty is depicted in Fig. 1.3. The penalty grows from a relatively negligible level at the lower clock rates of the 1980s to a much less tolerable level in the 1990s. This interconnect performance gap is driving the need for new cost-effective packaging and interconnecting solutions.

The density of integrated circuits is also increasing in response to a desire for increased functionality and performance. Rent's Rule, which relates increasing semiconductor device gate count complexity to the number of supporting input/output (I/O) terminals, rationalizes the evolution of integrated circuit packaging (see Fig. 1.4).

As semiconductor device density has increased, so has the number of I/O signal terminals. This has led the new device packaging and interconnections that are steadily replacing dual in-line packages (DIPs) with pin-grid arrays (PGAs) and fine-pitch surface-mount technology (SMT) devices, such as chip carriers and flat packs.

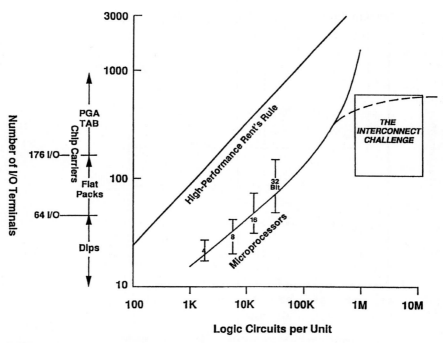

Figure 1.4. High-performance Rent's Rule.[4]

The cost per terminal also has continued to increase as the number of I/Os per semiconductor die has increased in high-performance interconnections. Thus the challenge is to break off from the single-packaged-device I/O increases predicted by Rent's Rule by integrating sufficient circuit functions into multichip packaging schemes.

In the VLSI era of the 1980s, there was a large spectrum of applications from megabit dynamic random-access memories (DRAMS) to high-density microprocessors and high-speed emitter-coupled logic (ECL) devices. They all had special requirements and applications. Consequently, the I/O requirements of these products varied greatly, and the optimal solution for chip termination and packaging also varied.[4]

As shown in Fig. 1.4, the highest DRAMS and static random-access memories (SRAMS) are projected in the 1990s to require a maximum of 40 I/O terminals; these can be satisfied easily by conventional wire bonding in small-outline SMT packages. At the other extreme are the high-performance random-logic devices that have a voracious appetite for I/O terminals.

With the projected growth of integrated circuits on a chip and the assumption that Rent's Rule will continue to be valid, up to 1000 I/Os per chip is probable as the interconnection requirement of a logic device in the mid-1990s. This will necessitate the use of new die termination techniques and, in many cases, will preempt the suitability of single-chip packaging.

The middle region from 100 to 500 I/Os remains an area for active die termination and packaging competition. Microprocessors, complementary metal-oxide semiconductors (CMOS), and many random-logic devices happen to fall into this I/O count region.

1.4 Substrate Price versus Density[5]

The entire spectrum of electronic circuit interconnections ranges from simple one-sided printed boards and basic thick-film hybrid circuits to sophisticated integrated circuits. In order to encompass them on a single graph and also to point out trends in electronic packaging, Fig. 1.5 compares substrate density with substrate price. Some price/density trend lines are plotted on this graph, as are the locations of some selected interconnection systems.

The x axis gives the value of the total wiring channel capacity of all the signal layers of a substrate (expressed in inches per square inch of substrate). The y axis gives the prices for the entire structure (expressed in \$0.01 per square inch of substrate), i.e., including ground and power distribution planes and surface land layers. On average, a typical structure will contain twice as many total layers as signal layers.

Figure 1.5 provides information for the total conductive capacity of a substrate, but it does not show the distribution, i.e., the number of conductors per inch located on each layer of the substrate, or the number of layers needed to meet the required total interconnection density. Any combination producing the required total can be used. Therefore, Fig. 1.5 does not provide precise prices for a given type of substrate, and their locations are given only for illustration purposes.

The difference between the total theoretical wiring capacity obtainable in a system (x axis) and the actual interconnection wiring is the efficiency of the wiring achieved in a given system. It is obvious that actual interconnection wiring cannot occupy 100 percent of every available wiring channel. From empirical observations and actual wiring length calculations of various substrates, the prevailing wiring efficiency is assumed to be about 50 percent.

In some multilayer printed boards, due to an excess of via blockages,

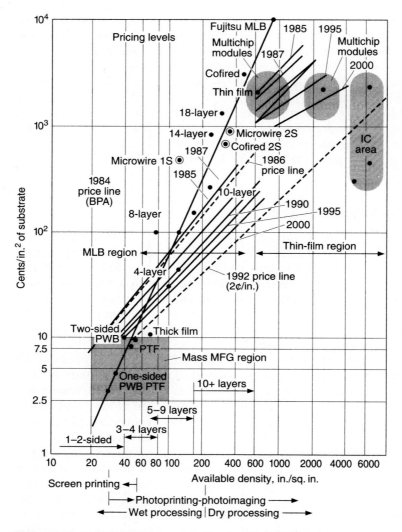

Figure 1.5. Substrate price versus density relationships.[5]

the wiring efficiency may be reduced to 40 to 45 percent of the available channel capacity. With some of the more specialized substrates, values up to 60 percent have been achieved. Still, a good universal number for wiring efficiency is 50 percent, and this value is used here; i.e., the theoretical wiring capacity of 200 in/in^2 in a system will generally result in a 100 in/in^2 of actual wiring length on a substrate.

Figure 1.5 shows that in the mid-1980s, the prices of substrates were increasing as the square of the interconnection density. It also indicates, however, that with time, due to the "experience curve" effects and general market dynamics, the price/density relationship is constantly changing. As a result, the "1992 price line" shows substrate prices increasing linearly with density increases. (It should be noted that this graph is based on a generalized derivation and therefore is only an approximation. It is best used to understand the relative positions of interconnection technologies in terms of one another and price trends as they become more mature.)

1.5 Evaluating the Alternatives[6]

An integral part of the process of selecting an electronic packaging technology for high-density applications is to evaluate the critical properties and determine the weighting factors of each of the items. Within this list, some of the items can be more important than others depending on the end product. Some critical properties to consider in the evaluation are

- Cost
- Performance
- Reliability
- Manufacturability
- Testing
- Service
- Rework

A myriad of options is available to the electronic packaging engineer for selecting the optimal packaging scheme. Packaging engineers can choose from component-level, to board-level, to system-level solutions in order to make the right choice. Table 1.1 can be used to aid in determining the impact of technology on packaging density.

1.5.1 Selection Procedure

Since the electronic packaging engineer must decide on the type of technology to use for a particular application, it is beneficial to have a selection procedure so as to simplify the task. The secret behind this is

Table 1.1. Packaging Technology versus Density[6]

Technology	Packaging density			
	Low	Medium	High	Ultra
Through hole	*	*		
Surface-mount technology (SMT)	*	*	*	
Molded-circuit interconnect	*	*		
Fine-line boards			*	*
Fine-pitch components		*	*	
Daughter boards		*	*	*
Hybrid plug-ins		*	*	*
Flex circuit interconnects			*	*
Flex circuit with components			*	*
Chip on board (COB)		*	*	*
Tape automated bonding (TAB)		*	*	*
Multichip module (MCM)			*	*
3D silicon				*
3D modules				*

to evaluate the highest rated or most critical parameters for each one of the technologies. Once this rating has been accomplished, the electronic packaging engineer will be guided toward the next higher level of system packaging. The selection process should continue until the final options have been provided.

1.5.2 Captive versus Subcontract Facilities

One of the key areas that needs to be addressed on any new packaging implementation is how that technology is going to be brought into the company, i.e., whether it will be manufactured in-house in a captive facility or whether any or all of it will be subcontracted to an outside source. In either case, ramifications of product life and equipment availability will be constant concerns.

If the technology is going to be used for high-density packaging and is going to be manufactured in-house, then the cost of capital equipment becomes more of a concern. For example, if the company has a surface-mount assembly manufacturing facility with pick-and-place equipment that does not have vision-recognition capability, then the incorporation of high-I/O fine-pitch components into a new design would probably require an upgrading of equipment to provide this capability. Thus the use of fine-pitch components for packaging reasons would have to be based on the ability of the company to justify such an investment.

However, if subcontract assembly services can be used, there are several more options as far as what technology can be designed into a new product. The manufacturing investment ramifications then could become less significant. In this case, the important features to look for are

- The number of vendors available to do the new technology.
- Whether the vendor is qualified in terms of the original equipment manufacturer's (OEM's) procurement requirements.
- The location of qualified vendors relative to the OEM's corporate strategy, i.e., offshore versus domestic.
- What type of premium cost is charged for the subcontract service.

1.5.3 Challenges

Anytime a new technology is being implemented (or an existing technology is stretched to its limits), there will usually be resistance by some organizations within the company. This reluctance to change often can be attributed to one or more of the following:

- Management might not want to bring in a technology because of the risks involved.
- Manufacturing might not want to bring in a new technology because of the costs involved.
- Electronic engineering might not want to bring in a new technology because of the end-product performance risks involved.
- Packaging engineering might not want to bring in a new technology because of the low confidence level as to whether or not the new technology is reliable or because of a concern that there are no standards or specifications available for the new technology.

All these challenges or hurdles can be overcome by following a methodical and logical implementation plan. Historically, this has been the case with many successful electronic product companies who have achieved improved high-speed performance along with

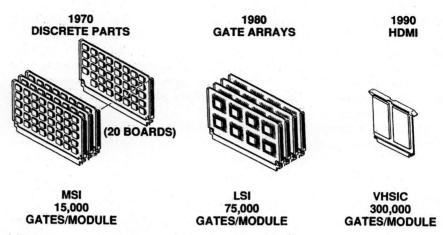

1970 **DISCRETE PARTS**	1980 **GATE ARRAYS**	1990 **HDMI**
MSI **15,000** **GATES/MODULE**	**LSI** **75,000** **GATES/MODULE**	**VHSIC** **300,000** **GATES/MODULE**

Figure 1.6. Three generations of packaging technology.[7]

miniaturization, cost reduction, and increased performance (payload) capability.

For example, as shown in Fig. 1.6, at the system level, 28 printed-board through-hole assemblies with dual in-line package (DIP) components in 1970 were reduced to four surface-mount assemblies with gate arrays in chip carriers in 1980 and subsequently were redesigned in 1990 as a high-density multichip module (MCM).

References

1. Gerald L. Ginsberg, Component Data Associates Inc., "Multichip Modules Gather ICs into a Small Area," *Electronic Packaging & Production,* October 1988, pp. 48–50.

2. Steve Stephansen, nCHIP Corporation, "Density, Speed Drive Multichip Modules," *ASIC Technology & News,* August 1990, pp. 1, 12, and 23.

3. T. A. Krinkle and D. K. Pai, Control Data Corp., "Advanced SMT–Packaging Concept–Multichip Modules," *Proceedings, Surface Mount International,* August 1991, pp. 823–835.

4. N. G. Koopman, T. C. Reiley, and P. A. Totta, IBM Corporation, "High Density Chip Interconnections," *Proceedings, International Symposium on Microelectronics,* October 1988, pp. 295–300.

5. George Messner, PCK Technology Division, "The Impact of Multichip Modules on Printed Boards," *Proceedings, Printed Circuit World Convention,* Technical Paper No.A11/3, June 1990.

6. Bruce Inpyn, Pitney Bowes Corp., "Selecting a High Density Electronic

Packaging Technology," *Proceedings, Surface Mount International,* August 1991, pp. 113–118.

7. Richard P. Himmel and James J. Licari, Hughes Aircraft Co., "Fabrication of Large-Area, Thin-Film Multilayer Substrates," *Proceedings, International Symposium on Microelectronics,* October 1989, pp. 454–460.

2
General Multichip Module Considerations[1]

The primary driving force behind the use of multichip modules (MCMs) is the increased system performance resulting from decreasing the length of wiring needed to provide interconnections between integrated circuit devices (chips). Not only is "time of flight" reduced, but, particularly for important complementary metal-oxide semiconductor (CMOS) systems, parasitic capacitance and resistance are also reduced. Circuit output drivers on custom devices can be tailored to drive these reduced parasitics so that driver speed increases.

In some cases, overall performance can be improved if the chip input/output (I/O) is redesigned for use in a multichip module (see Fig. 2.1) such that signals take less time to go from chip to chip than they do to go a substantial distance on an individual chip.

Integrated circuit device power also can be reduced because of the reduction in required output driver capability. This results in a dramatic increase in system performance.

In some cases, electronic system size is a critical factor. The use of multichip modules can help to eliminate the large mismatch between integrated circuit device interconnection density and the achieved functional density of the next level of packaging, e.g., a printed circuit board assembly, that is the result of using single-chip packages such as dual in-line packages (DIPs), pin-grid arrays (PGAs), or flat packs. In some instances, system size reductions on the order of from 5 to 10 are achievable. Thus, even though MCM substrates are several times the

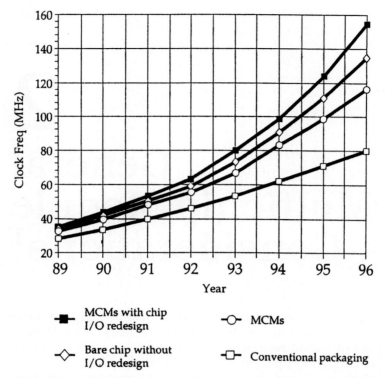

Figure 2.1. Microprocessor performance trends.[2]

cost of conventional packaging substrates on a per-unit-area basis, the resulting assembly size and associated hardware reductions can sometimes result in actual reductions in overall system cost.

The decision as to when and where to use MCMs and what type to use is a complex one. It involves making in-depth tradeoffs among the constraints of wiring density, power consumption, electrical performance, thermal management, bare-die termination, size, cost, reliability, test methodology, and many other considerations.

2.1 Multichip Module Types[3]

The Institute for Interconnecting and Packaging Electronic Circuits (IPC) considers multichip modules (MCMs) to be a relatively new electronic packaging technology and not a descendant from existing interconnection methods. Basically, the IPC has established a distinct and separate position for MCMs in the electronic packaging hierarchy that is between those for application-specific integrated circuits (ASICs) and application-specific electronic assemblies, e.g., printed-board assemblies.

The IPC further subdivides MCMs into three general types differentiated primarily with respect to the MCM interconnecting substrate's signal-layer dielectric and other distinguishing characteristics. Thus,

- Type MCM-C has fireable materials as part of multilayer ceramic dielectric substrates (see Chap. 6).
- Type MCM-D has deposited metals and unsupported deposited dielectrics on top of a variety of base materials (see Chap. 7).
- Type MCM-L has clad/plated copper conductors as part of multilayer, reinforced, organic laminate dielectric substrates (see Chap. 8).

The International Society for Hybrid Microelectronics (ISHM) recognizes the same three basic MCM designations but takes a slightly different approach to describing them. ISHM also identifies subdivisions of the MCM-C and MCM-D types (see Table 2.1).

2.2 Packaging Efficiency[4]

A figure of merit that can be used to differentiate between MCMs and conventional die-packaging techniques is the efficiency rate of using the bare-die interconnecting substrate. In this approach, the total area of the semiconductor dice is divided by the MCM substrate area. This relationship, expressed as a percentage, is sometimes called the *packaging* or *active silicon efficiency rating*.

The characteristic efficiency for typical die-packaging technologies is shown in Fig. 2.2. For example, the traditional bare-die hybrid microcircuit and chip-on-board technologies have less than a 30 percent active silicon efficiency, whereas all the more advanced high-density MCM interconnection (HDMI) techniques exceed this value. Thus all MCM applications are directed toward achieving a high substrate efficiency rating.

2.3 Relative Merits of MCM Technology[5,6]

The use of MCMs is based on the advantages and disadvantages of using an unpackaged chip assembly technique as opposed to using conventional surface mount and, to a lesser extent, through-hole mount

Table 2.1. Multichip Module Types and Basic Properties

	Multichip module identifier types (substrates)				
	MCM-C (ceramic)		MCM-D (deposited thin films)		MCM-L (layered)
Properties	Low-ε ceramics	Cofired ceramics	Semiconductor-on-semiconductor	Low-ε polymers	
Interconnect substrate	Low-ε ceramics	Cofired ceramics	Semiconductor-on-semiconductor	Low-ε polymers	Printed wiring boards
Possible materials	Porous ceramic, SiN, BeO	Al_2O_3	SiO_2	Polyimide, BCB, PPQ	Composites of fiber and epoxy
Dielectric constant	2.7–6.9	8.9–10.0	3.8	2–10	2–7.2
Subsubstrate materials	Aln	Al_2O_3	Silicon, GaAs, diamond, SiC	Ceramics, Si, metals, diamond	FR4, etc.
Power dissipation	High to very high	High	Very high	Very high	Poor
Line width (µm)	125	125	10	15	750
Line separation (µm)	125–375	125–375	10–30	25	2250
Line density per layer (mm/mm)	20	40	400	200	30
Pinout (mm^{-2})	1500–6000		800–3000		1500–3000
Typical size (mm)	100–150	150	100		660
Substrate costs	High	Moderate	Moderate		Low

SOURCE: ISHM.

LINEWIDTH (um)

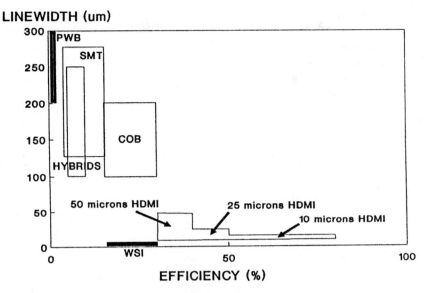

Figure 2.2. Electronic packaging efficiency.[4]

assembly technologies. It is also predicated on the relative differences in performance that can be achieved by the packaging alternatives.

2.3.1 Potential Benefits

The potential benefits of using MCMs include the ability of MCMs to handle integrated circuit dice with high I/O counts, provide denser interconnection matrices (which act as "density transformers"), and to ensure enhanced electrical performance.

2.3.1.1 Electrical Performance. In many instances, the most important MCM benefit is improved electrical performance that results from drastically shortening interconnection lengths. Thus the corresponding reduction in signal delays reduces signal "time of flight" and results in having faster circuit switching speeds. Degrading noise and crosstalk are also minimized, and there can be improved impedance control. A lowering of line capacitance also makes it possible to reduce power consumption.

2.3.1.2 Wiring Capacity. It also has been observed that in more complex electronic systems, printed-board designs are usually wiring capacity–limited and not component size–restricted. This is rarely the case with MCM technologies that provide very high wiring channel capabilities. As a matter of fact, almost all currently reported MCM designs can accommodate all required interconnections on only two MCM-D thin-film signal layers.

2.3.1.3 Flexibility. Another very desirable characteristic of MCMs is their ability to mix chips of different integrated circuit families into one "packaged" device. Digital and analog functions also can be integrated into one MCM, a process that can be difficult and expensive to achieve on a monolithic chip.

It also should be noted in this regard that MCMs do not necessarily interconnect only complex dice. Rather, they are quite useful for packaging all types of devices, in any combination, i.e., microprocessors, memories, and "glue" circuits. In this respect, they can be called precursors of wafer-scale integration (WSI).

2.3.1.4 System Reliability. MCMs also can considerably improve system reliability. This is so because the use of MCMs decreases the overall number of discrete terminations between chips. It is the number of discrete terminations (soldering or wire bonding) that significantly affects system reliability.

2.3.1.5 Product Development. The development time for an MCM can be shorter than that for the corresponding fully custom monolithic (ASIC) chip because the circuit is divided into more manageable smaller devices. The individual chips of an MCM can be fabricated, tested, and debugged separately. This makes the development effort easier while achieving the desired product development in a much shorter period of time.

Components from several different vendors can be used in MCMs. In many instances, most, if not all, of the devices in an MCM can be "off the shelf" or at least made from existing or slightly modified tooling.

2.3.1.6 Potential Cost. The cost of a large, complex ASIC can be much higher than that of the corresponding MCM chip set. This is due to the nature of chip-level yields. (The package choice for the monolithic chip also can cause a considerable variation in cost.)

Achieving this lower cost potential depends on how fast MCM volumes (quantities) develop. If the pace of MCM development is significant, it will be possible for MCM manufacturers both to achieve economies of scale and to move further down the learning curve.

2.3.1.7 End-Product Size and Shape. Lastly, the physical size and shape of end-product electronic equipment can benefit from the increased use of MCMs. Thus the ability to achieve reduced end-product weight, size, and packaging (z axis) profile can be enhanced by the use of MCMs. In fact, many such products would not even exist if traditional packaged-component technologies were used to implement them.

2.3.2 Disadvantages

As with any packaging technology, especially those which are somewhat new and relatively immature, there are distinct disadvantages to the use of MCMs. However, as MCM technology gains maturity, the relative significance of these drawbacks will diminish. Until then, these issues can drive up the cost of using the MCM approach to electronic equipment packaging.

2.3.2.1 Bare Die. The availability of a "known good die" is a major consideration in the development of an MCM product. The semiconductor industry does not yet routinely manufacture devices in bare-die form that have been tested (and possibly burned in) to the level that is required for use in MCMs.

2.3.2.2 Infrastructure. An industry infrastructure has not yet developed to the point where everything required for an MCM is readily available. In fact, it is still not clear what basic MCM technologies and which MCM fabrication companies will be part of the ultimate MCM industry. (High-volume manufacturability and reliability must be demonstrated before this can happen.)

2.3.2.3 Computer-Aided Tools. Most of the required computer-aided design (CAD), manufacturing (CAM), and testing (CAT) tools are still under development or are in the early stages of introduction to a broad base of users. This is due in part to the wide variety of MCM concepts being considered by original equipment manufacturers (OEMs) and, again, to the relative immaturity of the industry.

2.3.2.4 Heat Transfer. One of the most difficult tasks of electronic packaging is the extraction of the heat generated by the thousands of devices on integrated circuit chips. As will be discussed in Chap. 10, heat-sink structures that sometimes dwarf the bare die are often required to cool devices with the use of high-thermal-conductivity materials, moving air, and/or special heat-transfer liquids.

Thus achieving improvements in high-density performance with MCMs comes with the corresponding disadvantage of increased thermal management concerns. However, on the positive side, the miniaturization achieved in MCMs affords the heat-transfer mechanisms the ability to get closer to the initial source of the heat, and the use of improved materials provides the opportunity for achieving more efficient thermal management.

2.4 Multichip Packaging Considerations[7]

There are many choices and design tradeoffs involved in the consideration of an MCM for system packaging. The following is a summary of the major packaging and material issues associated with making these tradeoffs. Note that most of the criteria are interrelated.

2.4.1 Substrate Choice

The substrate-selection options are many (see Chap. 3). In addition to the many substrate-selection considerations that deal with design and performance, there is a significant dependence on size and processing considerations. For example, the imaging method chosen may dictate maximal substrate size limits because of the equipment being used and the ability to resolve features with the required precision over a certain surface area.

2.4.2 Die Attachment

Integrated circuit dice up to 12.5 mm (0.500 in) that dissipate 30 W or more are envisioned. These large die sizes and heat levels pose die attachment problems with respect to the need for mechanical (shock and vibration) stability, thermally uniform thin and void-free bonds, and processes that are stable over wide temperature ranges (see Chap. 3). Also, the die attachment techniques and materials used with ceramic substrates are well understood, while the use of organic substrates (printed boards) can require modifications to the processes and materials used.

2.4.3 Die Termination

Input/output terminations (microinterconnects) to the bare die by wire bonding, tape automated bonding (TAB), and flip-chip (face) bonding have been used in multichip modules (see Chap. 4). While having an obvious influence on electrical and thermal issues, concerns for integrated circuit availability, testing at both the bare-die and substrate level, process yield, and substrate compatibility are also major issues to be addressed when choosing a microinterconnect method.

2.4.4 Interconnect Density

MCM interconnecting substrate minimum feature sizes (conductor width/spaces, vias, and lands) and number of conductor layers must be consistent with the circuit technology and mechanical sizing to satisfy system needs. They also must be selected based on existing requirements and future needs.

Controlled-impedance connections are becoming necessary with high-speed circuitry even over relatively short intramodule distances. This further complicates signal interconnect density by necessitating the use of reference planes, orthogonal conductor routing, and controlled conductor spacing. Thus design, as well as process compatibility, plays a major role in cost-effectively achieving high-density interconnections.

2.4.5 Electrical Performance

The microinterconnect method used and the need to maintain a uniform thermal environment are critical to circuit noise control. Thus the selection of MCM dielectric materials also plays an important role in electrical performance.

Intercircuit propagation delay accounts for a significant percentage of system speed. This, too, is a direct function of the properties (i.e., dielectric constant) of the MCM signal interconnection media dielectric materials.

2.4.6 Power Distribution

The use of high-conductivity metals is essential for MCM power distribution, since interconnection resistance must be minimized. The output circuit distribution system may be separated from the logic circuit power distribution and reference planes in order to improve noise control, but this adds to MCM cost and complexity.

In order to minimize the coupling of power-distribution system noise with the system output circuitry, high-speed integrated circuits require power-supply decoupling (or filtering) that generally uses multilayer ceramic capacitors that are in close proximity to ouput circuits. This may require that the decoupling mechanism be contained within the MCM.

2.4.7 Thermal Management

The need for having low semiconductor junction temperatures can create severe thermal management problems both within and outside the MCM (see Chap. 10). The associated thermal, mechanical, and electrical tradeoffs are much more complex in high-performance MCMs than they are with conventional single-chip packaging technologies.

2.4.8 Next-Level Interconnections

Various approaches are used to make practical interconnections between MCMs and the next level of system packaging. These include the use of both perimeter and area arrays of I/O terminals. The terminals can be either of the leaded or leadless types that are suitable for through-hole or surface-mount soldering or separable (solderless) connection to high-density/high-performance sockets/connectors or special cabling (see Chap. 9).

2.4.9 Modification and Repair

In all but the simplest modules or in those with very regularized interconnections, e.g., memory modules, it is often important to have provisions for changing MCM interconnections in order to be able to cost-effectively correct logic errors, replace failed circuits, and/or alter terminations. This is so because even with the use of a high degree of simulation, test, and design aids, MCM and system circuits with millions of logic gates can have undiscovered "bugs" that must be compensated for or corrected.

While it is not practical to correct on-chip logic errors, it is often possible to have practical high-density techniques for MCM modification and repair. Thus, in some instances, the MCM also should provide spare I/O terminals, termination sites, and decoupling sites for future use.

2.5 Standards[8]

The principal thrust for MCM size standardization by the IEEE Computer Packaging Society is the coming maturity of MCMs in general and the MCM-D type in particular. Thus primary attention was given to MCM sizes that would be compatible with the use of either silicon interconnect substrates or MCMs that have organic insulation interconnect layers directly on a nonsilicon substrate, such as alumina, aluminum nitride, silicon carbide, and copper-molybdenum-copper composites.

2.5.1 Silicon Size Considerations

In theory, any silicon substrate size could be used in an MCM up to the capability of the silicon wafer, i.e., up to 200 mm (8 in). In practice, however, some MCM sizes would be less expensive than others depending on how many could be fabricated efficiently from a silicon wafer.

Accordingly, five silicon MCM substrate sizes were determined to be the most cost-effective to be made from 100-, 125-, 150-, and 200-mm (4-, 5-, 6-, and 8-in) wafers. They are nominally 40, 48, 62, 81, and 97 mm (1.6, 1.9, 2.4, 3.2, and 3.8 in).

2.5.2 Perimeter-I/O Considerations

The inner cavity of the MCM package obviously has to be larger than the substrate size and, when appropriate, also must be able to accommodate supplementary wire bonding or TAB. Consideration also was given to avoiding going over the 115-mm (4.5-in) size for the largest standard surface-mount package handling tray.

Thus the MCM package sizes that were selected for standardization by the IEEE task force were nominally 55, 65, 80, 100, and 115 mm (2.2, 2.6, 3.1, 3.9, and 4.5 in) on a side. [A 45-mm (1.8-in) size also might be added.] Although the size determinations were based primarily on silicon-substrate considerations, the recommended standards also were deemed suitable for use with other substrates by the IEEE task force.

2.5.3 Area-I/O Considerations

The MCM package size can be somewhat smaller for the same substrate size if the I/O is in the form of an area array of terminals (pins or pads), since the inside cavity clearance can be reduced. With this in mind, the recommended standard area-I/O package sizes were chosen to be nominally 52, 62, 77, 97, and 112 mm^2 (2.0, 2.4, 3.0, 3.8, and 4.4 in^2).

2.5.4 Final MCM Package Standardization

The final standardization determination for MCM packages will be made by the Joint Electronic Device Engineering Council (JEDEC). This is the same organization that gave impetus to surface-mount technology by its efforts to develop "chip carrier" standards.

JEDEC's efforts will result in specific package details, including terminal details for each package size standard. JEDEC also will take into account input from sources other than the IEEE Computer Packaging Society. However, in all probability, JEDEC's initial effort will result in from 5 to 10 perimeter- and area-I/O package standards for MCM applications.

2.6 Industry Challenges[1,9]

The speed with which MCMs establish themselves as the new level of electronic packaging technology depends on the ability of the electronics industry to overcome some dominant technical and business challenges. However, each of the challenges will be solved because the use of MCMs is the only way that the electronics industry will be able to sustain the phenomenal cost-effective growth in end-product performance that it has achieved since the late 1950s.

Thus the industry's infrastructure of design, fabrication, assembly, and testing suppliers of original equipment manufacturers is working on obtaining solutions to these problems. The solutions will revolve around interfaces between the design tool and the package and the semiconductor manufacturer's ability to work together with the end user.

2.6.1 Design Tools

Traditional integrated circuit/ASIC, hybrid microcircuit, and printed circuit board computer-aided design (CAD) tools do not meet the needs of MCM designers. For example, digital gate-level models, analog characteristics, and the thermal characteristics of various MCM substrates must be modeled accurately if increasingly complex designs are to be effectively simulated or prototyped during design cycles that are usually short in duration. Additionally, as the operating frequencies of systems increase, analog effects, which would otherwise be ignored, must be considered.

2.6.1.1 Integration CAD Tools. As MCM complexity increases, effective design tools must integrate design capture, component placement, conductor routing, electrical and functional simulation, design-rule checking, test-development methodologies, and manufacturing capabilities with materials databases. The design tools therefore must combine attributes of integrated circuit CAD simulation with printed circuit board CAD physical component placement and conductor routing capabilities, in addition to supporting designs of mixed logic family and component packaging technologies.

Failure to do so relegates the MCM designer to the use of a number of incompatible tools. The result will be repetition of design and data input tasks, reliance on empirical design verification methods, and longer product development cycles. Thus, without integrated CAD tools, multichip module OEM users cannot hope to reduce their products' "time to market."

2.6.1.2 CAD/CAM Linkages. Existing CAD tools also lack the critical linkages to provide the important data needed to drive computer-aided manufacturing (CAM) operations, such as mask preparation and the downloading of test programs. The challenge is to provide integrated CAD/CAM tools that can work in existing OEM design environments to support the new packaging and interconnecting manufacturing methodologies.

2.6.1.3 Thermal Analysis. Having an integrated thermal analysis capability as part of a CAD environment is much more critical for MCMs than it is for integrated circuits. In addition, the development of thermal management approaches that are more cost-effective for general applications than those now being used for very specific applications is very desirable.

2.6.2 Bare-Die Availability

Semiconductor manufacturers have historically provided individual, fully tested packaged integrated circuits to their customers, the OEMs. However, MCMs require furnishing the OEMs (or their MCM vendors) with fully tested unpackaged dice. These can be provided to the MCM customer in either complete wafer or individually diced form.

The availability of fully tested integrated circuits that satisfy full specifications (temperature, voltage, speed, etc.) is a critical issue facing the MCM industry. However, this challenge is gradually being met as semiconductor manufacturers begin to realize the significance of MCM technology to their major customers and the inevitability of MCMs achieving a major place in the electronics industry.

2.6.2.1 Burn-In. Similarly, the burn-in of integrated circuits has always been performed after the devices are individually packaged. To complicate matters, the development of a methodology to burn in a bare die is a significant technological challenge.

The burn-in of a bare die in an MCM after assembly is also somewhat less practical. This brings about the question, If only one integrated circuit in an MCM requires burn-in, should the entire MCM be burned in?

Burning in the entire MCM subjects additional dice to harsh, life-shortening processes, thereby affecting manufacturing yield and life-cycle costs. Conversely, not burning in the MCM may negatively affect product reliability.

2.6.2.2 Delivery and Handling. The shipment of integrated circuits in either a singulated bare-die or wafer form raises numerous problems. For example, the shipping of individual dice requires additional handling and process steps which increase the probability of device damage and reduce die traceability. Conversely, semiconductor manufacturers are reluctant to ship complete wafers because of the proprietary test structures that are usually incorporated on them.

2.6.3 Assembly Capability

In most instances, the techniques required for MCM assembly are essentially the same as those for packaged integrated circuits. However, these are generally specialized processes. The equipment performing these assembly operations has been designed specifically for use by the semiconductor industry. Thus, in most instances, extensive modifications are required in order to handle MCMs.

As the equipment is modified, MCM fabrication techniques must be developed that integrate the various assembly processes, including the establishment of operating procedures and personnel training. The variety of MCM requirements also dictates that assembly facilities maintain a greater variety of capability. Maintaining this flexibility involves a considerable investment in acquiring equipment and the use of experienced personnel.

2.6.4 Rework Capability

Rework is a critical element of an MCM manufacturing operation. The total cost associated with the fabrication of an MCM is often too high to justify the scrapping of a defective unit. Thus once a faulty integrated circuit is detected, it must be removed, replaced, and the MCM retested prior to use.

This is in contrast to the practices associated with the use of packaged devices. When a defective integrated circuit is found, it is scrapped along with its package. It is not cost-effective to rework it. Consequently, MCM-specific rework equipment and/or proven rework techniques are only now being developed, since nothing can be borrowed or modified from existing industry facilities. For example, one of the critical technical challenges associated with MCM rework is having the ability to isolate a specific die from the others while it is exposed to the elevated temperatures that are usually associated with the die removal process.

2.6.5   Testing Capability

A significant industry challenge is to establish the ability to test "at speed" fully assembled MCMs while also providing fault isolation to a specific integrated circuit in the event of a failure. The ability to test substrates and modules in high-volume production applications is also needed.

2.6.5.1   Functional Complexity.   The significant size reductions realized by MCMs are allowing what were once system-level functions to be incorporated at the module level. For example, this means that the module manufacturer must be able to test the essential functions of the central processor of a workstation.

Adding to the challenge is the fact that a typical MCM might contain not only processors, cache memory, and associated controllers but also drivers to interface with peripheral devices. The testing requirements then must encompass mixed device types, especially in terms of diagnostic capability.

2.6.5.2   Test Fixturing.   MCMs present testing challenges that are similar to those associated with printed circuit board assemblies. Historically, printed circuit board assembly manufacturers have used automatic test equipment (ATE) with "bed of nails" fixturing. However, this is not sufficient for testing assembled MCMs because of the close proximity of the integrated circuits to one another and to the package cavity and because of the significant reduction in feature size.

Equipment being developed to test MCM high-density interconnection substrates typically employs "noncontact" test techniques. Further modifications are also required to support high-volume MCM production and large MCM assemblies.

2.6.5.3   Design for Test.   Attention is being given to the use of "design for test" (DFT) techniques in order to help meet the challenge of testing fully assembled MCMs. However, in order to be effective, all the integrated circuits of an MCM must have DFT structures built into them. The use of DFT principles also adds significantly to the development and procurement costs of the integrated circuits, thereby increasing the cost of the MCM.

2.6.6 Infrastructure

Just as significant to the long-term viability of the MCM industry is the ability to meet the various business challenges that are encountered. Most of these challenges are associated with establishing a new level of electronic packaging activity that can cost-effectively coexist with existing design, fabrication, assembly, and testing disciplines.

The MCM industry must further develop its infrastructure so that it can progress and mature. Establishing such an infrastructure will involve the concerted efforts of the business, engineering, and financial communities.

2.6.6.1 Corporate Relationships. As MCMs grow in applicability, new corporate relationships must develop. Historically, the electronics industry is dominated by large, vertically integrated companies with mostly captive capabilities. This is so because the sophisticated technology and manufacturing costs have precluded many smaller companies from entering the market.

However, in addition to systems houses and semiconductor manufacturers themselves, new kinds of companies are emerging that specialize in MCM technology. These so-called MCM companies generally specialize specifically in one or more of the various aspects of MCM design, substrate manufacture, device assembly, and testing.

2.6.6.2 Specialized Companies. The emergence of such companies could significantly affect the infrastructure of an MCM-related electronics industry. One the one hand, the dominant electronics firms are moving away from having predominantly in-house capabilities. This is due in part to the desire to minimize investments in capital equipment and to be able to direct company resources elsewhere.

Another factor to be considered is the wide variety of MCM technologies. There are several different substrate and die attachment combinations, each of which is best suited for particular applications. Thus, unlike with surface-mount technology, it is conceivable that many OEMs will opt for having end-product flexibility and will not make a long-term commitment to any one MCM technology. Each application will use the technology best suited for it.

The end result could be that as the MCM industry matures and gains a broad base of acceptance, there will be a strong dependence on subcontract services for many aspects of product development and fabrication. The OEMs will then concentrate more on their role as system houses and less on their role as subassembly fabricators. Some of the specialized MCM companies could then act as the new intermediaries between the semiconductor foundry and the ultimate system MCM user.

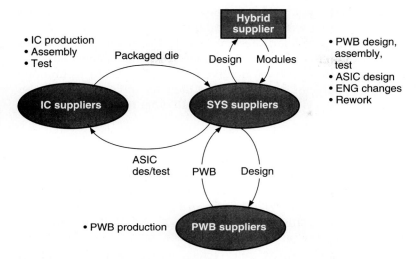

Figure 2.3. Traditional industry supplier relationships.[1]

2.6.6.3   Supplier Relationships.   The current industry relation-ships between suppliers are reflected in Fig. 2.3. Printed wiring board (PWB) and hybrid microcircuit assemblies are specified by the system manufacturer. The OEMs typically control the substrate and ASIC designs, furnish test criteria, and assemble the components onto the sub-strate.

This works well in the situation where the interfaces of technology and manufacturing are well defined and all the necessary skills are resident in each end-product manufacturer's organization. However, these traditional supplier/OEM user relationships are not structured to meet the demands of MCMs and, therefore, must be restructured in order for the OEMs to realize the benefits that MCMs offer.

2.6.6.4   Concurrent Engineering.   Technically, the MCM process steps involved integrate well with each other in order to maximize per-formance. Every step in the process must logically follow previous steps and precede subsequent steps.

Consequently, these distinct corporate entities, including appropri-ate suppliers, each specializing in its own area, must be organized within a concurrent-engineering environment that is based on having close working relationships to facilitate the interchange of the informa-tion necessary for the design, fabrication, assembly, and testing of the MCMs.

2.6.6.5 Proprietary Concerns. Below the surface of revenue and profitability issues, however, are fundamental proprietary concerns, such as die yields, proprietary designs, and test strategies that must be known on a wider basis in order to achieve a realistic business environment. Thus the various entities involved, including MCM technology suppliers, must share information about their technology to a greater extent than that which is commonly done with other technologies.

References

1. William Steingrandt and Michael F. Ehman, Alcoa Electronic Packaging, Inc., "MCMs' Impact on User-Supplier Relationships in the 1990s," *Hybrid Circuit Technology*, March 1991, pp. 31–37.

2. Steve Stephansen, nCHIP Corporation, "Density, Speed Drive Multichip Modules," *ASIC Technology & News*, August 1990, pp. 1, 12, and 23.

3. "Guidelines for Multichip Module Technology Utilization," *Institute for Interconnecting and Packaging Electronic Circuits*, IPC-MC-790, 1992.

4. John J. H. Reche, Polycon Corp., "Multichip Modules: Buzzwords or Bonanza?" *Circuits Manufacturing*, June 1989, pp. 46–50.

5. George Messner, PCK Technology Division, "The Impact of Multichip Modules on Printed Boards," *Proceedings, Printed Circuit World Convention*, Technical Paper No. A11/3, June 1990.

6. Michael Gulett, "Monolithic or Multichip?" *ASIC & EDA*, May 1992, pp. 24–26.

7. Daniel I. Amey, DuPont Electronics, "Thick Film Ceramic Technology for Multichip Modules," *Proceedings, International Microelectronics Conference*, 1990.

8. John W. Balde, IDC Corporation, "Proposed MCM Standard Sizes—A Report of the IEEE Task Force," *Proceedings, National Electronic Packaging and Production Conference*, February 1992, pp. 467–478.

9. Terry L. Ritter, High Density Integration, Inc., "Challenges Facing the MCM Industry in the Next Decade," *Proceedings, National Electronic Packaging and Production Conference*, February 1991, pp. 817–823.

3

Basic Elements of Multichip Modules[1]

Electronic circuits produced using multichip module (MCM) technology are intrinsically more reliable than their surface-mount and through-hole counterparts that use single-chip packages. This is true primarily because there are fewer levels of interconnection and the active devices are placed closer together.

Thus the number of reliability-reducing terminations and the amount of interconnection wiring are kept to a minimum. For example, for the two devices to communicate with one another, a signal will have to pass through a number of "segments" of interconnection, as indicated in Fig. 3.1.

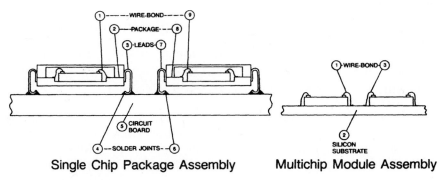

Single Chip Package Assembly   **Multichip Module Assembly**

Figure 3.1. Elements of electronic device interconnections.[1]

It can be seen that with conventional packaged single-chip technology there are nine segments in the path connecting the two integrated circuits. The equivalent MCM interconnection path has only three segments. This reduction in segments minimizes the number of opportunities for failure, thereby enhancing the potential reliability when using MCMs.

Major performance benefits are derived from the degree of circuit miniaturization. However, this miniaturization places a greater emphasis on the use of "known good" die and the selection of appropriate materials, interconnection wiring, device termination technique, and overall MCM package.

3.1 Known-Good Die[2,3]

A key aspect of achieving a high degree of MCM fabrication yield (see Fig. 3.2) is the ability to begin the assembly process with good integrated circuit chips, i.e., "known good" die. The ideal definition for *known-good die* implies that there is a high (e.g., 99.9 percent) confidence level that the integrated circuits meet their stated specifications, are free of "as received" defects, and will remain defect-free when subjected to (as appropriate) burn-in "infant mortality," environmental stress screening (ESS), the MCM assembly process, and lifetime field exposure.

Procuring bare integrated circuit die that are in accordance with the requirements of MIL-STD-883 generally provides reliable devices. However, bare die are usually given only a direct-current (DC) test by the integrated circuit fabricator; typically, they are not fully tested "at speed" or burned in by the device manufacturer.

3.1.1 Integrated Circuit Supplier Concerns

Important goals of the integrated circuit fabrication process are

- Delivery of quality parts that meet the specified performance and reliability levels.
- Production of the devices in a cost-effective manner.

The exact die-fabrication "recipe" used to achieve these goals is often unique to the integrated circuit manufacturer, the device function (memory, microprocessor, etc.), the technology (CMOS, bipolar, etc.), the device geometry, and level of integration (small scale, large scale, etc.).

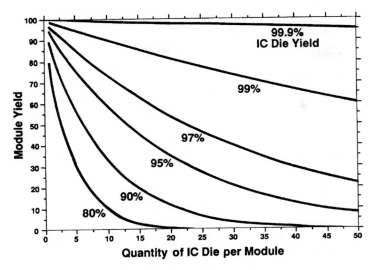

Figure 3.2. MCM yield versus bare-die yield.[2]

Since most integrated circuit production lines have always been set up to produce packaged devices, providing bare die can disrupt the manufacturing procedure and process flow. Thus the manufacturer undertakes an increased risk (and decreased revenue) when supplying unpackaged devices.

There is also a reluctance to sell bare die because the integrated circuit manufacturer is geared toward performing final quality checks and burn-in while handling packaged devices. The ability to conduct other evaluations and postprocessing is also limited.

3.1.2 MCM Vendor/User Concerns

The concerns of the integrated circuit supplier inevitably affect the vendors/users of the MCM, especially when they want to go beyond the prototype stage of product development. For vertically integrated electronics companies, a solution is to control all aspects of MCM manufacturing and assembly, including the making of the integrated circuit. Unfortunately, most companies are not capable of doing this or do not desire to do so.

Thus systems houses will continue to design and manufacture products while using both off-the-shelf and custom parts in order to achieve the desired balance of end-product function and cost. These companies are going to be dependent on vendors to provide various lower-level services.

3.1.3 Quality Assurance

There are a few basic approaches that can be taken to help ensure that known-good die are used in the MCM assembly process, including

- Purchasing integrated circuits from a semiconductor manufacturer that will guarantee meeting specific performance (confidence) levels.
- Purchasing integrated circuits from a third-party bare-die supplier that will guarantee meeting specific performance (confidence) levels.
- Doing in-house testing prior to device assembly.

The first approach is the ideal long-term solution for high-volume applications. However, one of the other two approaches is probably best suited for leading-edge, low-volume or startup applications until the volumes justify taking the first approach.

There are obviously alternate or supplementary approaches that can be taken either prior to wafer dicing or thereafter, such as

- *Design for testability.* This involves including as part of the design process functions and features that facilitate subsequent bare-die evaluation. The use of built-in self-test (BIST) features, boundary-scan capability, extra sacrificial lands, etc. is suitable for this purpose.
- *Process improvement.* This involves achieving high yields by placing an emphasis on achieving "six sigma" processing.
- *Wafer-level screening.* This involves the comprehensive pretesting of all chips by probing the wafer under various temperature, speed, and loading conditions, along with burn-in or wafer-level reliability testing.
- *Statistical sampling.* This involves sorting chip lots by evaluating a statistically sufficient number of devices in order to adequately ascertain the acceptability of the whole lot.
- *Testing every chip.* This involves pretesting all chips while using either metallurgical techniques (e.g., TAB) or temporary pressure-contact techniques (e.g, anisotropic conductive-film/adhesive and membrane probing) to improve test-point accessibility.

The effectiveness of the various screening and testing techniques, whereby all good die are separated from defective chips, depends first on having an appropriate applied environmental stress that is sufficient to reveal most defective devices. It then depends on having electrical test fault coverage that is adequate to reveal operational defects.

3.2 Materials[1,4]

The materials used in MCMs must satisfy the following requirements:

- Small conductor size demands high electrical conductivity.
- Dielectric materials must provide adequate insulation and protection for the conductors under a variety of environmental conditions.
- The coefficient of thermal expansion (CTE) of the substrate dielectric materials should match that of the integrated circuit in order to reduce thermally induced stresses.
- The thermal conductivity of all materials should be as high as practical, and dielectric thicknesses as small as practical, in order to help minimize thermal management concerns.
- Substrate base materials should have a high Young's modulus in order to minimize warp and bow.
- Adhesives, when used, should have adequate structural strength under a variety of environmental conditions while allowing for device removal and replacement without excessively degrading MCM quality and reliability.
- Encapsulation and conformal coating materials, when used, should be compatible will all other MCM materials. They also should induce negligible stresses on device terminations under a variety of environmental conditions.

3.2.1 Circuit Conductor Materials

The most common MCM circuit conductor materials are copper, gold, aluminum, nickel, and solder. Typical properties of these materials are shown in Table 3.1.

Copper and aluminum are normally used as the primary conductor. Nickel is used as a diffusion barrier over thin-film copper conductors. Gold and solder are used as the metallization on the device termination lands.

Table 3.1. Typical Properties of Conductive MCM Materials[4]

	Resistivity (ohm-cm $\times 10^{-6}$)	Thermal conductivity (W/cm K)	Coefficient of thermal expansion (ppm/K)
Copper	1.7	4.01	16.6
Gold	2.4	3.18	14.2
Aluminum	2.8	2.37	25.6
Nickel	7.8	0.91	13.0
Solder Sn63:Pb37	17.0	0.51	24.5

3.2.1.1 Printed Circuit Board Conductors. The traditional multilayer printed circuit board (print and etch) technology is generally capable of producing copper conductors as narrow as 0.13 mm (0.005 in) on internal layers of a large 0.6 × 0.6 m (24 × 24 in) panel. The use of new photoresist materials and advanced photolithography techniques makes it possible to reduce the conductor width down toward 0.05-mm (0.002-in) levels on smaller 0.3 × 0.3 m (12 × 12 in) panels (see Fig. 3.3).

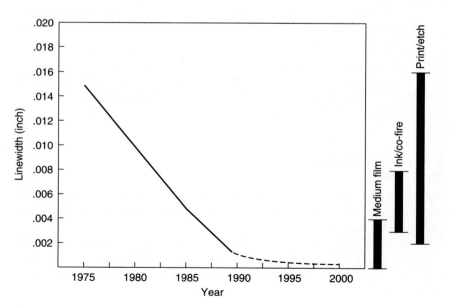

Figure 3.3. Conductor width technology trends.[4]

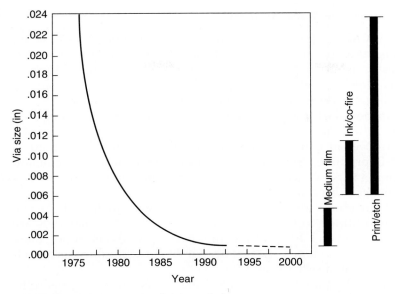

Figure 3.4. Via size technology trends.[4]

The corresponding via size limit is approximately 0.25-mm (0.010-in) diameter for large panels and 0.01-mm (0.004-in) diameter for the smaller panels (see Fig. 3.4). These small-panel feature sizes are generally considered to be sufficient to satisfy high-density multichip module (MCM-L) requirements.

3.2.1.2 Thick-Film Conductors. Thick-film conductive inks on cofired substrates, which use screen printing and firing techniques, can achieve 0.13-mm (0.005-in) conductor widths (see Fig. 3.3) and 0.25-mm (0.010-in) vias (see Fig. 3.4). When advanced "direct write" imaging techniques are used, these features can be reduced down toward 0.08-mm (0.003-in) conductor widths and 0.15-mm (0.006-in) vias, which are more compatible for multichip module (MCM-C) requirements.

3.2.1.3 Thin-Film Conductors. Thin-film technology provides the smallest possible MCM conductive features. The fabrication techniques used to make conventional semiconductors can readily be used to produce MCM-D medium thin-film conductor features (see Figs. 3.3 and 3.4) on the order of 0.015 mm (0.0006 in) and less, i.e., 0.005 mm (0.0002 in), if required.

3.2.2 Substrate Base Materials

The basic MCM substrate materials depend on the type of MCM being used. Thus alumina, the mainstay of the traditional hybrid microcircuit industry, is often used as the base substrate material for MCM-C products. However, advanced high-thermal-conductivity ceramics, such as silicon carbide, beryllia, and especially aluminum nitride, are gaining in popularity for high-power-dissipation applications (see Chap. 6).

Several different materials are used as the base substrate materials in MCM-D products. Silicon itself is used when thermal expansion mismatch is a major concern. The MCM-C ceramics and various metals and composites also can be used.

MCM-D products also use a supplementary deposited dielectric material in addition to the base substrate material. The materials are usually one of several different polyimides or new advanced polymers that have been developed specifically for MCM-D applications, such as benzocyclobutane (BCB) (see Chap. 7).

Conventional printed wiring board materials, such as glass-reinforced epoxies and polyimides, are used in MCM-L products. In some instances, the reinforcement is one of the materials developed for advanced surface-mount applications, such as aramid fibers (Kevlar) and quartz (see Chap. 8).

3.2.2.1 Thermal Conductivity. Thermal conductivity values for various MCM substrate and packaging materials are shown in Fig. 3.5. It is readily apparent that the popular MCM-D materials silicon and aluminum nitride are in the group of materials that exhibit relatively high thermal performance. It also should be noted that the thermal conductivity values for these materials are in the same range as those for materials which are generally selected for heat-sinking or heat-spreading purposes, e.g., aluminum. Other interesting new materials for MCM applications include silicon carbide, graphite composites, various metal-matrix composites, and metallurgically bonded "sandwiches" of various wrought metals.

3.2.2.2 Coefficient of Thermal Expansion. Mechanical stresses may be induced in integrated circuits and/or the interconnecting substrate as a result having a thermal expansion mismatch. The problem is exacerbated by the generally large size of the substrates used in MCMs, whereby even small differences in the materials' coefficient of thermal expansion (CTE) can result in significant dimensional differences between parts when they are moved through a broad temperature range.

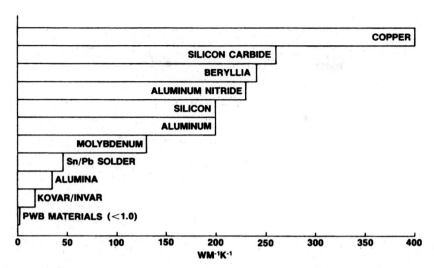

Figure 3.5. Room-temperature material thermal conductivity values.[1]

The mechanical stress level may be reduced by imposing compliant material between the mismatched elements. However, this will generally impede achieving good heat transfer, because the compliant materials (buffers) usually have poor heat-transfer characteristics.

Figure 3.6 provides CTE values for the various candidate MCM substrate materials. From the data, it is apparent that silicon, aluminum nitride, and silicon carbide have nearly identical CTE values and would thus be closely compatible in any combination as MCM materials.

Since the purpose of an MCM is basically to interconnect integrated circuits made from silicon, the merits of selecting an MCM substrate that has expansion properties that closely match those of silicon can hardly be considered unfavorably. If the substrate also has good thermal conductivity, then mechanical stresses arising from temperature gradients also will be minimized.

Using the same reasoning, aluminum nitride is an excellent choice for use in type MCM-C products. Aluminum nitride's adaptability to being used in multilayer/cofired structures, coupled with its good thermal conductivity and CTE, makes it particularly attractive for use in rugged package bases with electric feedthrough.

However, many other factors must be taken into account when selecting MCM substrate materials, especially cost. Therefore, although traditional printed wiring board materials do not generally have good thermal conductivity values (but do have good CTE val-

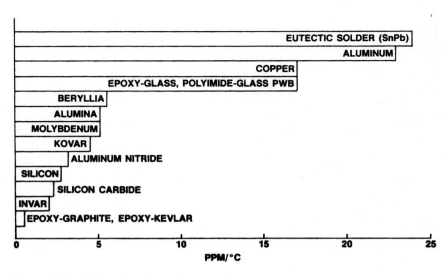

Figure 3.6. MCM material coefficients of thermal expansion.[1]

ues), MCM-L products definitely have applications for which they are ideally suited.

3.2.3   Die-Attachment Materials[5]

Traditionally, bare semiconductor die are attached to substrates by one of the following methods:

- *Eutectic bonding,* where high temperature and mechanical pressure produce a molecular bond line between the die and the substrate.

- *Solder bonding,* where soft solder (paste or solid wire) is applied at the solder's melting temperature in order to produce a metallic bond line between the die and the substrate.

- *Adhesive attachment,* whereby the adhesive is applied in its noncured (soft) phase between the die and the substrate and is then brought to its cured phase through exposure to elevated temperatures.

- *Tape bonding,* where a precut thin tape is placed between the die and the substrate and is then made to produce the necessary adhesion through the application of mechanical pressure and heat.

There are specific properties and advantages associated with each of these methods, which, in turn, determine the range of possible applications. However, the die-attachment method with adhesives has become dominant in a wide range of applications. Thus the use of adhesives has replaced, to a certain extent, the eutectic bonding method in ceramic-substrate bare-die assemblies. Bonding with tape is a rather new technology that has not yet reached the maturity of the other methods.

3.2.3.1 Stress Management.[6]

Almost all MCM assemblies will include some highly functional die that are generally very large, i.e., over 1 cm^2. Traditional integrated circuit packaging under this size can be made functional and reliable using conventional adhesives.

It has been demonstrated, however, that when the size exceeds the 1-cm^2 level, the stress might become excessive for such methods to be used reliably. The stress is associated with the differences in the coefficients of thermal expansion (CTEs) of the die (silicon), the adhesive, and the substrate. The stress exerted on the die-substrate junction can be calculated as the strain multiplied by the modulus of the adhesive.

There are two ways to address the potential stress problem. The first approach matches the CTE values of the die, the adhesive, and the substrate. However, the difficulty of this approach is obvious from the tabulation of the CTE values of some materials, as shown in Table 3.2.

The other approach involves adhesive modulus reduction. Since the moduli of adhesives can differ by as much as 2 to 4 orders of magnitude, they are primarily dependent on the glass transition temperatures (T_g) and cross-link densities of the materials.

Table 3.3 shows the moduli of materials that are commonly used in electronic applications. While some of the materials might seem usable, their applications are usually limited. For example, silicones can be used for some applications, but their relatively low solvent and chemical resistance and molecular "migration" can cause bonding and soldering problems. Similarly, polyurethanes are generally good in terms of stress reduction, but because of a lack of stability at temperatures above 126°C, their sensitivity in handling, and their isocyanate's toxic and carcinogenic potential, they have limited application.

3.2.3.2 Adhesives.

Adhesives for die-attachment purposes are suspensions of metal particles in a carrier. The metal particles (mostly silver) are several micrometers in size and have the form of thin flakes. The carrier provides the adhesion and mechanical strength in the bond line, while the metal particles provide electrical and thermal conductivity. The most commonly used adhesives contain about 75 percent metal (by weight) suspended in viscous fluids.

Most die-attachment adhesives use one of the following as a carrier:

Table 3.2. CTE Values of Common Materials[6]

Material type	CTE (ppm/°C)
Silicon	3
Gallium arsenide (GaAs)	3
Molybdenum	5
Alumina	7
Aluminum nitride	4
Kovar	6
Copper	17
Aluminum	27
FR-4 (*xy* plane)	16
Polyimide (*xy* plane)	12
Tin/lead solder	26
Indium solder	42
Gold eutectic	15
Silver-glass	17
Silver-epoxy	45
Alumina-epoxy	33
Silver-polyimide	40

- Epoxy resin
- Polyimide
- Glass frit plus organic carrier

The first two react chemically at elevated temperatures to form polymer chains, where the silver-glass reacts at higher temperatures to produce a sintered, inorganic-matrix glass-metal.

Die-attachment adhesives are applied to substrates in their "wet," noncured form by means of either stamping, screening, or dispensing. The technology of dispensing can be divided into two categories that represent two different approaches:

- The *"print" method* results in having a complete adhesive pattern in one step through the use of a dedicated dispensing tool. The tool (nozzle) determines the printed pattern.

- The *"write" method* uses a single dispense tube (monotube nozzle) to

Table 3.3. Typical Moduli of Various
Die-Attachment Materials[6]

Adhesive material	Tensile modulus (10^5 lb/in^2)
Tin-lead solder	10.0
Indium solder	5.0
Gold eutectic	10.0
Silver-glass	12.0
Silver-epoxy (T_g @ 100°C)	1.0
Alumina-epoxy (T_g @ 100°C)	2.0
Silicone	0.015
Polyurethane	0.020
"Stress-free" epoxy*	0.017

*A.I. Technology ME7159.

dispense beads or continuous lines of adhesive, while the substrate or nozzle is moved to produce the desired pattern.

The "write" process has significant advantages, since it allows more flexibility with programmable patterns and a single tool. Yet it is a relatively slow process in comparison with the "print" method, especially with large die.

3.2.4 Bare-Die Protection Materials[7,8]

Increasingly, many applications are requiring that the MCM assembly protect the chips from the atmosphere (i.e., that the chips be sealed, hermetically when practical) and protect the chip and terminations to it from mechanical shock, moisture, and various chemicals used in the MCM manufacturing process and to which the end product might be exposed during its functional lifetime. The means for doing this fall basically into two categories, ("glob top") coatings and lids.

3.2.4.1 Selection Criteria. The choice of a coating/encapsulating material for MCM assembly applications must be based on several criteria, including

■ Type of application

- Special application requirements that are not common to single-die packaging
- Special criteria needed to satisfy more stringent interpretation of industry specification requirements
- Type of environment against which the MCM must be protected
- Method of product application
- Cost

Any material intended for direct contact with a bare die also must be free of water-extractable ions and other corrosive agents. It must have controlled flow and form a void-free shell around the device without breaking fragile soldered/bonded terminations to the chip.

Additionally, moisture resistance and electrical insulation characteristics are significant. These two properties are interrelated because moisture absorption seriously degrades the dielectric constant and loss factor.

Handling and curing considerations have a significant impact on yields and throughput, and chemical resistance is important to processing and performance. A suitable coating material also must not swell or otherwise be affected by MCM cleaning solvents. In selecting the technique to be used for the seal, several important properties must be considered, namely:

1. *Sealing temperature (and time).* The technique chosen must be able to form a seal at a low enough temperature and in a short enough time to minimize the heating effects on the chip and board components.

2. *Thermal expansion.* The thermal expansion of the sealing material/device also should closely match that of the board in order to minimize thermal stresses and thus maintain the integrity of the seal.

3. *Hermeticity.* The seal must provide the degree of hermeticity required and maintain this level when exposed to the equipment operating and storage environment.

4. *Cost.* The sealing technique must be cost-effective not only with respect to material cost but also with respect to application and replacement costs, when applicable.

5. *Repairability.* If it is necessary to be able to replace a chip or repair a wire/lead termination after the chip has been sealed, it is important that the sealing technique be such that it can be readily "broken" and replaced.

6. *Stability.* When coatings are used, they should be sufficiently stable that they do not tend to excessively stress the wire/lead bonds or the die-attachment bond when exposed to the equipment operating and storage environments.

3.2.4.2 Silicone Coatings. Typical room-temperature-vulcanizing (RTV) dispersion coatings are one-component, room-temperature-vulcanizing (RTV) silicone-rubber coatings that are supplied as a xylene dispersion. (No mixing is required.) The curing process uses a cross-linking mechanism that generates methanol during cure. Once applied and exposed, the material vulcanizes by reaction with moisture from the air to form a soft, resilient elastomeric coating.

Silicone gels have found continued, and in some cases increased, use in bare-die protection applications. Silicones formulated especially for use with integrated circuits are now employed by many manufacturers of high-reliability products. This is so because, among other things, they exhibit excellent dielectric thermal stability properties.

Curing noncorrosively, silicone gels bond satisfactorily to the surface of bare silicon die, as well as to various MCM substrates. In fact, the performance of some silicone gels and comparable materials is being seriously considered for use in "reliability without hermeticity" (RwoH) applications in lieu of using expensive hermetic bare-die packaging.

Critical MCM requirements that silicones can satisfy include

- High dielectric strength
- High surface and interface resistivity
- Low dielectric constant
- Nonexothermic cure cycles without corrosive by-products
- Ability to withstand long-term exposure to temperatures as high as 250°C (482°F)
- Short-term temperature endurance to 316°C (600°F)
- Resistance to ozone, corona, moisture, and weathering

Special controlled technology can yield a silicone gel that affords the nonflowable permanence of a solid but also give the freedom from large mechanical and thermal stresses of a fluid. Chemically, a typical silicone gel is very similar to silicone fluids, but with just enough cross-linking to prevent separation of the individual polymer chains and give nonflow thermal-set properties. The fully cured dielectric gel is a soft, jelly-like material that exhibits tenacious pressure-sensitive adhesion to virtually any substrate.

3.2.4.3 Epoxy Coatings.   Epoxy coatings are also available for chip-on-board (COB) self-crowning or "glob-top" applications. Typical materials are two-component liquid epoxy–anhydride systems that have been formulated for their superior thermal shock performance, substrate adhesion, moisture resistance, and glass-transition temperatures in the range of 165 to 180°C.

The so-called third-generation epoxies are suitable for relatively high reliability bare-die coating/encapsulating applications. This is so because their moisture resistance, product purity, and thermal cycling characteristics are significantly better than their first- and second-generation predecessors.

These newest epoxies can be used to serve as both I/O junction coatings and bare-die mechanical/chemical protection overcoatings, particularly in high-volume/low-cost MCM-C and MCM-L applications. This is so because their ionic purity is on a par with that of the widely used die-attachment adhesives. Their greatly improved thermal expansion characteristics have resulted in minimal I/O termination degradation during thermal cycling.

3.2.4.4 Sealing Lids.   Metal lids can be used to seal individual chip sites. For MCM applications, soldering is generally used to attach the lid to the MCM substrate.

The use of preforms is often the most convenient method for applying the solder, in addition to the solder coating on the board. The heat required to reflow the solder can be applied using one of the soldering processes that is associated with conventional surface-mounting technology.

3.3 MCM Packages[9]

While integrated circuits and high-density substrates are key elements of MCMs, it is often also necessary to provide some form of mechanical housing (package) to complete the assembly. Such packages serve to protect the sensitive integrated circuits from damage due to physical handling or environmental contamination, supply a solderable interface for I/O signal and power terminations to the next-level assembly, and provide thermal paths between the MCM and its environment.

The selection of a suitable MCM package depends on several factors

Table 3.4. MCM Package Options[9]

Parameter	Quad flat pack	Pin-grid array	Pad-grid array
Terminal count	Limited	Medium	High
I/O pattern	Peripheral	Surface	Surface
Mounting	Surface	Through hole	Surface
Assembly	Conventional	Conventional	Special

(see Table 3.4). Most desirable is to have an MCM with an I/O terminal pattern that is compatible with existing high-density through-hole [e.g., pin-grid array (PGA)] or surface-mount technology [e.g., quad flat pack (QFP)] components. Thus common next-level printed circuit board design, assembly and testing equipment, hardware, and software can be used with both single-chip and multichip packages.

With small multichip packages and low I/O terminal requirements, it is possible to duplicate existing land patterns. However, special packages are often needed even in these instances because MCM substrates need larger package cavities than do individual bare die.

3.3.1 Flat Packs

Problems occur when multichip module I/O requirements exceed those for conventional single-chip packages, which is usually the case. The surface-mount flat pack becomes pin-limited first. Additionally, signals can be handled by increasing package size and/or decreasing I/O terminal pitch.

Large packages can reach a size whereby it is difficult to control lead planarity. Conversely, going to finer lead pitches can cause manufacturing problems with respect to lead/land alignment and obtaining defect-free assemblies.

3.3.2 Grid Arrays

Higher I/O terminal counts and larger MCM substrate cavities are possible with grid-array packages that use the bottom surface of the package, rather than its perimeter, to provide the interface with the next level of packaging. However, use of the more conventional pin-grid array (PGA) package has associated with it all the relative disadvantages of using through-hole technology instead of surface-mount technology for the method of component assembly.

Surface-mountable pad-grid array packages without pins or with very short pins can be used to overcome these disadvantages. However, the use of pad-grid arrays presents some unusual challenges. An obvious drawback is the need to accommodate mostly hidden or "blind" solder joints that can be difficult to make and inspect visually. However, as with flip-chart technology, time will tell if leadless grid array packaging will become generally accepted, especially for MCM applications.

References

1. John C. Mather and John K. Hagge, Rockwell International Corp., "Material Requirements for Packaging Multichip Modules," *Proceedings, National Electronic Packaging and Production Conference,* February 1990, pp. 1135–1142.

2. Carl Cleveland, Boeing Defense and Space Group, and Marshall Andrews, Microelectronics and Computer Technology Corp., "Development of Multichip Module Packaging for the Military Environment," *Proceedings, National Electronic Packaging and Production Conference,* February 1992, pp. 479–501.

3. Russell J. Wagner and John K. Hagge, Rockwell International Corp., "Improving MCM Assembly Yields Through Approaches for Known-Good ICs," *Proceedings, International Electronics Packaging Conference,* September 1991, pp. 882–897.

4. T. A. Krinkle and D. K. Pai, Control Data Corp., "Advanced SMT–Packaging Concept–Multichip Modules," *Proceedings, Surface Mount International,* August 1991, pp. 823–835.

5. Uri Sela and Hans Steinegger, ESEC, "Dispensing Technology: The Key to High-Quality, High-Speed Die-Bonding," *Microelectronics Manufacturing Technology,* February 1991, pp. 47–52.

6. Kevin Chung, Garrett Dreier, Andrew Boyle, Pat Fitzgerald, Jeffrey Sager, and Martin Lin, A.I. Technology, "MCM Die Attachment Using Low-Stress Thermally-Conductive Epoxies," *Surface Mount Technology,* May 1991, pp. 42–45.

7. Art Burkhart, Dexter Corp., "Considerations for Choosing Chip-on-Board Encapsulants," *Electri•Onics,* September 1985, pp. 67–69.

8. Robert C. Antonen and Gust T. Kookootsedes, Dow Corning U.S.A., "Silicone Coatings for IC Protection," *Microelectronic Manufacturing and Testing,* April 1985, pp. 15–16.

9. Bill Blood and Allison Casey, Motorola, Inc., "Evaluating MCM Packaging Technology," *ASIC Technology & News,* 2d of 2 parts, August 1991, pp. 22–24.

4

Bare-Die Termination Techniques[1,2]

Each multichip module (MCM) for each specific application requires the appropriate bare-die termination (chip-to-substrate interconnection) technology. Unfortunately, there is no universal solution for all applications. Each method offers distinct advantages and disadvantages (see Table 4.1).

The three basic bare-die termination techniques or derivatives thereof, i.e., wire bonding (chip-and-wire), tape automated bonding (TAB), and flip-chip (controlled-collapse) soldering, have been used in some cases for over 20 years in semiconductor packages and hybrid microcircuit assemblies. More recently, they have been refined and improved to the point where they are also suitable for chip-on-board (COB) applications.

While performance issues must be addressed in selecting an appropriate interconnection scheme from the chip to the substrate, cost is an equally important consideration. However, because of the number of variables that affect the cost of a finished module, cost issues are not easily determined.

4.1 General Considerations[3,4]

The selection of the method of connecting bare dice to substrates is the primary decision in the physical design of the MCM. The die termination technique must be compatible with other parts of the module.

Table 4.1. Bare-Die Termination Technique Features[3]

Technology feature	Wire bond	TAB	Flip chip
Maturity	Very good	Good	Good
Chip availability	Very good	Fair	Poor
Peripheral bond pitch	4–7 mil	3–4 mil	10 mil
Area-array bond pitch	N/A	N/A	10–15 mil
Max I/O count	300–500	500–700	>700
Footprint size (chip+)	20–100 mil*	80–600 mil†	Clearance
Repairability	Poor	Fair	Good
Thermal path	Substrate	Substrate	Lid/substrate
Chip burn-in/test	Poor	Good	Fair

*Depends on cavity or no cavity.
†Depends on outer lead bond pitch.

In particular, the technique chosen will dictate to a large extent the type of substrate and the heat-dissipation thermal path that are optimal for the application. The die termination technique also must provide suitable electrical performance and often is required to accommodate several hundred I/O interconnections at very small pitches.

Chip-level interconnections are generally of either the peripheral or area-array types (see Fig. 4.1). Peripheral termination techniques are based on the use of bonding lands that are spread around the periphery of the die. Wire bonding and conventional TAB are the most important technologies used in MCMs for this purpose.

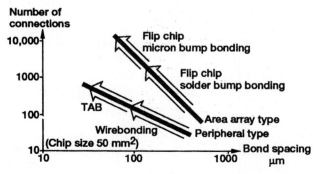

Figure 4.1. Peripheral and area-array technologies.[4]

Area-array termination techniques are based on the use of bonding lands that are spread over the entire surface of the die. Flip-chip technology is the most important technology used in MCMs for this purpose.

In principle, area arrays provide far more interconnections per chip. This is extremely important in very high I/O multichip module applications. However, almost all high-volume/low-cost single-chip semiconductor packaging and lower-cost MCM assemblies utilize peripheral terminations.

4.2   Wire Bonding[5,6]

There are basically three types of wire-bonding (chip-and-wire) technologies, namely, thermocompression, ultrasonic, and thermosonic. They derive their names from the method the energy source employs to terminate very small diameter gold or aluminum wire, approximately 0.018 to 0.25 mm (0.0007 to 0.010 in) for MCM applications, between the die and the substrate.

The general parameters associated with the general application of the three basic wire-bonding techniques are compared in Table 4.2.

4.2.1   Thermocompression Wire Bonding[7]

Thermocompression wire bonding is one of the most frequently used bonding processes. The basic method actually encompasses three different bonding process, i.e., wedge, ball, and stitch.

The principle is to join two metals using heat and pressure but without melting. The elevated temperature maintains the metals in an annealing state as they join in a molecular metallurgical bond. The process is quite involved (see Fig. 4.2), but generally speaking, the softer the metals, the more readily do they bond together.

A major disadvantage associated with thermal bonding, however, is that many of the materials cannot withstand the high temperatures required. Aluminum, for example, is difficult to bond by thermal techniques because a hard oxide forms at temperatures of 250 to 300°C, thus inhibiting bondability.

4.2.1.1   Thermocompression Wedge Bonding.   The oldest form of thermocompression bonding is *wedge bonding*. This method is very useful with small-diameter wires. It is also quite simple to produce two bonds between the wire and the pad/land, thereby improving joint reliability.

Table 4.2. Wire-Bonding Methods[1]

Parameter	Thermocompression (gold wire)	Automatic thermosonic (gold wire)	Ultrasonic (gold and aluminum wire)
Develop and control	May be difficult to control melt to tip	Easiest to control	Must control acoustic energy and force
Speed (bpm)*	≈6	≈600	≈240
Heat required†	Pulse capillary heated work stage optional	150°C work stage (maximum)	No heat required (typical)
Force required†	Most	Less than for other methods	Less than for thermocompression
Direction	Omnidirectional (360°)	Omnidirectional (360°)	Straight line ($\pm 7.5°$)
Looping	Some control	Best control	Good control
Bond pad size (25 µm/0.001 in diameter)	Ball size dependent (2 to 5 × diameter)	Ball size dependent (2 to 5 × wire diameter)	Wedge size dependent (1.2 × wire size)
Bond-head clearance	Largest head size (maximum clearance required)	Smallest head size (minimum clearance required)	Large head size (deep access available)
Contamination	Most sensitive	Less sensitive	Least sensitive

*Bonds per minute (each wire requires two bonds).

†Parameters such as heat and force may be adjusted for specific applications.

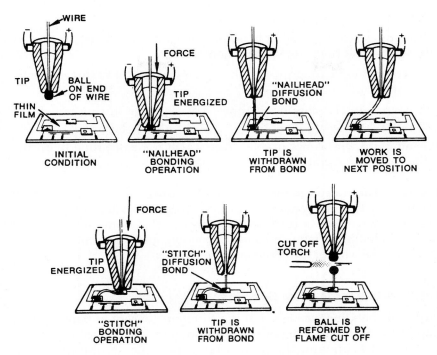

Figure 4.2. Mechanics of pulse-heated thermocompression bonding.[8]

4.2.1.2 Thermocompression Ball Bonding.

A technique suitable for high bonding rates is known as *ball bonding*. With this method, the wire to be bonded is fed through a capillary that is usually heated to between 300 and 400°C. An open flame or spark discharge then melts the end of the wire to form a small ball. The bonding tool then forces the ball onto the land, and the termination is made. Wire cutoff is achieved by a "flame-off" operation that also produces the ball used at the next wire termination.

The advantages of thermocompression ball bonding are

- It is omnidirectional; i.e., after the first bond is made, the bonding head may move in any direction to make the second bond.
- No unique fixturing is required during bonding.
- It is the easiest process to develop and control.

The disadvantages are

- It requires a high working temperature.

- It requires relatively large bonding lands and wire-bond clearances for high-yield/high-rate production.

- It is the wire-bonding process that is most sensitive to surface contamination.

- It has relatively slow bond times, i.e., the time during which the bonding force is applied.

- Aluminum wire is not usable, since it will not ball properly during the flame-off operation.

4.2.1.3 Thermocompression Stitch Bonding. Thermocompression *stitch bonding* is a compromise between the wedge and ball methods. It uses a cutoff arrangement in place of the flame-off. This allows for the use of gold and aluminum wire and smaller bonding areas. The cutoff process also forms the wire for the next bonding operation.

4.2.2 Ultrasonic Wire Bonding[7]

Ultrasonic bonding (see Fig. 4.3) is a different concept of bonding that employs a rapid scrubbing or wiping motion in addition to pressure as a means of achieving the molecular bond. The scrubbing action removes any oxide films that might be present. A slightly larger area of contact is necessary because of the scrubbing action. Also, extreme care must be taken so as not to damage the chip during the ultrasonic wire-bonding operation.

Because ultrasonic bonding can create bonds between a wide variety of dissimilar materials, it is an extremely flexible process. Thus both gold and aluminum wire are compatible with this technique. Void-free junctions are produced by ultrasonic wire bonding with relatively few foreign material inclusions, making it a desirable means of creating high-quality, low-resistance electrical junctions. Also, bonding dissimilar metals at low temperatures eliminates or greatly decreases the formation of intermetallic compounds and allows bonds to be made in the immediate vicinity of temperature-sensitive components without adverse effects.

The advantages of ultrasonic bonding are

- It is a room-temperature process.

- It is the wire-bonding process that is the least sensitive to surface contamination.

- It is workable with smaller lands than thermocompression ball

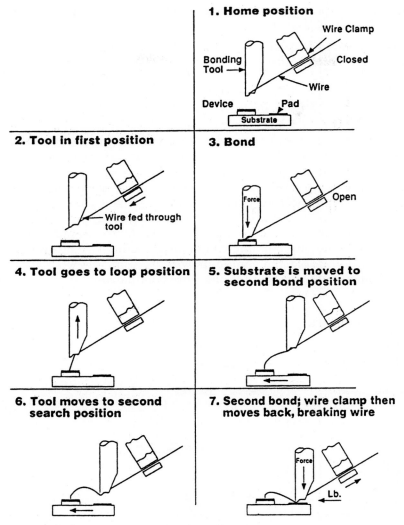

Figure 4.3. Mechanics of ultrasonic wire bonding.[7]

bonding; e.g., for a wire with a diameter of 25 µm (0.001 in), a land size of 38 × 75 µm (0.0015 × 0.003 in) is practical.

The disadvantages are

- It is unidirectional; i.e., after the first bond is made, the bonding head must move in only one direction toward the second bond site.

- Component- or package-wall proximity must allow for bonding-tool and wire-clamp clearances.
- Acoustical energy measurement problems make the process difficult to characterize and control.

4.2.3 Thermosonic Wire Bonding

Ultrasonic energy is commonly used with the thermocompression wire-bonding methods, resulting in a technique known as *thermosonic wire bonding.* This technique (see Fig. 4.4) relies on vibrations created by ultrasonic action to scrub the bond area to remove any oxide layers and also to create the heat for bonding. This, combined with the pressure of the tool forcing the wire into the bonding land, provides the final bond. Since this can take place at temperatures around 120 to 150°C, thermosonic wire bonding can be done with low-temperature materials, including gold and aluminum wire.

The advantages of using thermosonic wire bonding are

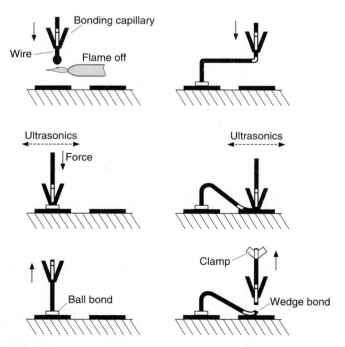

Figure 4.4. Mechanics of thermosonic bonding.[7]

- It uses moderate bonding temperatures.
- It is omnidirectional.
- It is less sensitive to surface contamination than is thermocompression wire bonding.

The disadvantages are

- It requires a minimum land size of 0.1 × 0.1 mm (0.004 × 0.004 in).
- The process requires the control of acoustical energy.
- Special fixturing is required.
- It has some wire-looping limitations.

4.2.4 MCM Considerations[3,4]

The wire-bonding approach used in MCMs is an extension of single-chip packaging technology. Thus, as a well-defined mature technology, wire bonding offers the lowest MCM assembly risk. However, wire-bonded dice cannot be tested "at speed" or be burned in prior to mounting, and repair is difficult.

Extending this technology to MCMs, however, presents some unique challenges. For example, advances in integrated circuit technology have rapidly increased device I/O count and reduced I/O spacing. This has created many challenges in wire-bonding operations by driving pad sizes to be smaller, lead widths to be narrower, and bonding pitches to be finer.

The driving force toward having a finer bonding pitch is the potential savings on die cost for "pad-limited" devices. Thus die cost is expected to be halved by reducing pad pitch from 0.16 to 0.11 mm (0.0062 to 0.0045 in).

Several key requirements for the successful bonding of such devices include

- Higher bond placement accuracy with smaller and consistent bond imprints capable of location and bonding on fine-pitch lands.
- Stable low-loop wire profiles that have minimal sagging or deflection over longer spans that can, when appropriate, withstand mold sweep (i.e, the forces exerted by the flowing encapsulation resin).
- Wire layout improvement with respect to the lead and bonding pad in order to help avoid interference between the bonding tool and adjacent (previously terminated) wire.

■ Real-time process monitoring and control in order to achieve higher wire-bonding/packaging yields.

Probably the biggest disadvantage of using this technique in MCMs is that the need to attach the die to the MCM substrate prior to wire bonding complicates thermal management. Heat generated by the die must then be initially conducted through the die-attach adhesive to the substrate and from there to the ultimate heat sink. However, most MCM substrates are poor conductors of heat.

Some substrates also have coefficients of thermal expansion (CTEs) that are sufficiently different from that of the bare die (silicon) that there can be potential thermal stress problems. Thus wire bonding is generally best suited for use in MCMs containing a few low-power integrated circuits.

4.2.5 Processing Considerations[4]

In so-called shrunk chips, bonding areas that are reduced from 120 to 80 μm (0.005 to 0.003 in) impose a new set of demands on the accuracy of wire bonders. In fact, it is envisioned that in a few years, 55-μm (0.002-in) bonding pads will be used with wire that is 12 μm (0.0005 in) in diameter.

4.2.5.1 Wire-Bonding Accuracy. Fortunately, recent advances in wire bonders have improved their accuracy to approximately 5 to 10 μm (0.0002 to 0.0004 in). These new wire bonders feature linear xy motors and frictionless bonding heads with precision synchronization of x-, y-, and z-axis movement. The mapping of xy table inaccuracy against a known reference and the use of software to correct inaccuracies further enhance system performance.

Software can provide features such as autocentering of the ball on the pad during the "teach" mode and can eliminate aim error by the operator. Better control of the bond-head touchdown and force and digitally controlled electronic "flame-off" (EFO) systems have significantly reduced "ball squash" variations. Because of this, reasonably good yields can be obtained with bonding gold wire that is 25 μm (0.001 in) in diameter on pads that are on a 120-μm (0.005-in) pitch. However, unlike the use of mass bonding techniques, individual wire-bonding yield is directly proportional to the number of wires being terminated. Thus wire bonding sophisticated high-I/O integrated circuits in MCMs can be a significant processing challenge.

4.2.5.2 Process Control. For MCM wire bonding to have a reasonable yield, some form of in-process quality monitoring is essential. For this purpose, most wire bonders are equipped with wirebond monitoring systems that employ a small current to perform continuity checks and to detect nonsticking conditions and broken wires.

In more advanced wire bonders, bonding process analyzers are used to monitor real-time force and power at the point of bonding. Such machines automatically shut down if these parameters are outside the preprogrammed control window. Such closed-loop process monitoring helps to ensure the uniformity and quality of each wire bond.

4.3 Tape Automated Bonding[9]

The continuing trend toward increasing the complexity of an integrated circuit die to its ultimate limit by maximizing the number of circuit elements and putting as many interconnections as possible on the die where they cost the least is creating a cost/density gap that conventional wire-bonding technology has difficulty meeting. The use of smaller die feature sizes and the resulting increase in I/O terminals have created further pressures on MCM packaging that can be satisfied by the use of a cost-effective, high-speed/high-density packaging technology such as tape automated bonding (TAB).

4.3.1 Advantages

The use of advanced TAB technology provides MCM packaging engineers with options that can possibly enhance the cost-effectiveness and performance of the end product being developed. The following reflect some of the reasons for this.

4.3.1.1 Density. TAB die-bonding patterns can be up to one-half the size and pitch of those associated with wire bonding, i.e., 0.1-mm (0.004-in) pads on 0.2-mm (0.008-in) centers. Thus smaller die often can be used or more I/O terminals can be provided on the same die size; the packaged devices also will be significantly smaller using TAB.

4.3.1.2 Electrical Performance. As compared with wire bonding, TAB is characterized by shorter lead lengths and lower impedances, which can result in less propagation delay and smaller signal distortion. The rectangular beam leads of the TAB tape provide superior high-speed circuit electrical performance at operating speeds above 40 MHz.

Power and ground leads can be "fatter," thereby lowering the TAB interconnection's already low resistance. The use of TAB tape with two metal layers can further enhance electrical performance by providing a ground plane that is especially useful for controlled-impedance transmission-line applications.

4.3.1.3 Reliability. The die-bonding pad areas on each TAB device are sealed by a thin-film metallization. This, plus the use of "bumped" dice, provides a high degree of protection against contamination from moisture and chemicals to achieve longer die life and improved end-product reliability.

4.3.1.4 Productivity. Through the use of "gang" or "mass" bonding, TAB provides a higher assembly throughput. Also, by reducing the number of terminations between the integrated circuit die and interconnecting substrate from three to two (for wire bonding), TAB can significantly reduce "first pass" yield.

TAB eliminates the integrated circuit production problem of "lead wash" in bare-die assembly processes involving cleaning and coating high-lead-count devices, wherein wire bond leads tend to be moved so as to touch (short) adjacent wires.

4.3.1.5 Automation. TAB's use of reel-to-reel or reel-to-carrier principles makes it highly suitable for integration into a manufacturing facility that emphasizes the use of automation.

4.3.1.6 Low Profile. TAB can provide a packaging profile that is as low as 0.08 mm (0.032 in) or less because it does not have to contend with the strain-relief "service" loop associated with wire bonding.

4.3.1.7 Testing and Burn-In. TAB devices, usually individually placed (singulated) in carriers after inner-lead bonding, can be tested and burned in prior to excising the die for next-level assembly. Thus, when required, more reliable devices can be attached to the interconnecting substrate. However, the use of the TAB carrier does eliminate further reel-to-reel processing.

4.3.1.8 Thermal Management. In some applications, TAB provides another thermal management option over wire bonding through the use of the increased mass/conductivity of the copper TAB leads and ground planes.

4.3.2 Disadvantages

The use of tape automated bonding is not without its disadvantages. Thus the following considerations also must be taken into account.

4.3.2.1 Equipment and Tooling. A significant capital investment is required to set up a TAB production facility and for personnel training. Also, equipment availability is limited to a small number of suppliers that are located throughout the world, and each TAB product requires new tooling. Conversely, many companies have extensive experience in wire bonding and have the necessary equipment in place for MCM packaging.

4.3.2.2 Die Availability. Semiconductor manufacturers are sometimes unwilling to invest the necessary resources to accommodate an unpackaged device TAB market. They are also generally not prepared to supply the special metallization and assembly features associated with the use of "bumped" dice. However, as TAB and MCMs gain in use, bare-die availability is increasing.

4.3.2.3 Planarity. To achieve successful TAB gang bonding with "hard" metallurgical systems, very tight planarity must be maintained consistently so that the large forces involved are distributed evenly to each bonding site. However, single-point TAB bonding can be used to overcome this problem.

Also, to dissipate heat properly, solid contact is generally required between the TAB-bonded die and the MCM substrate, acting as a heat sink. This is particularly critical with large silicon dice, which are more sensitive to temperature and thermal management.

4.3.2.4 Handling. Blank etched TAB tape must be handled with care to avoid mechanical displacement of the delicate leads. If care is not taken, stress problems can occur whenever silicon dice are in contact with other materials that have a different coefficient of thermal expansion.

4.3.2.5 Cost-Effectiveness. All things considered, TAB is presently an expensive technology with costs that are often difficult to quantify unless all the device and assembly-level cost savings are measured.

4.3.3 TAB Process Overview

TAB is an electronic integrated circuit die "fine pitch" packaging technology that uses fine-line conductor patterns on a flexible printed circuit or on bare copper. The most common TAB construction is a tape carrier/interconnect product that has special features to facilitate reel-to-reel processing (see Fig. 4.5).

The tape used is similar to photographic film. Many applications use a two-layer (copper-polyimide) or three-layer (copper-adhesive-polyimide) combination. The tapes come in standard widths ranging from 8 to 70 mm (0.315 to 2.756 in).

Unlike conventional flexible printed circuits, TAB tapes have precision sprocket holes along their edges. This provides them with a "movie film" feature to accommodate the reel-to-reel processing.

An opening, appropriately called a *window,* is formed near the center of the conductor array in the dielectric base film if one is present. (One-layer TAB tape has no dielectric base.) The window permits the etched conductor leads to extend over the opening to create the essential beam-type interconnect array.

A process unique to TAB, known as "bumping," is performed to provide a raised surface at the die-bonding sites. The bump can be formed either on the semiconductor wafer or on the tape carrier. The integrated circuit wafer, with or without bumps, is scribed or sawed to separate the individual dice. In the initial bonding process, the TAB tape unwinds from one reel and is taken up by another.

A die is selected and positioned under the window in the tape. The chip-to-tape connections are accomplished using an inner-lead bonding (ILB) machining. The ILB machine precisely aligns the patterned tape to the die and then descends to the die. The ILB tool mass "gang" bonds the TAB tape leads to the die by either a thermocompression or solder/eutectic technique. This results in having a sprocket-driven tape with bonded die that can be mounted directly onto a printed board or readied for use as a packaged integrated circuit component.

After the plating busses have been disconnected from the individual leads, testing of the bonded die can be performed while it is still on the TAB tape. This affords the opportunity to remove poorly bonded dice from the TAB tape so that they do not proceed further along the assembly process, thus enhancing the yield and reliability of the end product.

The bonded die is then usually protected by applying a "glob" of organic potting compound. To perform the final bonding of the tape to the printed board, an outer-lead bonding (OLB) machine is used. OLB requires that the TAB interconnection area be "blanked" or excised from the tape.

The excised TAB device is bonded to the surface of the printed board by aligning the TAB outer-lead frame with corresponding sites on the land pattern and then applying energy. The OLB is usually a

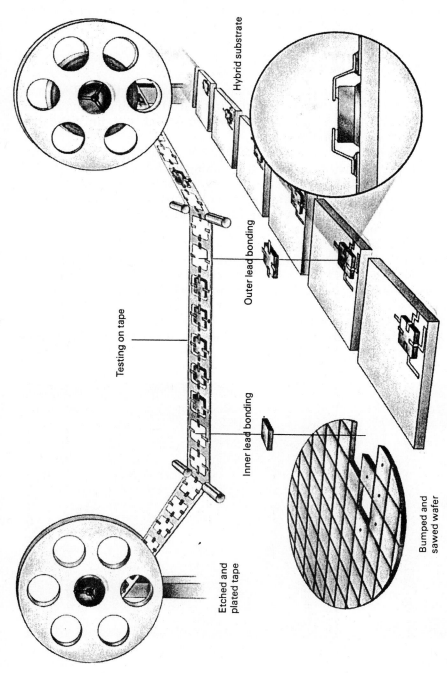

Figure 4.5. Typical "bumped" wafer TAB processing (Farco).

Hybrid substrate

Outer lead bonding

Testing on tape

Inner lead bonding

Etched and plated tape

Bumped and sawed wafer

65

gang or single-point (one-lead-at-a-time) thermocompression or reflow soldering operation.

4.3.4   TAB Tape Carriers[10]

The tape carrier provides three important functions to the TAB production process. It carries dice after inner-lead bonding, provides the interconnection leads, and allows for testing and burn-in of the dice while they are still on the tape.

In addition to providing adequate physical support for the dice, the tape carrier must be capable of maintaining critical die location during repeated movements through a variety of sprocketed transport production equipment. In addition, the tape must provide a circuit pattern, usually etched copper foil, with lands to accommodate probes for the testing and burn-in process.

Depending primarily on the tape width and die size, a wide range of lead I/O counts can be provided that vary from a very few to well over 200 (see Fig. 4.6). In general, the three most commonly used basic types of TAB tape carrier constructions are single-layer, two-layer, and three-layer.

Each TAB tape construction offers certain advantages over the others, and each construction has its limitations. It remains for the design-

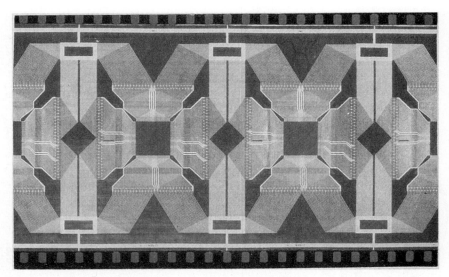

Figure 4.6. A 70-mm TAB tape with 224 leads [0.08 mm (0.003 in) wide on 0.15-mm (0.006-in) centers].[10]

er to choose the construction (and materials) most suited to a specific application to obtain optimal results. An understanding of the choices available in base materials, conductors, plating, adhesives, and construction will help the designer to choose wisely.

4.3.4.1 TAB Tape Materials.[11] Tape materials and the metallurgy of the bonding site are critical to the overall reliability of the TAB assembly. Thus projects are being undertaken to further improve tape materials and bump metallurgies to afford maximal bond reliability and product manufacturability. Attempts are also being made to more tightly control the material systems so that process repeatability is optimized.

Tape Base Dielectric. By far the most widely used TAB tape base dielectric material is polyimide film. Some applications use the less expensive polyester and epoxy-glass dielectrics. However, polyimide is preferred because it has a proven dimensional stability, it is not flammable, it withstands high temperatures, it has controllable shrinkage, it resists chemicals well, and it has excellent electrical properties.

Polyimide film is usually used in a 0.05-mm (0.002-in) thickness for two-layer TAB tape constructions where it must be etched and in a 0.125-mm (0.005-in) thickness for three-layer constructions because of its mechanical strength and controlled-environment dimensional stability.

The potential disadvantages of using polyimide film, in addition to cost, include the possibility of pinholing and dimensional instability when the material is temperature- and humidity-stressed. Also, future high-speed/controlled-impedance applications may be better for new low-dielectric-constant materials that are being developed for stripline and microstrip configurations.

Copper Foil. Although some work has been done with materials such as Kovar, aluminum, and additively plated copper, copper foil is by far the most commonly used TAB tape conductor. It is used in both the rolled and electrodeposited types, each of which has distinct characteristics which the user may or may not want. (Oxygen-free copper is of interest to TAB users who expect the best possible electrical conduction at higher frequencies.)

The significant characteristic produced in copper by the rolling operation is the very smooth surface with a pronounced "horizontal" grain structure. This provides the user with a dense, ductile, pinhole-free metal that allows maximum control in imaging and etching and has a uniform resistivity.

Rolled annealed copper foil has been used in the manufacture of high-reliability circuits for many years and is the most common choice for single-layer TAB constructions. Its uniformity in thickness and smooth surfaces are desirable when making "bumped" tape by a subtractive process.

The version of electrodeposited (ED) copper foil used widely in making printed wiring boards also can be used to make three-layer TAB constructions. ED copper foil has a marked "vertical" grain structure that is more likely to allow oxidation to penetrate deeply into the foil than is the horizontal grain of the rolled copper. Pinholes are also more likely to appear in thin ED copper foil than in rolled copper, and the vertical grain boundaries can become stress concentration points for fractures.

Finishes.   Typical finishes for TAB tape products are either solder, immersion tin, or gold. In the case of solder and gold, the tapes must be electrically bussed so that electroplating can be done, and of course, the electroplating must be done in a continuous reel-to-reel manner.

Immersion tin also has been a very successful metallurgy for TAB tape. In any case, the substrate materials used must be capable of withstanding the plating or chemical operations involved without exhibiting delamination or contamination of any kind.

Adhesives.   In any three-layer TAB tape, the adhesive is a critical element. It must bond the conductor to the base dielectric material without deterioration through all the solvents and chemical baths involved in stripping of photoresist, plating, and cleaning.

The major adhesive groups used in the manufacture of TAB tape are acrylic, epoxy-amide, phenolic butyral, and polyester. The acrylics and epoxy-amides have good insulation resistance but have a rather high moisture absorption and lower than desired temperature resistance. Phenolic butyrals are extremely low in moisture absorption, and because they are thermosetting in nature, they resist softening at bonding temperatures. The polyesters are generally lower in desirable qualities than the others, but they serve well when used with polyester TAB tape carrier materials.

Polyimide shows promise as a TAB tape adhesive because of its very high temperature capabilities. Compared with the other adhesives used for TAB tape, polyimide is the only adhesive that can withstand 350°C for 10 minutes and remain dimensionally stable and retain its mechanical properties. Although polyimide is more costly than the others, its use is being evaluated for high-temperature TAB usage.

4.3.4.2 Single-Layer Construction.   The single-layer ("all-copper") TAB tape construction consists of a copper tape into which the interconnection pattern and support structure have been etched. A rolled or electrodeposited copper foil either 0.07 or 0.005 mm (0.0028 or 0.002 in) thick is normally used for this product.

The copper foil is coated with photoresist in a continuous processing operation (on one or both sides), imaged, and etched by the processes normally used in the manufacture of printed wiring boards. However, the etching is a much more difficult task than is usually encountered because of the fine lines involved and because the TAB beams are unsupported. Typically, beam widths of 0.075 mm (0.003 in) are utilized that also require careful handling and inspection.

Single-layer tape is the least expensive TAB construction and can be used with standard dice if the tape is bumped. Its main disadvantage is that all the leads are electrically interconnected by the supporting structure, thus prohibiting device testing or burn-in while on the tape.

4.3.4.3 Two-Layer Construction. Two-layer TAB tape construction makes use of a base dielectric material, usually polyimide, to support the metal conductive pattern. The most common combination of materials for this type of structure is obtained either by casting a polyimide film on copper foil (usually of the same thickness used in single-layer tape) or by depositing copper directly onto the polyimide film.

The two-layer tape is manufactured in a manner that is similar to that for the single-layer construction but with the added steps needed for etching the base dielectric material. In addition, careful indexing between the conductive pattern and the base dielectric material is required, as difficult as this may be.

Since the features in the polyimide are formed by chemical etching, a support ring can be left inside the window containing the free-standing TAB beams. Use of this support ring is especially necessary for high-lead-count devices.

A further advantage of using two-layer TAB tape as compared with the three-layer construction is that no adhesive is used between the conductive and dielectric materials. This means that if part of the dielectric base material structure, such as the support ring, is left in the end product, no organic epoxy or acrylic material will be present.

Proponents of the additive two-layer TAB tape construction process claim that it has some significant advantages over both the subtractive/copper foil two-layer and three-layer types. First, lead shape can be closely controlled, instead of having the undercut sidewalls associated with subtractive etching processes. Also, the additive process permits the fabrication of high-aspect-ratio leads, i.e., higher than they are wide, which permits increased current-carrying capabilities without compromising lead spacing.

4.3.4.4 Three-Layer Construction. Three-layer TAB tape construction is the original TAB technique that has been utilized since the

1970s. In this construction, an adhesive-coated base dielectric material, usually polyimide, is first mechanically punched and sprocketed. Copper foil is then laminated to the film/adhesive combination. Lastly, the tape is imaged and etched.

Reported advantages of using the three-layer tape include having a stronger bond strength between the base dielectric material and the copper foil, good insulation resistance, and low moisture absorption as a consequence of using the adhesive layer. Owing to the expense of the hard-tooled punching equipment, three-layer tape is generally used only in the 35- and 75-mm widths.

4.3.4.5 "Multilayer" Construction.   Multilayer tape is an extension of TAB technology that allows for multiple die attachment to a single substrate for increased packaging density. It consists of a base dielectric material, usually polyimide, with a conductive layer on both its sides which are connected by means of vias. (*Note:* In printed circuit board terminology, use of the word *multilayer* in this regard is somewhat of a misnomer; *double-sided* would perhaps be a better term to use.)

Multilayer TAB tape is manufactured using a process that produces an "adhesiveless" metal-dielectric-metal construction. Since this process does not use an adhesive in the manner that three-layer tape does, vias interconnecting the conductive layers can be formed by chemical processing rather than by mechanical means. Because the conductor-via patterns are photoimaged onto the tape, the registration of the layer is superior to that achievable by mechanical processes.

Dice are mounted directly to the tape and coated with a polymer for protection. Then the tape is bonded to a stiffener in order to increase rigidity. In this respect, multilayer tape differs from the other constructions, since most TAB applications are used in conjunction with other kinds of packaging.

A patented "multiple-level" TAB tape construction (Fig. 4.7) is also available for multiple die attachment by having from two to four tapes assembled back-to-back onto a middle layer of film. The top tape has the bonding land patterns; the bottom tape(s) provides a conductive pattern to facilitate die interconnections. The center film's thickness is dimensioned to control die seating and thermal requirements.

Interconnections between conductive layers are accomplished by single-point bonding of cantilevered leads through punched holes. Thus the entire process is accomplished without plated through holes.

4.3.4.6 Area-Array Tapes.   As die lead counts begin to increase, it is inevitable that I/O pads within the perimeter of the die will be used to supplement those traditionally used on its periphery. To accommodate

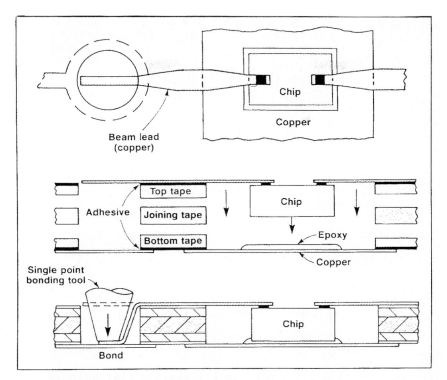

Figure 4.7. "Multiple-level" TAB tape construction.[8]

this trend, TAB technologists have devised a scheme called *area-array TAB* (Fig. 4.8).

A single- or two-layer TAB tape that interconnects to two peripheral rows of bonding pads fits this need. However, more generally, an area-array tape consists of multiple layers of metal sandwiched between layers of dielectric material.

4.3.5 "Bumping"[12]

In addition to making a choice of the TAB tape construction, the TAB user must determine what type of "bumping" is most appropriate for the application. "Bumping" refers to the addition of thick metal bumps to either the bonding pad sites of the individual dice while they are still together on the integrated-circuit fabrication wafer or to the bonding sites on the land pattern of the TAB tape.

Sometimes called *BTAB*, this is done to facilitate the inner-lead bonding process.

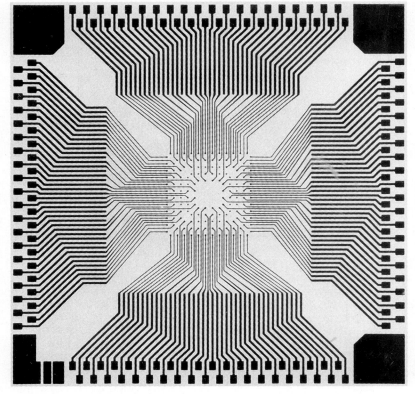

Figure 4.8. Area-array structure.[10]

4.3.5.1 Wafer "Bumping." "Bumping" of the die bonding sites on a wafer requires the fabrication of bonding pads that are raised above the planar surface of the wafer. These bumps facilitate the inner-lead bonding without having the TAB tape touching the surface of the die.

The initial stage of the "bumped" wafer preparation is much the same as that for wire-bonded dice. A pinhole-free silicon nitride passivation layer (or silicon dioxide or polyimide in some cases) is deposited at low temperatures. The passivation is selectively removed to expose a good portion of the aluminum bonding pads.

At this point in the preparation of the TAB wafer, a barrier metal (such as titanium-tungsten) is deposited over the exposed aluminum and over the passivation on the periphery of the pad. These steps, plus the addition of 25-μm-high (0.001-in-high) gold (or sometimes copper) bumps and subsequent electroplating, hermetically seal the chip to help ensure the reliability of the inner-lead bonding termination.

The lack of commercially available wafers or dice in low quantities, reduced yield, and the additional (15 to 20 percent) cost are often cited as disadvantages associated with the use of TAB technology.

However, the "bumping" technology is relatively straightforward, and good wafer "bumping" equipment is becoming readily available for barrier-metal deposition and bump plating for both production and laboratory applications.

4.3.5.2 Tape "Bumping" (BTAB). There are a few different ways to create the desired inner-lead bonding bump on the TAB tape. The most common method is to subtractively etch a relatively thick copper foil on the tape so as to expose the bumps in the land-pattern areas. This approach suffers from variations in the etching process and from misregistration owing to the fact that at least two photolithic stages are used in the BTAB manufacture.

Another approach to achieving a testable "bumped" TAB tape system uses semiadditive fabrication techniques that overcome most of the disadvantages of the subtractive etching method. This approach starts with a relatively thin foil to which the bump is added by electrodeposition. Also, by making the bump from a more compliant material, one of the major difficulties of BTAB systems, bond reliability, is overcome.

A radically different method first forms the bumps on a substrate by means of gold plating. Then the bumps are transferred from the substrate onto each corresponding land-pattern bonding site. The bump transfer is carried out by means of pressure application under elevated temperature.

4.3.6 Initial Assembly[12,13]

The initial TAB assembly processing begins with inner-lead bonding (ILB). As applicable, ILB is followed by burn-in, testing, and encapsulation or molding of the attached semiconductor die.

4.3.6.1 Inner-Lead Bonding. ILB is the technique for connecting the inner portion of the TAB tape leads to the die. The type of bond produced depends primarily on the metallurgies at the tape-die interface and the ILB method employed.

Common combinations are gold to gold, gold to tin, and copper to copper. Each ILB combination offers different advantages (low cost, ease of processing, low bonding force, etc.) that must be matched with each particular application. For example, solder bumps offer a low-cost/low-bonding-force option but cannot be spaced as tightly as gold bumps because of the needed volume of solder.

Thermocompression Bonding.   Thermocompression ILB is a popular TAB assembly technique. A diamond- or synthetic diamond–tipped steady-state thermode is the most widely used bonding tool for the thermocompression mass-bonding technique. The diamond has been chosen because of its heat uniformity. The system produces a very strong and reliable bond in approximately 200 to 250 ms.

The metallurgy generally consists of electroless gold on copper bumps joined to bare-copper leads. A second metallurgy that is rapidly increasing in use is the joining of gold-plated leads to gold bumps.

The advantage of thermocompression technology is the ability to join similar metals. This results in excellent bonds because the possibility of intermetallics is eliminated. The joining process is basically simple and permits a fairly wide range of bonding schedules.

Furthermore, when gold is used, the total metallurgy system is inert and unaffected by the environment. (This is not true with all-copper metallurgies. Thus they must be overmolded or protected due to copper's oxidizing and corrosive properties in an open environment.)

The disadvantages include the relatively high bonding temperature and pressure required, the latter of which may damage the integrated circuit die if proper bump design is not employed. Another disadvantage is that the gold on the TAB leads requires electroplating. Therefore, the lead fingers initially must be electrically interconnected, and a means must be provided for their separation prior to electrical testing.

Eutectic Bonding.   Eutectic bonding normally requires a gold-tin eutectic or solder configuration of some sort. The gold-tin eutectic ILB is very often done with a pulsed thermode rather than with a constantly heated thermode, as is used for thermocompression bonding.

The gold-tin eutectic occurs at a lower temperature than does the gold-to-gold thermocompression bond. Although the bond itself is usually considered to have a less reliable metallurgy, it has the advantage of requiring less heating of the die and can be done with lower applied pressure.

Reflow Soldering.   Solder "bumped" die with electroless tin-plated TAB tape have been used successfully for inner-lead bonding. In these reflow soldering applications, the ILB has primarily been accomplished using a pulse-tip thermode.

Because of the molten solder interface during the bonding cycle, bonding tool and die planarity considerations are not major concerns. Unfortunately, the bonding time cycle for this method is approximately 4 to 6 s, considerably longer than that for the thermocompression ILB technique.

It is recommended that the solder "bumped" die have a pedestal beneath the solder. The pedestal keeps the beams from coming into contact with the die surface in order to avoid cracking of the passivation during the bonding operation. An excellent metallurgy for the pedestal is a chrome–copper sputtered layer for adhesion and an electroplated copper to define the pedestal.

The assembly of solder-plated TAB tape to "bumped" die has not been done successfully because of the inadequate control of the sagging reflowed solder on the bottom portion of the ILB beam during mass bonding. Thus the sagging solder can touch the edge of the die and cause short circuits.

The solder used for ILB reflow soldering may be any of the commonly used reflow bonding solders. However, consideration must be given to the outer-lead bonding (OLB) method when selecting the appropriate solder. Most users choose an ILB solder that has a higher melting point than required for the OLB operation. A solder flux is typically used for all solder reflow operations, and it should be applied to the die prior to the solder reflow process.

Reflow/Thermocompression Bonding. The combination of reflow soldering and thermocompression bonding has been a very popular ILB method to date. It uses electroless tin-plated TAB tape and gold "bumped" dice. The resulting bond is achieved most successfully using a heated steady-state thermode.

Pulsed-tip thermodes have been used, but the prolonged heating during a pulsed-reflow operation causes heating of the surfaces away from the bonding area. Also, heating of nonreflowed electroless tin in an open environment causes tin oxides to be generated that later cause problems with the outer-lead bonding operation. However, there have been few problems associated with using the pulsed-tip thermode when the tin has been reflowed prior to bonding.

This combination bonding system is an excellent ILB technique when all the parameters are properly controlled and the end product is not placed in a humid environment without proper protection from corrosion.

Single-Point Bonding. Mass ("gang") bonding has been the traditional method for implementing the ILB techniques described above. This has been primarily because of the higher throughput achieved by bonding all the TAB tape leads simultaneously. Unfortunately, with gang bonding, flatness of the bonding surfaces is critical.

The need for increased planarity and pressure has created applications that are better suited to single-point ILB, especially when using larger dice and higher lead counts. Single-point bonding is a "one at a time" process that uses a small, wedgelike tool. It can be employed equally well for making both inner-lead (ILB) and outer-lead (OLB) terminations.

Features that are unique to single-point bonders include

- The height of each lead is measured during bonding in order to eliminate the need for having a high degree of planarity between the bonding tool and the integrated circuit die.
- A consistent force is applied to each lead.
- Individual leads can be reworked.
- A variety of ILB and OLB configurations can be terminated readily by the same machine without significant tooling modifications.

4.3.6.2 Testing and Burn-In. Testing and burn-in are done electrically by contacting test lands on the TAB tape. The test lands are produced by the same procedure used to define the leads on the tape.

Testing can be performed with the tape in a reel-to-reel mode or by utilizing "slide carriers" that hold one tape site and which are compatible with either socket or common test handlers. However, TAB users generally acknowledge that burn-in can only be done in a slide carrier and socket configuration.

4.3.6.3 Die Protection.[11] One of the more recent developments in TAB involves encapsulating (or molding) the die for environmental protection. This protection can be provided on automatic reel-to-reel machines.

General practice is to apply a liquid encapsulant to the active circuit side of the die and then cure the material. Encapsulants include epoxies, silicones, and polyimides.

Criteria for selecting the encapsulant are dictated by the specific application, especially with respect to solvent resistance, cure schedule, ease of dispensing, mechanical properties, and level of ionic contaminants. For low-volume production, the encapsulation can be done semiautomatically using a positive-displacement dispenser that controls the volume of material applied. Fully automated encapsulating machines are also available that are typically robot-driven dispensers and integrated curing ovens.

4.3.7 Final Assembly[10,12]

The final TAB assembly processes are excise and form, followed by outer-lead bonding.

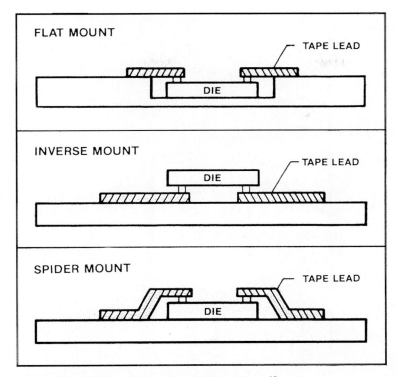

Figure 4.9. TAB lead/mounting configurations.[10]

4.3.7.1 Excising and Lead Forming. *Excising* refers to the punching out (excising) of the TAB device from the TAB tape or TAB carrier. The unsupported TAB leads can then be bent (formed) or left straight (see Fig. 4.9). In conventional TAB, the leads are formed into a compliant "gullwing" shape so that they can withstand thermal and mechanical stresses.

4.3.7.2 Outer-Lead Bonding. Outer-lead bonding (OLB) is typically done using a gang or single-point bonder (see Fig. 4.10). As with inner-lead bonding, OLB can be done by reflow soldering, thermocompression, or thermosonic bonding, depending on the metallurgical system involved. (Single-point OLB is also done with ultrasonic bonding.)

OLB equipment is often customized because of the wide variety of substrates involved. However, for a given class of substrates, only the excising tool, thermode, lead-forming tool (when required), and work fixtures need to be customized.

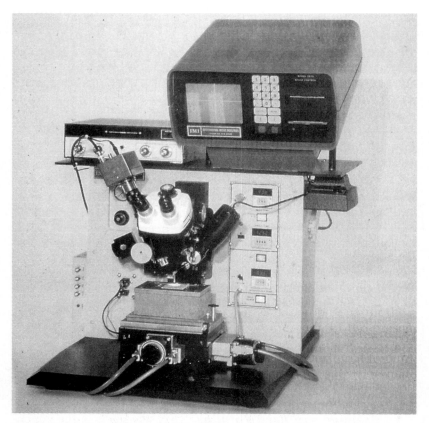

Figure 4.10. Single-point outer-lead bonder.[10]

4.4 Flip-Chip Technology[14,15]

Conventional flip-chip technology employs soldering directly between the integrated circuit die "face" and the interconnecting substrate. Thus it is often also referred to as *face bonding, controlled-collapse soldering,* or *controlled-collapse chip connection* (C-4).

Since flip-chip bonding does not use bonding wires or beam leads to land patterns outside the die's perimeter, it can be used to achieve the highest ratio of active silicon surface to MCM substrate area. Thus interconnection conductor lengths can be minimized and circuit performance maximized. It also can be used to achieve a very high number of fine-pitch I/O terminations per chip. For example, the 6.5 × 6.5 mm (0.256 × 0.256 in) integrated circuit die

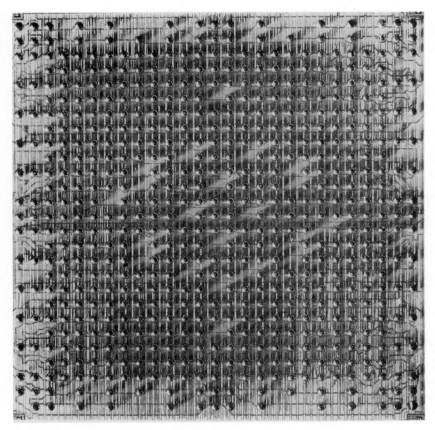

Figure 4.11. A 549-I/O bipolar-logic flip chip.[15]

in Fig. 4.11 has 549 flip-chip "bumped" I/O pads on 0.25-mm (0.010-in) centers.

The original flip-chip concept employed small, solder-coated copper balls sandwiched between the chip termination lands and the appropriate lands on the interconnecting substrate. The resulting solder joints were made when the unit was exposed to an elevated temperature. However, the handling and placement of the small-diameter balls was extremely difficult, and the operation was costly.

In a more-advanced concept, a raised metallic bump or lump, usually solder, is provided on the chip termination land. This is normally done on all lands of all the chips while they are still in the large-wafer form. The individual chip is then aligned to the appropriate circuitry on the substrate and bonded in place using reflow soldering techniques. In this way, the interconnection bonds between the chip and the substrate are made simultaneously, thus reducing fabrication costs.

4.4.1 Advantages

The use of flip-chip technology has associated with it the advantages already enumerated that are associated with packaging circuits with bare chips instead of with packaged devices. In addition, the primary advantages of using flip-chip technology and face-bonded die in MCMs as opposed to using wire bonding or TAB include

- Best circuit performance because of having the shortest interconnect distances
- Highest packaging density with the most efficient use of the substrate area
- Inherently better reliability by simplifying the path between the chip and the substrate

4.4.2 Disadvantages

The use of flip-chip technology also has associated with it the disadvantages already enumerated that are associated with packaging circuits with bare chips instead of with packaged devices. In addition, the primary disadvantages of using flip-chip technology and face-bonded die in MCMs as opposed to using wire bonding or TAB include

- The need for highly specialized assembly processing
- The inability to visually inspect all the assembled chip
- The limited availability of specially designed area I/O chips
- Difficult flux removal
- Potential thermal management complications
- The inability to pretest/burn in the chip prior to assembly

4.4.3 Manufacturing Flip Chips

The manufacturing steps for conventional integrated circuits and flip chips are similar through most of the processing steps until they reach the passivation step. Integrated circuits are normally passivated, i.e.,

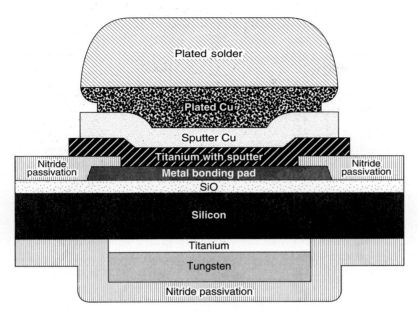

Figure 4.12. Cross section of a typical solder bump.[16]

coated with a protective silicon nitride layer, and then readied for testing and encapsulation. Flip chips require more processing that includes an additional coating, backside marking, and solder bump-formation steps (see Fig. 4.12).

4.4.3.1 Backside Marking. Backside part numbers and orientation markings can be applied to nitride-coated silicon wafers by sputtering on a pattern of titanium tungsten. The markings also can be coated with a thin layer of silicon nitride to protect them and to enhance their contrast with the underlying silicon.

4.4.3.2 Bump Formation. The bumps, which are composed of a series of metal layers, are formed over the integrated circuit aluminum bonding I/O pads. In a typical application, a layer of titanium is first sputtered over the I/O pads to enhance bump adhesion.

This is generally followed by a sputtered copper layer that acts as a transition layer for the solder. This layer is etched to form a pedestal on which the solder bump rests. The pedestal shape distributes bump stress so that the adjacent silicon nitride protective coating does not crack.

Another layer of electroplated copper is added, and this is followed by an electroplated layer of tin-lead solder. Finally, the "bumped" wafers are heated to permit solder reflow. The end result is the formation of controlled-height solder bumps over each I/O bonding pad.

4.4.4 MCM Substrate Preparation

The MCM substrate must be prepared as shown in Fig. 4.13 prior to mounting of the flip chip. In a typical process, the MCM substrate and its conductive pattern are first precleaned. Next, a solder paste is stenciled onto the substrate's land pattern at locations that correspond to the locations of the solder bumps on the flip chip.

It is important to deposit the proper amount of solder paste on the lands. Too much solder paste can cause bridging during reflow, while too little will compromise the termination.

It is often recommended that the solder paste should contain a mildly activated rosin-based flux (RMA) and 45- to 75-µm-diameter spherical particles of 10% tin, 88% lead, and 2% silver alloy.

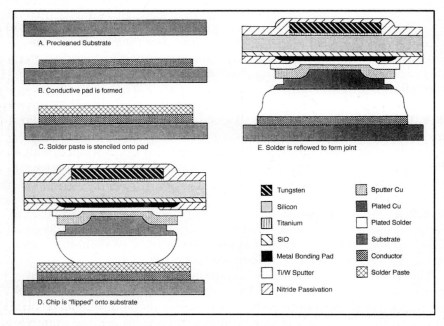

Figure 4.13. Typical flip-chip assembly process.[14]

4.4.5 Flip-Chip Mounting

Flip chips can be mounted on the MCM substrate either manually or automatically. This operation is often the gating activity in the entire assembly process.

The flip chips are usually supplied by the integrated circuit manufacturer in waffle packs. They also have some sort of identification marking and mounting orientation designators.

If the assembly is being done manually, the operator simply removes the individual die from the waffle pack using a vacuum pencil. Each die is then positioned over its MCM substrate land pattern, which was previously covered with a tacky solder paste flux. The solder paste will hold the chip in place until the soldering reflow operation.

If the assembly process is automated, there are several "pick and place" machine options. If the bare dice are provided in precision waffle packs, the assembly machine can either remove the individual dice and place them directly onto the MCM substrate or they can be transferred automatically to a holder prior to final component mounting.

Whether the dice are placed manually or automatically, their positioning with respect to their land patterns may be off by as much as slightly less than one-half the pad pitch. This is so because the surface tension created during the reflow soldering process will be sufficient to force the proper alignment between flip-chip pads and MCM substrate lands.

4.4.6 Reflow Soldering

Once all the dice are in place, the entire MCM assembly is placed in an oven to drive off any flux residues. Then the MCM assembly can move through an infrared reflow soldering oven within an inert nitrogen atmosphere.

The thermal profile of the reflow soldering oven will vary depending on the equipment being used. The critical factors are the magnitude of the peak temperature and the duration of time the MCM assembly is exposed to it in the reflow soldering oven. If solder reflow has been accomplished correctly, the flip-chip solder joints will be columnar, smooth, and shiny.

The adhesion of the solder bump can then be determined quantitatively using a shear tester. Good adhesion is indicated if the shear strength exceeds 0.8 N per bump.

4.4.7   Solderless Flip Chip[16,17]

As microelectronic devices continue to move toward miniaturization, the need for flip-chip devices becomes more apparent. Also apparent is the need for new and innovative technologies for the manufacture of flip-chip assemblies that can improve flexibility and reliability yet offer lower manufacturing costs than the traditional solder bump approach.

The use of solderless conductive polymers is being advanced for these applications. These new adhesives provide mechanical bonding and the electrical interconnection between the flip chip and the MCM substrate.

References

1. Gerald L. Ginsberg, Component Data Associates, Inc., "Advanced Electronic Packaging and Interconnection Technologies," *Electronic Packaging and Interconnection Handbook,* Chapter 10, Charles A. Harper (ed.), McGraw-Hill, New York, 1991.

2. E. Jan Vardaman and Lee H. Ng, TechSearch International and IBIS Associates, "A Cost/Performance Analysis of Multichip Module Interconnects," *Proceedings, International Symposium on Microelectronics,* October 1991, pp. 27–32.

3. Bill Blood and Allison Casey, Motorola, Inc., "Evaluating Multichip Module Packaging Technology," *ASIC Technology & News* (1st of 2 parts), July 1991, pp. 26–27.

4. Walter Nehls, ESEC SA, "Gold Wire Bonders for the Nineties," *Solid State Technology,* June 1991, pp. 59–62.

5. Gerald L. Ginsberg, Component Data Associates, Inc., "Chip and Wire Technology: The Ultimate in Surface Mounting," *Electronic Packaging and Production,* September 1985, pp. 78–82.

6. Claudio Meisser, ESEC SA, "Bonding Techniques for Plastic MCMs," *Semiconductor International,* October 1991, pp. 120–124.

7. *Hybrid Microcircuit Design Guide,* ISHM-1402/IPC-H-855, October 1982.

8. Hughes Aircraft Co., *Hybrid Repair Station,* SL 41487, March 1984.

9. Gerald L. Ginsberg, Component Data Associates, Inc., "TAB Enters Multichip Modules for the Next Step in High-Density Packaging," *Electronic Packaging and Production,* October 1989, pp. 64–68.

10. Philip W. Rima, International Micro Industries, "TAB Gains Momentum," *Connection Technology,* August 1987, pp. 28–32.

11. Howard W. Markstein, Western Editor, "TAB Rebounds as I/Os Increase," *Electronic Packaging and Production,* August 1986, pp. 31–33.

12. Paul Hoffman, Mesa Technology, "TAB Implementation and Trends," *Solid State Technology,* June 1988, pp. 85–88.

13. Jim Morris, Cross Technology, "An Introduction to Tape Automated Bonding (TAB) the Next Generation in High-Density Packaging," *Proceedings, International Electronic Packaging Conference,* October 1987, pp. 360–366.

14. Barbara Gibson, Cherry Semiconductor Corp., "Flip Chips: The Ultraminiature Surface Mount Solution," *Surface Mount Technology,* May 1990, pp. 23–25.

15. V. L. Gani, M. C. Graf, R. F. Rizzolo, and W. F. Washburn, "IBM Enterprise/9000 Type 9121 Model 320 Air-Cooled Processor Technology," *IBM Journal of Research and Development,* Vol. 35, No. 3, May 1991, pp. 342–351.

16. Frank W. Kuleza and Richard H. Estes, Epoxy Technology, Inc., "Solderless Flip Chip Technology," *Hybrid Circuit Technology,* February 1992.

17. Zymet, Inc., *Introducing Flip Chip Adhesives,* Product Information Bulletin, 1992.

5
Design Considerations[1,2]

Historically, interconnections between both active and passive electronic components have been dominated by the printed wiring board. This process has been characterized typically by a fully packaged integrated circuit (dual in-line, flat pack, PGA, etc.) mounted on a conventional printed wiring board (PWB). Increases in system speeds and system requirements forced designers to move from MSI to LSI to VLSI design rules, and individually packaged chips could no longer interconnect and communicate with the outside world efficiently. Hybrid packaging was developed to answer this need, using single or multiple chips mounted on a single substrate. Although both PWB and hybrid packaging technologies remain in wide use today, they provide only an active silicon-to-substrate efficiency of 10 to 15 percent. Multichip modules (MCMs) and the associated technology answer these design needs.

5.1 Design Tradeoffs

The electronics packaging engineer has several choices to make when considering MCM design and packaging. The success or failure of an MCM design depends on many interrelated considerations. Substrate materials, processing techniques, packaging method, and the module supplier will be selected on the basis of cost objectives, volume needs, electrical circuit performance goals, operating environment, and other factors. Following consideration of these issues and the selection of a technology, the design must be based on a specific set of design rules.

From an end-product use standpoint, the impact on the design by the following parameters should be considered:

- Equipment environmental conditions such as ambient temperature and heat generated by the components.
- Process allowances such as etch factor compensation for conductor widths, spacings, bonding site, fabrication, etc.
- Manufacturing limitations such as minimum etched features, minimum plating thickness, module shape and size, etc.
- Materials selection.
- If the module is to be repairable and maintainable, consideration must be given to chip density, the selection of coating materials, and placement for accessibility.
- Testing/fault-location requirements that might affect placement, conductor routing, connector contact assignments, etc.

5.2 Materials[1-3]

The primary concern with materials is the interrelationship of materials with each other within an MCM. Careful consideration should be given to the materials in a design to determine if the proposed design is prone to failure mechanisms. For instance, nonconforming materials can result in failure of the circuit as a result of one or more of the following conditions:

- Differences in thermal coefficients of expansion
- Ionic contamination
- Improper adhesion
- Intermetallic formation
- Galvanic corrosion

5.2.1 Substrates

The mechanical base and electrically insulating material used in MCM fabrication, the substrate material, affects the processes used in fabrication of the module, as well as the reliability of the final circuit. It must be compatible with the process used, as well as be compatible with the other materials in the MCM. Factors critical in selecting a sub-

Table 5.1. Substrate Materials[4]

Mechanical/Thermal/Electrical Properties (Typical Values)

Substrate	Young's modulus (Mpsi)	CTE (ppm/°C)	Thermal conductivity (W/m · K)	K (@ 1 MHz)	Dielectric strength (kV/cm)
Si	29	3.5	120	12.0	100
SiC	83	3.8	270	4.0	0.7
BeO	45	7.5	250	6.5	100
AlN	39	4.1	100–220	8.8	155
Al_2O_3	52	6.5	20	8.8	100

strate are materials compatibility, dielectric strength, thermal conductivity, surface finish, thermal coefficient of expansion, and camber. The substrate may form an integral part of the MCM package, or it may require properties compatible with other package materials.

Materials are chosen based on their compatibility with the particular process employed. Young's modulus is the most important mechanical property. Cured dielectric films used in the module fabrication process can exert compressive stresses on the substrate. Also, the substrate can exert a tensile stress on the dielectric film. Thermal properties are also important, since the coefficient of thermal expansion (CTE) should be close to that of the other parts of the MCM such as the silicon or GaAs die.

Substrate materials for MCMs include ceramics such as alumina, aluminum nitride, beryllia, silicon carbide, glass-ceramics, silicon, and glass. More exotic materials such as quartz, oxidized silicon, and sapphire are sometimes used for high-frequency applications. Also used on some occasions are FR-4 glass-epoxy and other printed wiring board materials, films, or composited materials.

Critical requirements placed on the substrate material for use in MCMs are the mechanical integrity and the thermal conductivity. For this reason, silicon and ceramics are the most often selected materials. Table 5.1 gives some typical mechanical, thermal, and electrical characteristics of commonly used substrate materials.

5.2.2 Conductive Materials

A large number of materials is used as conductive materials, depending on the process. Conductors are used for both signal lines and power distribution. Major factors that contribute to metal conductor choice for MCMs include

- Good corrosion-resistance properties
- Chemical inertness
- Low resistivity/high electrical conductivity
- Good adhesion to the substrate, dielectric, and other metals

The most common MCM circuit conductor materials are copper, gold, aluminum, nickel, silver, tungsten, molymanganese, and solder. Copper is ideal because it can be both sputtered and plated. Copper and aluminum are usually used for the primary conductor. Sputtered aluminum is used in several technologies, but conductivity is somewhat less than copper, line thickness is limited, and vias are usually staggered. Tungsten and molybdenum are common in cofired ceramic MCMs. Chromium and titanium are used for barrier or adhesion layers. Tin, lead, and tin-lead (solder) are used for surface attachment.

Nickel is used as diffusion barrier over thin-film copper conductors and is also useful for filled, stacked vias. Gold and silver are traditional thick-film materials; gold is often plated as metallization on the device termination leads. Palladium is useful for barrier or surface layers. Electrical conductivity is an important property in all cases. Adhesion and other process-compatible issues such as exposure to process chemicals or subsequent high temperatures are critical. Table 5.2 summarizes the advantages and disadvantages of some of these conductors.

Table 5.2. Metal Conductors in MCMs[4]

	Advantages	Disadvantages

Gold (Au)	Chemically inert
	Good corrosion resistance
	High electrical conductivity
		Poor adhesion to
		  polymer dielectrics
		Sputtering targets
		  are expensive

Copper (Cu)	High electrical conductivity
	Good solderability
	Inexpensive
	Can be electrolytically or
	  chemically plated
		Poor adhesion to
		  polymer dielectrics,
		  particularly polyimides
		May require barrier
		  or adhesion layers

Aluminum (Al)	Good adhesion to polymer
	  dielectrics
	Forms an inert native oxide
	Well understood by IC
	  processing engineers
		Lower conductivity
		  than Au or Cu

5.2.2.1 Thin-Film Metallizations. Normally, thin-film metallizations are gold or aluminum. The choice of the metallization depends on
the technology used for the MCM and also may be limited because of producibility problems. Gold is the primary thin-film material and is normally
deposited by vapor deposition, sputtering, or evaporation. Normally, the
deposited film is further electroplated to increase its conductivity. A final
thickness of from 0.0025 to 0.005 mm of gold is usually employed.

Other conductor materials are used in thin-film applications, primarily for special process reasons such as cost, conductivity, and metallurgical compatibility. These conductors are aluminum, copper, and
palladium.

5.2.2.2 Thick-Film Metallizations. Thick-film conductors, used
in MCM technology where density is not a factor, are typically compositions of metals with glass frits and other additives to accommodate the
manufacturing process. They are typically gold or silver and alloys of
these materials with either palladium or platinum. Emerging as a newer
low-cost technology are copper- and nickel-based thick-film pastes.

5.2.2.3 Metallic Coatings and Platings. Commonly used in
MCM design, these conductors may be formed by selective deposition or
application of metallic foils or coatings. The more common materials are
electroless copper, electrodeposited copper, gold plating, nickel plating,
tin-lead plating, and solder coating.

5.2.2.4 Conductor System Attributes. Typical attributes for both
thick- and thin-film conductors are listed in Table 5.3.

5.2.3 Dielectric Materials[4]

A critical element in MCM manufacture is the dielectric material. The
first dielectric materials used in electronics were for sealing glasses
serving as environmental protection. The primary functions for dielectric materials now, however, are for insulators, either as crossovers or
capacitors or for multilayer uses. For the dense packaging required in
an MCM, use of a low-dielectric-constant material insulator between
multiple metal layers is essential to maintain a low dielectric constant.
Feature density of less than 25-μm lines and spaces requires the insulator to have a dielectric constant of less than 4. Conventional dielectrics
such as epoxy-glass and the usual thick-film ceramic dielectrics cannot
be used in this new technology. Low-K organic dielectrics, especially
alumina (SiO_2, have contributed greatly to the success and acceptance
of high-density MCM technology.

Table 5.3. Conductor System Attributes[1]

	Die bondability methods			Wire bondability		Solderability	Solder leach resistance	Corrosion resistance
Thick films	Eutectic	Solder	Organic	Gold	Aluminum			
Au	Good	Poor	Excellent	Excellent	Good	Poor	Poor	Excellent
PtAu	NG	Good	Excellent	Fair to Poor	Fair	Excellent	Good	Excellent
PdAu	NG	Fair	Excellent	Fair to Poor	Fair	Good	Good	Excellent
Ag	NG	Good	Excellent	Good	NG	Good	Poor	NG
PtAg	—	Good	Excellent	Good	NG	Good	Good	Good
PdAg	—	Good	Excellent	Good	Good	Good	Good	Good
PdPtAg	—	Good	Excellent	Good	Good	Good	Good	Good
Cu	NG	Good	Excellent	NG	Fair	Excellent	Excellent	Poor
Ni	NG	NG	Excellent	NG	NG	NG	Excellent	Excellent
Polymeric	NG	NG	Excellent	NG	NG	NG	NG	Good
W/MoMn	NG	NG	Excellent	NG	NG	NG	NG	Good
Thin Films								
Au	Good	NG	Excellent	Excellent	Excellent	Poor (with Ni undercoat OK)	Poor	Excellent
Cu	NG	Good	Excellent	NG	NG	Excellent	Excellent	Poor
Pd	NG	NG	Excellent	NG	NG	NG	NG	Excellent
Ag	NG	NG	Excellent	NG	NG	NG	NG	Poor
Platings								
Au	Good	Good	Excellent	Excellent	Good	Poor	Poor	Excellent
Cu	NG	Good	Excellent	NG	Fair	Excellent	Excellent	Poor
Ni	NG	NG	Excellent	NG	NG	NG	Excellent	Excellent
Pb/Sn	NG	Excellent	—	—	—	Excellent	—	—

Table 5.4. Properties of an Ideal
Organic Dielectric[4]

Low dielectric constant (2–4)
Excellent adhesion
Good mechanical properties
Chemical resistance
Thermally stable
Etchable
Ionically clean
Low moisture uptake
Low residual stress
High planarization
Capability of applying thick coatings (10 μm or better)

There are a number of demands placed on the organic dielectric for use in MCMs. Table 5.4 lists the "ideal" characteristics of a dielectric material for MCMs.

5.2.3.1 Thin-Film Dielectrics. For MCM-D products, thin-film dielectric materials such as boron nitride, silicon oxide, and silicon nitride are used most commonly, usually as dielectric separation between layers or as a protective overcoat. However, for thin-film dielectrics, these materials have limited uses.

5.2.3.2 Organic Dielectrics. A polyimide is the material of choice for an MCM dielectric for a number of reasons. It has most of the ideal characteristics for this application, it has good dielectric and electrical properties for microelectronic applications and superior and predictable thermal behavior in high-performance end use, and it is easy to apply, typically by dipping or spin or spray coating. For MCM-L products, rigid polymer materials such as epoxy or polyimide reinforced with fiberglass, aramid, or quartz cloth and nonreinforced polyvinyl or polyimide films are used commonly as a substrate, for interlayer dielectric isolation, and as a protective overcoat. Table 5.5 lists typical properties of film dielectrics.

5.2.4 Adhesives

Although the primary use for adhesives in MCMs is to attach the devices to the substrates and fulfill the bonding requirements, a sec-

Table 5.5. Dielectric Comparisons[1]

Parameter	Units	Glass-ceramic	Thin film	Polymer film
Insulation resistance range	Ohms	$<10^{11}$	$<10^{10}$	$<10^7$
Dielectric constant range @ 1 kHz	—	8–14	NA	4–6
Dissipation factor range	%	<3.5	NA	<5
Voltage breakdown range	Volts/mil	0.002-in film <500	≤100	Low
Temperature coefficient of capacitance	ppm/°C	<250	NA	NA
Hermeticity	—	Excellent	Fair	Poor
Thermal coefficient of expansion range	—	96% Al_2O_3	99% Al_2O_3	High
Conductor compatibility	—	PtAu, Au	Au	Cu, Ag
Resistor compatibility	—	Good	Good	Good
Capacitor value range (practical)	pF	≤1000	Small	Small
Trimability	—	Abrasive	No	Abrasive

Table 5.6. Properties of Adhesives[1]

Material	Tensile strength, MPa	Shear strength, MPa	Elastic modulus, Gpa	Hardness	Conductivity, W/m · K	Coefficient of expansion, ppm/°C	Resistivity, Ω · m	Dielectric constant @ 1 MHz
Silicone	10.3	—	2.21	20–90A	6.4–13 15 7.5	262	10^{13}–10^{15}	2.9–4.0
Urethane	5.5–55	15.5	0.172–34.5	10A–80D	1.9–8 4.6	90–450	3×10^8	5.9–8.5
Acrylic	12.4–13.8	—	0.69–10.34	40–90A	—	—	7×10^{11}	—
Epoxy silicone	—	11.7	—	—	—	—	—	—
Epoxy Novolac	55–82.7	26.2	2.76–3.45	—	—	13 16	10^{13}–10^{16}	3.4–3.6
Epoxy bisphenol A	43–85	—	2.7–3.3	106RM	—	14 16	19^{14}–10^{16}	3.2–3.8
Epoxy elec. cond.	3.4–34	—	—	—	0.17–1.5	—	10^{-6}	—
Polyimide modified	—	—	0.275	—	—	73	—	—
Polyimide	—	16.5	3.0	—	—	50	—	—
12 Epoxy polyimide	—	41	—	—	—	—	10^{12}	—
b Epoxy polyurethane	34	—	—	—	—	—	—	—

ondary function is to provide for thermal and/or electrical conductivity. Usually, the adhesives for die-attachment purposes are suspensions
of metal particles in some sort of carrier. Materials used for these purposes must be compatible with other components, especially those
which are temperature-sensitive. Some critical adhesive properties are
shown in Table 5.6.

5.3 General Design Considerations[4,5]

In many ways, the design of MCMs is similar to that for printed
wiring modules, except for the vast difference in interconnection density and methods of manufacturing. Leaning on the microelectronics
industry, MCMs are manufactured with such techniques as photoimaging, electroless plating and electroplating, sputter deposition,
and reactive-ion etching. In conventional digital design, the process
begins with specification and architecture and proceeds with detailed
electrical/physical layout, prototype development, and finally manufacturing and test. Normally, layout is performed independently of
electrical design, and downstream tasks such as maintainability and
reliability analysis are not considered beforehand by engineering. This
procedure is basically an open-looped process decidedly marked by a
lack of integration between design and layout tools, which severely
restricts the transfer of engineering "design intent." Figure 5.1 illustrates the conventional printed circuit board (PCB) design sequence

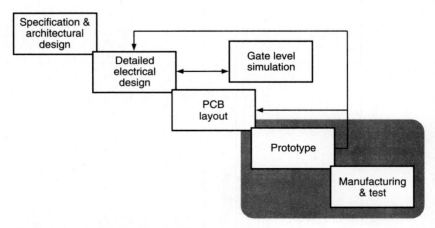

Figure 5.1. Conventional digital PCB design.[6]

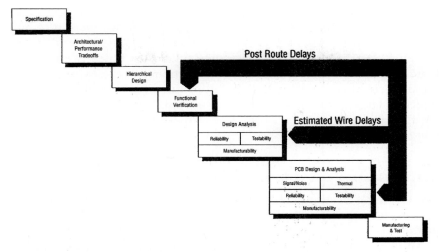

Figure 5.2. Integrated digital design process.[7]

and shows that it lacks the real-time analysis and also requires expensive feedback cycles.

It is no surprise that, similar to other packaging technologies, MCMs introduce a unique set of challenges into the physical design process. Design packages based on application-specific integrated circuits (ASICs) usually do not have the sophisticated autorouters and multilayer design tools needed. Traditional printed circuit board packages do not have the submicron database resolution of feature sizes required to support MCM designs. The increased popularity of MCM design technologies has resulted in the development of sophisticated design tools. These tools combine process accelerators, application tool sets, and process framework technology that serves to manage the increased complexity of electronic design more effectively, resulting in integrated application tools such as shown in Fig. 5.2.

5.4 Electrical Considerations[2,5,8]

MCM design has a number of challenges in the electrical design area. The engineer must take into account several design considerations for this particular application. At the very high operating frequencies seen in MCMs, signal lines need to be treated as transmission lines, and since these are thin conductor traces with high series resistance and capacitance, the delays are proportional to the square of the distance traveled. Further complications come with the choice of dielectric material. Signal speed is inversely proportional to the square root of the dielectric constant of the insulator. Since currents in MCMs are typically larger, while actual voltages are smaller and the corresponding tolerances are more narrow, power distribution is also an important consideration.

5.4.1 System Considerations

The electrical design problems facing an MCM designer are significantly more complicated than those normally associated with conventional electronic packaging design. The type of technology used in MCM-C, MCM-D, and MCM-L products can have an effect on the electrical design. For instance, MCM-D products involve IC-type processing using 20- to 75-µm line widths and tolerances. A low dielectric constant and short interconnection lengths ensure high-speed signal propagation. MCM-C products are characterized by a low-temperature cofired ceramic (LTCC) process that allows for interconnects of 100 to 400 µm, and a large number of layers are possible, that is, 40 to 100. A relatively high dielectric constant is prevalent, with longer interconnection lengths, reducing operating speeds as compared with MCM-D products. MCM-L products, really scaled down printed circuit boards (PCBs), are characterized by low direct-current (dc) resistance of the copper interconnects, which allows for good performance.

Increased signal frequency has been an important factor in changing the requirements of MCM design. High-speed complementary metal-oxide semiconductor (CMOS) circuitry formerly meant rise and fall times of 10 ns. Now, the speed has increased by a factor of 10, yielding rise and fall times in the neighborhood of 1 to 1.5 ns. The result is that if the signal propagates from a source to a load and back in more than one-tenth of the time it takes the signal to rise, then transmission-line effects need to be taken into consideration. This means that transmission-line effects are no longer negligible for the MCM designer. The most serious impacts of transmission-line effects on the system are ringing and reflections. Undershoots, overshoots, and pedestal and crosstalk effects are others. It is important to consider these factors in terms of avoiding serious device damage, unwanted logic transitions, and compromises in setup and hold times.

5.4.2 Electrical Characteristics

Electrical characteristics important for the MCM designer include the fundamental transmission-line characteristics of the interconnect as well as the dynamic behavior of signals propagating between chips. These electrical characteristics include the capacitance C, resistance R, inductance L, all per unit length, and the characteristic impedance Z_0 and propagation constant. These properties relate to the cross-sectional geometry of the interconnect, the electrical properties of the conductor and insulator, and the frequency of the signal. Critical dynamic characteristics include the propagation delay, the rise and fall times of the signals, noise from signal reflections, attenuations, and crosstalk (forward and backward) between lines. The transmission-line characteristics, along with the electrical properties of the driver and receiver circuits and other interconnect elements such as conductors, vias, wire bonds, and stubs, have a critical effect on the dynamic behavior of signals reaching the receiver circuits.

5.4.2.1 Signal Distribution.
The advent of high-speed circuits found in MCMs has imposed high-density interconnecting requirements on the designer, making it more important to consider dynamic characteristics of the signal distribution, not only the usual requirement that continuity be provided and that no shorts be permitted. Interconnection wiring, such as found in MCM design, has inductance, capacitance, and resistance and presents transmission-line environments with built-in characteristic impedance, propagation delay, and signal-line reflections. Each of these parameters is sensitive to high frequency and must be factored in to the electrical design. The higher the frequency, the more critical is the design. In high-speed systems, logic rise time and logic propagation delay are device characteristics of importance. With fast rise time of high-speed devices, along with the shorter propagation delays, special consideration needs to be given to the MCM design to avoid degrading the performance of the system.

5.4.2.2 Electrical Rules.[8]
Design tools must provide the designer with the ability to reflect electrical constraints in the final MCM design. These tools will be mapped into a set of physical rules for subsequent use by place and route algorithms. Types of electrical constraints include the following:

- *Topology control.* The ability to specify the method of interconnect to be used directly with the schematic. For example, will stubs be allowed, or daisy chaining? When routing the same signal to multiple loads, which load should be connected first, second, etc.?

- *Impedance control.* Designers need to specify impedance requirements for a single net or group of nets.

- *Balanced pairs.* Used in emitter-coupled logic (ECL) technology, balanced-pair routing requires that the designer be able to specify pairs of nets to be routed parallel to each other with their lengths matched.

- *Time control.* The engineer must specify the allowable interconnect delay to be assigned to a single net or group of nets; i.e., the designer may specify that 50 Ω impedance be maintained.

- *Shielding.* An engineer must be capable of specifying that a net or group of nets be shielded.

By inserting these electrical rule constraints into the front end of the design capture and later mapping them into a set of physical rules for the place and route algorithm, the initial physical representation will more closely meet the electrical performance requirements of the design.

5.5 Thermal Considerations[1]

Power dissipation has a major influence on the circuit partitioning and ultimate size of the MCM. Material and component operating capabilities are limited by their maximum operating temperatures (junction temperature), above which their performance may be degraded. For other components, the maximum body temperatures and hot-spot temperatures are commonly used as figures of merit. Since all components, active or passive, generate heat, the problem is to handle the heat as efficiently as possible to prevent deteriorating heat problems. Normally, a thick substrate is used for the best heat transfer, unless it is bonded to a heat sink, in which case a thin substrate should be used. The use of some "rules of thumb" for the number of devices that can be accommodated with a given technology would provide a starting point, along with thermal considerations, for deciding if a circuitry needs to be partitioned. Another deciding factor is the input/output (I/O) requirements of the circuitry.

Some general guidelines for thermal design for MCMs are as follows:

- Locate the high-power sources near substrate corners or edges unless heat sinking is provided in that vicinity.

- Distribute power sources as evenly as possible to reduce hot spots and to maintain a uniform thermal profile.

- Components should not be attached over other heat-dissipating components, e.g., chip capacitors over thick-film resistors.

- High-heat dissipating elements should be attached to the substrate so as to provide the lowest thermal resistance between the components and the substrate.

- For best thermal performance, make the junction between a back-side-mounted integrated circuit (IC) and the substrate with a material of low thermal resistance that is as thin as possible and provide a uniform contact area that is free from voids.

- In final packaging, you should (1) select a package configuration that will provide the best thermal conductivity for a specific application, (2) provide a good thermal conduction path between the substrate and the package case, and (3) avoid air spaces in the thermal conductivity path if possible.

The close proximity of high-performance dice in MCMs is apt to create hot spots. From a manufacturing standpoint, attachment technologies such as flip TAB and flip chip can effectively dissipate a module's heat. Also useful are thermally conductive materials such as polyimide, polymer, or silicon as well as diamond-filled epoxies with low electrical and high thermal conductivities. Finally, boards or heat sinks are the ultimate method, functioning as heat sinks or for any residual thermal activity.

5.6 Design Layout[1,9,10]

The obvious first step in the design process is to determine the appropriate component substrate (i.e., type of technology), component selection, interconnect technology, and package that will be required to meet the design requirements and end-use environment. The layout of the MCM requires its own planning and design. The electronics engineer and designer have several choices to make when considering MCM packaging. Substrate materials, processing techniques, and the module supplier must be selected based on the electric circuit performance goals, cost objectives, production needs, operating environment, and reliability goals, among others. Once these issues are addressed, the design must be based on a specific set of design rules.

5.6.1   Design Methodology[11]

MCM design begins with overall system partitioning and selection of the technology. System partitioning is accomplished by considering the system requirements. Partitioning may mix analog and mixed analog and digital circuits onto one or more MCMs. It is wise to determine which portions require high-speed digital processing, e.g., the central processing unit (CPU) and random access memory (RAM) memory circuit, data bus circuits, custom digital logic, and so on. When partitioning is done, circuit performance, cost, production volume, weight, environmental conditions, and other factors will determine selection of the technology.

Since MCM design is process driven, each technology determines a specific set of design rules which must be adhered to. Additionally, each substrate supplier will have rules and concerns which must be understood by the designer to come up with a cost-effective layout. The rules include

- Trace widths
- Trace clearances
- Via sizes and shapes
- Pad sizes and shapes
- Via stacking rules
- Metal plane construction
- Device or component attachment technology
- Maximum/minimum trace lengths
- Specific electrical rules (i.e., crosstalk, impedance, etc.)
- Rules applied to an area
- Rules applied on a layer-by-layer basis

5.6.2   Routing, Interconnect

An MCM with a large number of dice and fast clock speed poses challenging problems. Routing software must maximize the efficiency of the process to meet design constraints on the first design pass. To satisfy these high-speed design constraints, normally the software must preroute critical high-speed signals; use schematic data to control route lengths, stub size, and pair routing for timing purposes; and use directional control (X and Y) to precisely create the necessary routes for each layer.

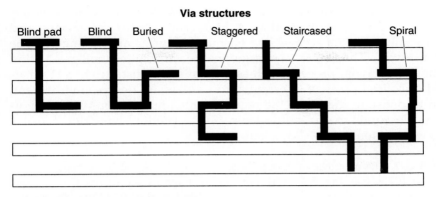

Figure 5.3. MCM via structures.[10]

Packing devices as closely together as in MCMs is advantageous from an area-use standpoint, but routing problems occur. For example, nonparallel traces are very popular in high-speed and MCM designs, since they minimize crosstalk. Single vias, however, can introduce a material mismatch in the package. To help connect complicated traces, MCMs can accommodate a wide variety of via structures. These include blind, buried, staggered, staircased, and spiraled structures, as shown in Fig. 5.3.

Staggered vias may be placed directly underneath each other, as long as they are separated by at least one dielectric layer. Conversely, staircased vias are laid out across the substrate in a stairstep fashion and do not generally fall underneath each other. Spiraled vias, like staggered vias, can be placed directly underneath each other, but must be separated by at least two dielectric layers. It is easy to recognize the problem with vias—they "eat up real estate"—and that conflicts arise—a staircased via can run directly underneath an already established staggered via. The sheer number and potential configurations of MCM vias make sophisticated routing software imperative.

5.6.3 Computer-Aided Design[8,11,12]

Automated design systems are evolving to handle the technology rules for MCMs. Many are simply converted printed wiring board layout tools, and only a few are true MCM layout tools. Not surprisingly, MCMs introduce new challenges into the physical design process. Traditional PCB packages do not have the submicron database resolution or feature sizes required to support MCM designs. Some issues such as blind and buried vias, etch analysis for reflections and crosstalk, and data accessibility for manufacturing and testing must be considered. The ability to retarget manufacturing technologies within the MCM layout process, such as from silicon substrates to a laminated or cofired package, is essential to a successful design environment. In response to these specific requirements imposed on MCM designers, electronic design automation (EDA) vendors have developed a new set of tools for MCM layout.

5.6.3.1 Evolution of EDA Tools.[7] The EDA industry began in the early 1970s (see Fig. 5.4) with companies such as Applicon, Calma, and Computervision developing computer-aided design (CAD) tools for the physical layout of PCBs and ICs. These were basically drafting systems. The 1980s introduced new tools, from companies such as Valid Logic, Daisy Systems, and Mentor Graphics. These tools included graphics editing for schematic capture as well as a number of design-verification capabilities. At the same time, the CAD industry was going through another major change in the approach to physical layout. Companies such as Cadnetix, Telesis Systems, Computervision, Redac, and Calay were developing physical layout tools that could be driven through a file system mechanism called *netlists*.

Throughout the 1980s, the improvements in the different CAE/CAD tools such as logic simulation for CAE, automatic place and route, and

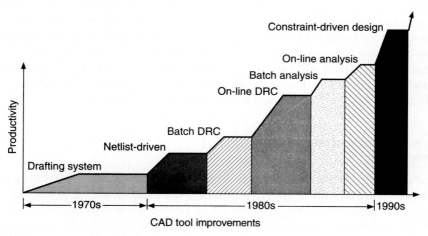

Figure 5.4. CAD tool improvements.

on-line design rule checks for physical spacing checks, etc. provided productivity improvements. Through mergers and takeovers (Valid/Telesis, Daisy Cadnetix, etc.), specialized EDA vendors were now becoming single suppliers of CAE/CAD products.

This restructuring and major focus on developing integrated tools influenced the development of the "rules driven" design methodology by which engineers could set specific design rules at the logic design level which would translate throughout the physical layout. Considered a "correct by verification" function because it checks placement and routing after the fact, in-process analysis set the trend for EDA tools for the 1990s.

5.6.3.2 Constraint-Driven Design. The next generation of EDA tools will be *constraint-driven design* (Fig. 5.5), a "correct by design" methodology that addresses many technologies (PCB, hybrid, MCM) and is based on a systems design approach integrating performance-driven CAD technology, independent design tools, and technology file definition. Technology files enable the capture of electrical, thermal, reliability, testing, and manufacturing design requirements to leverage the skills of the entire design team. When applied within the CAD tool, technology files speed up the layout while adhering to all performance and manufacturing specifications.

5.6.3.3 Performance-Driven CAD. Performance-driven CAD systems take the knowledge base from rules-driven design and move it into the earlier stages of the design process (see Fig. 5.6). This method improves the entire design process, reducing the total number of design iterations by highlighting problems early and by eliminating costly hardware prototyping. The design environment created supports constraint-driven placement and routing capabilities, including controlled impedance, controlled delay or timing skew, signal distortion, etc. Timing-driven placement and routing will now be a part of the standard design process.

Figure 5.5. Constraint-driven design.[7]

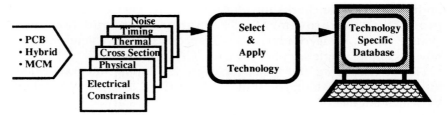

Figure 5.6. Performance-driven CAD.[7]

5.7 Manufacturing Considerations[13]

A certain characteristic of MCMs is the unstable, rapidly moving man-ufacturing environment. Changes are prevalent which influence the layout procedure used by the designer to describe the component and conductor geometries, as well as the method used to transmit the information to the manufacturer or foundry. Many conventional PCB design groups may not be familiar with the new fabrication require-ments introduced by MCMs. Another problem is that, as in other man-ufacturing processes, different foundries have different design rules and restrictions, and the designer must quickly accommodate these. Designers must have access to a system which can employ correct-by-design methodology. Designers also have a need to know where com-ponents are placed, how interconnections are made, and how data and information are communicated to the fabrication foundry.

5.7.1 Design for Assembly

Many types of component and attachment methods are used for MCMs, a possible combination of bare-die, imaged, packaged compo-nents. Assembly options include single-sided, double-sided, and cavi-ty-mounted. Component type used in a design can require different processing steps and could affect yield. Component spacing require-ments depend on the attachment method and whether manual or automated assembly is used. Automatic pick and place machines require less space for components than if manual attachment is used. The sequence of assembly of components also affects the design. Normally, imaged parts are added first, followed by chip and wire parts and then surface-mount components. Also affecting the spacing of components are test, rework, and inspection requirements. Heat-sensitive components should not be placed near parts having a high power dissipation.

A number of mounting methods are available for parts unpackaged or in bare-die form. The most common, chip and wire, attaches the bare die to the substrate, and a gold wire is welded to the pad on the die and to the pad on the substrate. Location and length of the bonding wire will have a direct bearing on the circuit performance as well as manufacturability. Bond wires should not cross and should be as short and straight as possible. The length of the wire should be long enough to clear the edge of the die without crimping and short enough so as not to droop and touch a conductor. When tape automated bonding (TAB) is used, enough space must be provided around the component to accommodate solder techniques. Another method used to attach the die is the flip-chip method. This allows greater density, since all the pins are under the die, but registration of the die to the pads can be an issue. Also, since the die is placed directly onto the solder bumps, coplanarity of the mounting surface is required to ensure that the die makes contact with all the pins. The HDI (high-density interconnect), or "chips first," method of attachment is the most process-intensive method of attaching components to the substrate. In this method, openings in the dielectric film allow contact between the pads on the die and the metal conductors. Although alignment can be adjusted between conductors and pads, there can be no bends or vias in the conductors within a certain perimeter around the die moat.

5.7.2 Design for Test

There are different test techniques and capabilities available for MCMs, depending on the type being designed. Prior to assembly, the die and substrate should have been tested. Testing the final assembly will confirm proper assembly and also will determine if there are any shorts or opens on the design. Test points may have to be provided for external probing, depending on use of a physical probe or a VCEB (voltage-constant electron-beam) tester. The test points could be selected from existing geometry on the design which meets the tester parameters for such criteria as test side, probe spacing, and minimum probe pad size. Bond pads may be oversized to allow access for probes, but if no geometry exists on the design, test points may need to be inserted onto the design.

5.7.3 Design for Fabrication

More so in MCMs than in PCBs, the fabrication requirements affect the design. Requirements range from technology-specific data such as manufacturing limitations, conductor spacings and widths, and legal via structures to design-specific data such as required impedances, delays on nets, maximum allowable crosstalk, and others. MCMs are difficult to model, since layer stackup rules to which they have to be designed can be very complex. The designer must have a good understanding of the module cross section as well as what output is needed for manufacturing. Since a main reason for the use of MCM technology is to improve circuit speed, this benefit is lost if connections are overly long. Also, certain nets such as clock nets will need to have matched lengths to provide simultaneous switching. As with PCBs, the conductor width and spacing are determined by current-carrying requirements and the amount of impedance desired, as well as the tolerance that the foundry can maintain while fabricating, which may vary from foundry to foundry. Although using minimum conductor widths and spacing will increase circuit density, they should be used only where necessary. Wider spacing and lines will improve yields. The design of vias in an MCM is very process-dependent. Vias are not typically drilled but are clearances in a dielectric level that allow connection between metal layers. To minimize thickness of the dielectric layer, it is not desirable to have a via transcend through multiple dielectric and conductor levels, which is known as a *stacked via*. Methods to avoid this are staggered and spiraled vias. A design rule specifies how many levels a via is able to transcend, and if a connection needs to be made through additional layers, vias are overlapped to make connection between vias on the same layer.

References

1. "Guidelines for Multichip Module Technology," Institute for Interconnecting and Packaging Electronic Circuits, IPC-MC-790, 1992.
2. Evan Davidson, IBM, "Designing Multichip Modules," *Electronic Packaging and Production*, October 1992, pp. 16–20.
3. Leonard W. Schaper, Alcoa Electronic Packaging, "Meeting System Requirements through Technology Tradeoffs in Multichip Modules," *Proceedings, International Electronics Packaging Society Conference*, September 1990, pp. 25–30.
4. Robert D. Rossi, National Starch and Chemical, "Multichip Modules: An Overview of Design, Materials and Processes," *Surface Mount Technology*, August 1990, pp. 17–21.
5. J. O. Hurlbrink, NCR, "NCR's Approach to Multichip Modules," IPC-TP-947, 1991.
6. Laurel A. Stanley, Valid Logic Systems, "A Concurrent Approach to Design Process Engineering for MCM's," *Surface Mount Technology*, April 1991, pp. 34–36.

7. Frank Boyle, Valid/Cadence, "CAD Tools: The Next Generation," *Proceedings, NEPCON*, 1992, pp. 89–96.

8. Jacob Ben-Meir and Jonathan Weiss, Mentor Graphics, "High Density, High Speed Design Focuses on Physical Performance Impacts," *Proceedings, NEPCON*, 1992, pp. 525–532.

9. John Isaac, "Staggered, Staircased and Stepped," *Printed Circuit Design*, February 1991, pp. 42–48.

10. W. T. Greer, Jr., Motorola, and John Isaac, Mentor Graphics, "Military Increasing Use of Multichip Modules," *Hybrid Circuit Technology*, April 1991, pp. 31–38.

11. Tony Mazzulo, Harris/Scientific Calculating Division, "An Introduction to Multichip Module Design, Materials and Processes," *Surface Mount Technology*, August 1990.

12. Laurel A. Bixby and Donald T. DiMatteo, Valid Logic Systems, "An Alternative Packaging Technology," *Hybrid Circuit Technology*, December 1990, pp. 9–12.

13. Debra Ives, Cadence Design Systems, "Design for Manufacturability of Multi-Chip Modules," *IPC Technical Review*, June 1992, pp. 21–24.

6

Ceramic-Dielectric Multichip Modules (MCM-C)

Representing the oldest of the multichip module (MCM) technologies, MCM-C is an extension of thick-film hybrid and cofired ceramic single-chip package technologies. In these cases, circuit chips are mounted on insulating substrates and interconnected using screened conductor pastes. Pioneered in the 1980s by many mainframe and supercomputer manufacturers, this approach was based on the conventional successive screen and fire technologies used by many manufacturers such as IBM, Univac, and others for highly dense packaging.

Basically, three distinct technologies are used to produce the circuits considered MCM-C. These are thick-film ceramic (TFC), high-temperature cofired ceramic (HTCC), and low-temperature cofired ceramic (LTCC).

MCM-C products consist of insulating materials with dielectric constants higher than 5 stacked between signal planes or signal or ground planes; conductors can be screen-printed thick-film conductors such as gold, silver, copper, or tantalum or metals such as tungsten or molybdenum. MCM-C modules are mostly designed using embedded chip and wire parts and surface-mount devices (SMDs) with bond wires connecting to signal layers.

Now a cofired ceramic substrate design that is an extension of the old single-chip packages, MCM-C design has become a highly proven, mature technology with well-established volume manufacturing procedures. With a layer count sometimes exceeding 30, and with large pitch traces of 250 to 450 μm, module performance is somewhat less when compared with other substrate technologies due to a high dielectric constant (*K*) of 8 to 10 and because of high line resistance with tungsten metal. Cofired ceramic is strong and inert to handling and environmental exposure, so it can be used for external module surfaces. It is a good technology for modules having pin-grid array (PGA) or land-grid array (LGA) interfaces to a circuit board because it has the ability to support electrical vias through the ceramic.

6.1   Technology Overview

Conventional multilayer ceramic technologies use a "silk screen" printing method for the formation of traces by the sequential printing, drying, and firing of conductive, dielectric, and resistive material on a ceramic substrate (Al_2O_3). The screen print process and the rheology of the thick-film ink have a limiting effect on the line resolution. Thick-film processes characteristically limit interconnect pitches to 15 mil as a result of the silk screen process used to make vias.

Obviously, this method cannot meet the requirements for a fine-line technology. Since it is a sequential process, adding layers (which adds process steps) increases cost and decreases yields. Because of the difficulty of fabricating thick-film hybrids with more than a few layers of interconnect, use of this technology is limited to low-density applications. Also, as the layer count goes up, the cumulative surface features layer by layer deteriorate the top-layer planarity, limiting resolution in printing and increasing the complexity of mounting IC chips. Other process steps necessary include via filling, dielectric layer printing, etc., all adding to the cost of the production.

Cofired ceramic hybrids are similar to thick film, with the exception that refractory metal thick-film conductor pastes are printed (by silk screen or other process) onto unfired (green tape) ceramic sheets of 90 to 94 percent Al_2O_3. Filling the vias, the paste also defines the required conductor pattern. Individual green sheets represent one layer, and layers are inspected, stacked, and laminated. Following firing, exposed metal is nickel and gold plated to provide pads for the interconnection of the IC die to the interconnect plane.

6.2   Technology Choices[1-3]

The primary difference between the traditional thick-film ceramic (TFC) and the cofired ceramic (HTCC and LTCC) modules is simply that the thick-film parts are processed layer by layer, or sequentially. Each layer of a thick-film ceramic circuit requires many printing and firing operations per layer. Thick-film ceramic parts require a mechanical support base and need a package or device passivation to protect active elements. Up to 60 firing steps may be required to produce 10 layers. In the cofired technology, however, a single step is required for the predefined layers in laminating and firing. The type of tape, or substrate material, used dictates the type of conductor that can be fired. In high-temperature cofired (HTC) substrates, the alumina tape used has to be fired at above 1500°C, which allows only refractory metals such as tungsten (W), molybdenum (Mo), and molymanganese (Mo-Mn) to be used for conductors. These materials must be fired in a reducing-atmosphere oven to prevent oxidation. Low-temperature cofired (LTCC) substrates use glass-ceramics, which allows lower firing temperatures (800 to 900°C), permitting use of noble metals such as gold, silver-palladium, or even copper. In effect, tailorable dielectrics can be used for LTCC modules, and they can be fired in a normal atmosphere. HTCC modules can use only alumina dielectrics. Table 6.1 shows a comparison of thick-film and high-temperature cofired technology.

6.2.1 Conventional Multilayer Thick Film

In conventional thick-film hybrid technology, each successive layer is built up by successive printing and firing of conductive and insulating layers. The pastes are applied by the conventional screen printing process, followed by drying at 90 to 150°C to remove solvents. Resistors, capacitors, and inductors can be patterned as well as conductors. As many as four dielectric printing and firing steps with accompanying via fill printing and firings may be required for each layer. Firing takes place at temperatures of 500 to 1100°C. This essentially sequential process becomes less cost-effective as the number of conductive layers increases. This is the most frequently used manufacturing technology for making multilayer hybrids. Current state of the art for screen printing in high-volume production operations is 200- to 250-μm vias and 150-μm lines and spaces. The substrate in this technology is a ceramic material which serves as a foundation for the thick-film circuit, usually 96 percent alumina. Conductors are printed, dried, and fired on the substrate, and dielectric (insulating) layers are printed and fired. This process continues for up to five layers. Following the firing of the dielectric, the vias are filled, dried, and fired.

Table 6.1. A Comparison of Thick-Film and High-Temperature Cofired Technology[4]

	Thick film	High-temperature cofired
Dielectric	Paste composition Glass + fillers	Tape 90–96% Al_2O_3
Dielectric constant	7–10	9.5
Conductor metallurgy	Ag, Au, Pd-Ag, Cu	W, Mo, Mo-Mn
Sheet resistance, $m\Omega/\square/12.5~\mu m$	2–4	16–30
Firing	800–950°C 45–60 min Air (precious metals) N_2 (Cu)	>1500°C >24 h H_2 Atmosphere
Vias	Screen printing 0.010 in diameter 0.025 in center	Punching 0.005 in diameter 0.010 in center
Line resolution, line/spaces	0.006/0.006 in	0.004/0.004 in
Multilayer proc.	Sequential, many steps	Cofired, fewer steps
Substrate required	Yes	No
Lead attach.	Direct	Plating required
Resistor compatibility	Yes	No
Capital investment	Low	High

In order to gain the advantage of finer lines and smaller vias, other methods of fabrication are required. These include techniques that can extend the "process envelope" to higher layer counts and smaller lines and vias. Methods for doing this include the photoimagable thick-film process for dielectric and conductors and diffusion patterning. The photoimagable thick-film process involves the use of a photoactive paste placed on a substrate and exposed through artwork or a mask to define circuit characteristics, lines, and vias. The materials are developed in an aqueous process and then fired using conventional thick-film methods. Both copper and gold metallizations are used, and layer counts of up to 10 circuit layers are possible. Figures 6.1 and 6.2 show the basic steps for this process. Figure 6.3 shows an application of an MCM-C module made using photoimaging.

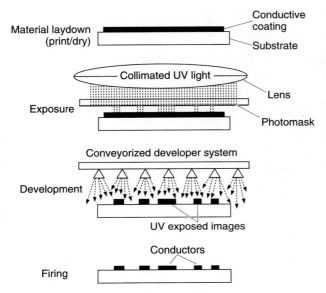

Figure 6.1. Photoimagable conductor patterning.[1]

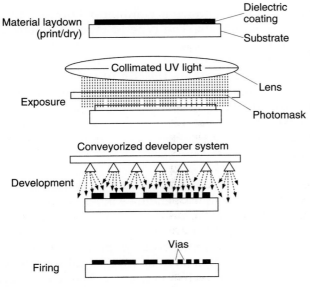

Figure 6.2. Photoimagable via patterning.[1]

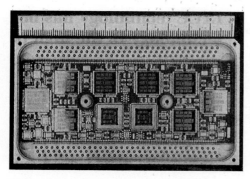

Figure 6.3. MCM-C photoimaging process.[5]

6.2.2 Cofired MCM-C Modules[3,4]

The basic element of this process involves the use of sheets of unfired green tape formed from alumina powder and glass with organic binders. The individual layers are punched with vias and then patterned using thick-film inks. Lamination of the entire circuit takes place; then the "stack" is fired.

Cofired multilayer ceramic substrates differ from thick-film substrates in that there is only one firing cycle. They have been developed to increase circuit density, shorten conductor lengths, and reduce the number of interconnects. The type of tape or material used dictates the type of conductor that can be cofired. In high-temperature cofired (HTC) substrates, the alumina tape used must be fired at or above 1500°C, which permits the use of only refractory metals such as tungsten or molybdenum, not the best conductors. Newer materials are now available allowing lower firing temperatures (800 to 900°C). These materials, called *glass-ceramics,* allow noble metals such as gold, silver, palladium-silver, and even copper to be used in the circuit.

6.2.2.1 High-Temperature Cofired MCM-C.[4] Not commonly used in the fabrication of MCMs, high-temperature cofired processes are restricted by the particular fabrication process required. High temperatures require the use of refractory metals such as tungsten or molybdenum, and a reducing firing atmosphere is needed to prevent the oxidation of these metals. Adding to the problem, the commercial sources of the high-quality alumina dielectric are becoming scarce. The sources for compatible metal conductor materials are also drying up. Metals such as molybdenum and tungsten have high sheet resistance and do not meet

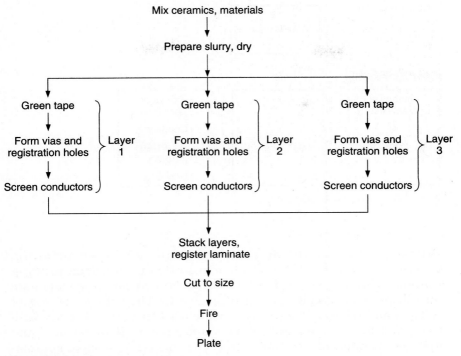

Figure 6.4. HTCC process flow.

the signal speed requirements for MCM-C designs. The process sequence for high-temperature cofired ceramics is shown in Fig. 6.4.

6.2.2.2 Low-Temperature Cofired MCM-C.[5-7] Low-temperature cofired ceramic systems allow use of precious metal conductors and incorporate air firing in conventional thick-film–type furnaces. A cofired process is different from conventional thick-film processes, where each successive layer, dielectric or conductor, must be fired individually. The material system consists of ceramic constituents mixed with binders and cast into "green tape," compatible conductor paste systems for conductors and via fill purposes, and thick-film conductors and resistors for postfiring (see Fig. 6.5).

The process flow for a low-temperature cofired process is illustrated in Fig. 6.6. The process begins with the mixing of alumina powder and glass frit in a predetermined formula and blending it with organic binder and solvents. This slurry is then cast on a Mylar carrier and dried to remove solvents. The tape is then cut to size, and holes are punched for vias. Vias are filled using a specially formulated high-

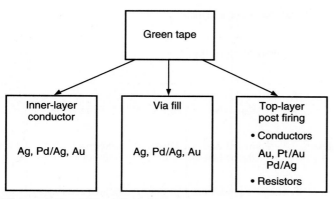

Figure 6.5. LTCC materials system.

solids-content conductor paste by means of screen printing. Conductors are printed using standard off-contact screen printing methods. The tape is then dried. Punched, printed, and dried tapes are then inspected and collated and registered for lamination. The sets of collated and registered layers are then placed in a special cavity with the dimension of the blanked sheet and laminated under heat and pressure. Laminated parts are placed in a convection oven at approximately 350°C and prefired for about 1 h. This removes the solvent. Firing consists of a higher-temperature firing (approximately 850°C for 15 min). Surface-layer printing includes any resistor printing, if required, as well as pad locations for component attachment. This is subsequently fired. An example of an LTCC MCM is shown in Fig. 6.7.

6.2.3 Multilayer Polyimide MCM-C Products[7]

A combination of conventional multilayer thick film and polyimide technologies, the multilayer polyimide process technology shown in Fig. 6.8 consists of a number of operations built up on a conventional thick-film multilayer circuit. Basically, the process begins with the selection of a substrate material such as silicon, glass, high-temperature cofired ceramic, low-temperature cofired ceramic, or conventional multilayer ceramics. The substrates are cleaned and coated with polyimide and cured. Following this, the substrates are than coated with a thin layer of sacrificial metal, which is then patterned using a high-resolution photoresist; this is the imaging mask for the next step, which is polyimide etching. The polyimide is etched to expose vias and chip

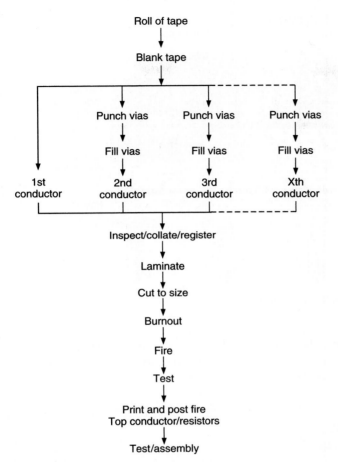

Figure 6.6. Low-temperature cofired ceramic process flow.

cavities, and the excess sacrificial metal is removed using a wet etchant.

Metal processing, which includes power, ground, signal, and/or I/O, begins with the evaporation of thin layers (less than 2500 Å) of a plate-up base metal over the entire substrate. Either chrome-gold (Cr-Au) or titanium-palladium-gold (Ti-Pd-Au) is used to be process-compatible with IC photolithography and to provide a good base for further metallization. The metal is then exposed to a high-resolution photoresist and defined for regions on the substrate to be metallized. Up to 8 µin of gold is electroplated directly onto the exposed regions of the substrate. The photoresist and the excess thin metals are then

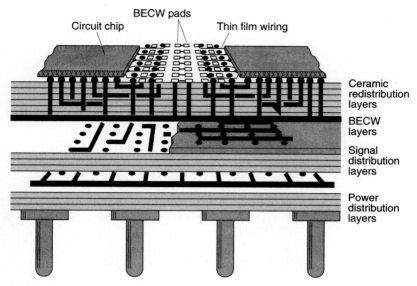

Figure 6.7. IBM ES/9000 module.[8]

removed with solvents and wet etchants, respectively. This process is repeated for multilayer structures. An example of the use of multilayer polyimide in an MCM is shown in Fig. 6.9.

6.3 Material Considerations[1,9]

6.3.1 Conventional Thick Film

6.3.1.1 Substrates. The substrate is the foundation of the MCM. It provides mechanical support for the module, controls the module's temperature, and provides a vehicle for the MCM's electrical performance. The substrate is normally pressed and fired in a variety of sizes and thicknesses, ranging from 0.008 to 0.060 in thick and up to 6 × 12 in in size. Normally, substrates are provided with laser scribing to facilitate breaking to size. The most popular ceramic material is aluminum oxide, or alumina (Al_2O_3). Although alumina ranges in purity from 88 to 99 percent, most of the thick-film substrates are 96 percent alumina, since it provides the best combination of properties required for this technology. Table 6.2 provides a summary of the most used substrate materials.

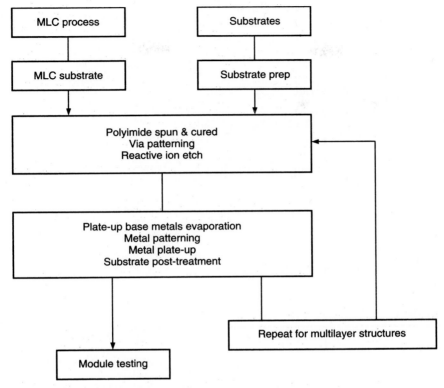

Figure 6.8. Block diagram of the multilayer polyimide process.[7]

Depending on the purity of the alumina ceramic, the coefficient of thermal expansion (CTE) ranges from 6.77 to 7.0. This is higher than some ceramics but does not eliminate alumina as a substrate material. The thermal conductivity of the material ranges from 19 to 34 W/m · K. The dielectric constant averages about 9.5, comparing well with other ceramic substrate materials. Aluminum nitride (AlN) has become a popular material for MCM substrates because of its high thermal conductivity and low CTE. The thermal conductivity of AlN is typically 170 to 190 W/m · K, and when it is coupled with the low coefficient of expansion of 4.5 to 5.0 ppm/°C, it makes it a good match for MCMs with large integrated circuits. AlN is a good material for high-power applications, since the thermal conductivity increases with temperature. Beryllia, or beryllium oxide, is also a popular material for high power dissipation, since it has a high thermal conductivity. The thermal conductivity of a BeO substrate is in the range of 260 to 290

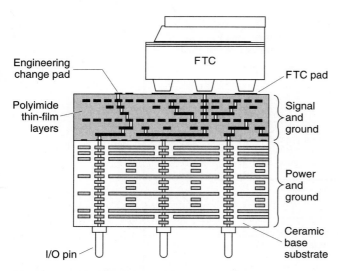

Figure 6.9. NEC SX-3 computer module.[11]

Table 6.2. Ceramic Materials Properties[9]

	Characteristics		
	Thermal conductivity (W/m · K at 25°C)	Coefficient of thermal expansion (ppm/°C; 40–400°C)	Dielectric constant (at 1 MHz)
Alumina—92%	19–20	6.77	9.5
Alumina—95%	34	7.0	9.9
Aluminum nitride	170	4.45	8.8
Beryllia	290	7.4	6.7
Silicon carbide	70–260	3.8	40–79
Mullite	5	4.2	6.8
Diamond	>1000–1500	1.0–4.0	5.7
Glass ceramic*	3–5	2.5–8	4.5–8

*Depending on substrate formulation.

W/m · K. The dielectric constant of BeO is 6.7, and the coefficient of thermal expansion is 7.4 ppm/°C, lower than alumina. A big problem with BeO however, is its toxicity, and for this reason, it requires special care in handling and processing.

6.3.1.2 Conductors. Thick-film conductors are typically silver, gold, and alloys of these materials with either platinum or palladium. These are the so-called noble metals. Other materials such as copper, aluminum, and nickel are also used, but copper is the primary of these used in thick-film technology because it is lower in cost and has other desirable attributes, such as high electrical conductivity and low loss at high frequencies. Thick-film conductors are composed of the metal powder plus vitreous or oxide powders and an organic material that acts as a binder and determines the processing characteristics of the material.

6.3.1.3 Dielectrics. Thick-film dielectric pastes are a combination of dielectric powders and an organic material that acts as a vehicle. The first dielectric compositions used were sealing glasses that served to cover other circuit elements from attack by atmosphere and other processes. For MCM-C modules, dielectric compositions are now established in four important classes: resistors, crossovers, insulating layers in multilayers, and capacitors. Resistor materials are normally ruthenium oxide mixed in a glassy matrix or a combination of a heavy metal (lead or bismuth) and ruthenate. Crossover dielectrics are low-dielectric materials used to insulate between conductors and lines in a single-layer thick film. The materials are low-melting-point glasses, typically lead-aluminum-borosilicates. Multilayer dielectrics are usually glass-ceramics specially developed for multilayer application. Not commonly used in MCM applications, capacitor dielectrics are usually combinations of barium titanate and glass.

6.3.2 Cofired MCMs[3,10]

6.3.2.1 Dielectric Materials. For HTCC products, the common dielectric material is 86 to 96 percent alumina with glass. The need for use of high-conductivity metals in thick-film processing led to development of the low-temperature cofired process. The use of high-conductivity metals is premised on the use of low-firing-temperature dielectric materials. These materials, basically alumina-filled glasses and vitrifiable glasses, have a firing temperature between 850 and 1000°C, permitting use of the noble metals for conductors, as well as copper. The foremost considerations for LTCC composition are low dielectric constant (5 to 7) and good sinterability at temperatures below 1000°C to permit the use of the noble metals and copper pastes. Other considerations are a low CTE (30×10^{-7} ppm/°C) and reasonable strength. The alumina compositions are the most widely used materials for cofired products, these being sin-

Table 6.3. Conductor Metals Used in Cofired Substrates[10]

Metal	W	Mo	Cu	Ag	Au	Ag-Pd
Bulk resistivity ρ ($\mu\Omega \cdot$ cm)	5.5	5.2	1.72	1.59	2.35	>20
Thick-film resistivity ρ ($\mu\Omega \cdot$ cm)	10–15	10–15	3–6	3–7	3.75	>20
Sintering temperature (°C)	>1500	>1500	<1000	<1000	<1000	<1000
Atmosphere	Reducing	Reducing	Reducing	Air	Air	Air
CTE ($\times 10^{-7}$/°C)	45	60	170	190	140	>190
Principal concern	Sintering atmosphere control	Sintering atmosphere control	Sintering atmosphere control	Sintering atmosphere control	Migration cost	High ρ

tered ceramics. The second class of ceramic compositions is a sintered composition of glass and ceramic. The sintered microstructure of these materials is characterized by a glassy matrix with dispersed ceramic grains. Typical materials are lead-borosilicate glass and alumina, glass-bonded mullite, and glass-bonded cordierite. The third category of material consists of the glasses, namely, the spodumene and cordierite compositions.

Mullite is another material used for MCM substrates. Comprised of a combination of alumina and silicon dioxide, mullite has a low dielectric constant, and its CTE is favorably closer to silicon's than most other ceramic compositions.

6.3.2.2 Conductors. Table 6.3 lists a number of metals that are used for cofired MCM fabrication. To minimize the dc losses in the substrate and to increase the permissible interconnection lengths, metals with high electrical conductivity are preferred, such as copper, gold, and silver. Gold has an advantage in that it can be sintered in air. Silver also can be sintered in air, but only in the silver-palladium alloy. The lower cost of copper is an attractive reason to use it, if not for the processing costs involved in preventing oxidation, and the losses that occur in paste formulation, screening, sintering, and subsequent operations.

6.4 Design Considerations (IPC)[8]

6.4.1 Layout

The initial diagram should show all components in their relative locations as they will appear in the final layout. This drawing or sketch is
usually termed the *preliminary layout*. The inputs to the layout process
should include special component position requirements if there is
interaction between the components that will affect the overall circuit
performance. In addition, process limitations should be considered in
the design. A typical sequence of events leading to a final layout is
shown in Fig. 6.10. The MCM designer is usually furnished with initial
circuit information in the form of a schematic diagram and a parts list
delineating component types and values, tolerances, and power and
ground information.

For layout, the designer must do the following:

- Review the schematic diagram for completeness.

- Determine the layout techniques that are needed to optimize circuit
  performance, such as locating matching resistors in close proximity
  due to tracking requirements, or special electrical restrictions.

- Identify components that must be placed in a particular relationship
  to each other so that they will be at the same temperature, will operate with minimum-time-delay signal processing, or can be shielded
  effectively.

Each technology determines a set of design rules that are process-
driven. Each manufacturer will have specific rules and desires that
must be understood by the designer. The rules for thick-film (TFC)
modules vary from those for the cofired (HTCC and LTCC) versions.

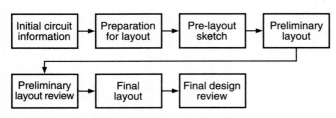

Figure 6.10. MCM layout sequence.[8]

Table 6.4. Dimensional Constraints for Thick-Film Conductors and Lands[8]

Conductor and land sizes and spacing	Minimum dimension, mm (in)	Nominal dimension, mm (in)	Maximum dimension, mm (in)
Conductor to edge of substrate for conductors ≤0.38 mm (0.015 in)	0.25 (0.010)	0.51 (0.020)	None
Conductor to edge of substrate for conductors >0.38 mm (0.015 in)	0.25 (0.010)	0.32 (0.0125)	None
Exit bonding lands (width and length)	0.25 (0.010)	0.32 (0.0125)	None
Wire bonding lands (width and length—one or two wires on same land) (preferred)	0.25 (0.010)	0.32 (0.0125)	None
Wire bonding lands (width and length—one wire per land) (special)	0.25 (0.010)	0.32 (0.0125)	None
Conductor width (preferred)	0.25 (0.010)	0.51 (0.020)	None
Conductor width (special)	0.13 (0.005)	0.25 (0.010)	None
Conductor-to-conductor spacing (preferred)	0.25 (0.010)	0.51 (0.020)	None
Conductor-to-conductor spacing (special)	0.13 (0.005)	0.25 (0.010)	None
Conductor-to-resistor spacing (on untrimmed side of resistor)	0.25 (0.010)	0.38 (0.015)	None
Conductor-to-resistor (on trimmed side of resistor)	0.38 (0.015)	0.51 (0.020)	None
Conductor-to-resistor spacing, top-hat configuration	0.76 (0.030)	0.89 (0.035)	None
Upper and lower conductor widths at crossover junction	0.25 (0.010)	0.38 (0.015)	None
Crossover conductor-to-connecting overlap-length	0.25 (0.010)	0.32 (0.0125)	None
Conductor crossover dielectric overlap	0.25 (0.010)	0.38 (0.015)	None
Dielectric to resistor spacing	0.51 (0.020)	0.51 (0.020)	None

Among the differences, other than material considerations, are the pitch of the conductors, via structure and orientation, and the allowable number of layers. Material differences also may influence the use of vias for thermal reasons.

A body of design rules exists for all hybrid ceramic technologies, including TFC and cofired technologies. Basically, the rules include the following:

- Conductor widths
- Conductor clearances
- Minimum/maximum conductor widths
- Trace routing rules
- Via configuration
- Via stacking
- Pad sizes and shapes
- Metal plane construction
- Chip attachment methods

Typical guidelines for design are shown in Table 6.4.

References

1. Daniel I. Amey, DuPont Electronics, "Overview of MCM Technologies: MCM-C," *Proceedings, NEPCON,* 1992, pp. 1–10.

2. Timothy L. Hodson, EP&P, "Using Existing Technologies to Process Multilayer MCMs," *Electronic Packaging and Production,* August 1991, pp. 48–50.

3. David Lischer and Joe Morabito, AT&T, and Rusty Capers, DuPont Electronics, "Low Temperature Co-Fired Multilayers Will Thrive in Multichip Modules," *Electronic Packaging and Production,* July 1990, pp. 48–49.

4. A. L. Eustice, S. J. Horowitz, J. J. Stewart, A. R. Travis, and H. T. Sawhill, E.I. duPont de Nemours & Co., Inc., "Low Temperature Co-Fireable Ceramics: A New Approach to Electronic Packaging," *Proceedings, 36th Electronics Components Conference,* 1986, pp. 37–47.

5. Steven Gallo, DuPont Electronics, "Technology Choices for Multilayer Hybrids," *Electronic Packaging and Production,* October 1992, pp. 42–44.

6. William R. Blood, Jr., and John S. Carey, Motorola, "Practical Manufacturing of MCMs," *Surface Mount Technology,* November 1992, pp. 16–22.

7. Gail Lehman-Lamer, Douglas Hoy, and Kathy Middo, Tektronix, Inc., "New Multilayer Polyimide Technology Teams with Multilayer Ceramics to Form Multichip Modules," *Hybrid Circuit Technology*, October 1990, pp. 21–26.

8. "Guidelines for Multichip Module Technology," Institute for Interconnecting and Packaging Electronic Circuits, IPC-MC-790, 1992.

9. Timothy Hodson, "Selecting a Ceramic Substrate for Multichip Modules," *Electronic Packaging and Production*, June 1992, pp. 66–70.

10. Ananda Kumar and Rao Tummala, IBM, "State of the Art, Glass-Ceramic/Copper, Multilayer Substrate for High-Performance Computers," *The International Journal for Hybrid Microelectronics*, Vol. 14, No. 4, December 1991, pp. 137–148.

11. Mary Wesling Hartnett and E. Jan Vardaman, Tech Search International, "Worldwide MCM Status and Trends: Material Choices," *Proceedings, NEPCON West*, 1991, pp. 1111–1120.

7
Deposited-Dielectric Multichip Modules (MCM-D)

A new technology designed to address the growing needs of increased packaging density for electronics, MCM-D modules are characterized by shorter interconnect lengths between chips, a smaller package, and lower system costs.[1,2] Although the term *MCM-D* is the industry description for a wide variety of modules using a thin-film technology with deposited dielectric, it is well known that this technology is the most important of the MCM types and certainly holds the most promise as a surviving technology for future applications.

The MCM-D type module is an electronic assembly using a base substrate with one or more deposited-dielectric and conductive circuit layers. The conductive layers furnish both electrical interconnect and device interface features. In addition, the materials selected for the substrate will influence both the device-attachment and terminal technology.

Type D multichip modules (MCMs) are produced by the deposition of thin-film circuitry on a variety of substrate materials. The thin-film elements are formed by sequentially depositing, by evaporation or sputtering, resistive and conductive materials from a source or target on a substrate (usually glass or ceramic) in a vacuum chamber. In the evaporation process, the source materials are heated to their vapor-phase temperatures and then allowed to condense onto the substrate. The conductor layers are separated by deposited dielectric layers, usually materials with low dielectric constants, such as silicon dioxide or polymers.

7.1   Technology Overview[3,4]

Although the processes used for fabrication differ widely, the basic method for making thin-film, or MCM-D, modules is a layer-by-layer process using organic films on silicon or ceramic. A typical example is the Honeywell system, illustrated in Fig. 7.1. Metal layers are sputter deposited on the substrate, where the barrier layers serve as an adhesion-barrier interface layer. Copper is the conductor material of choice

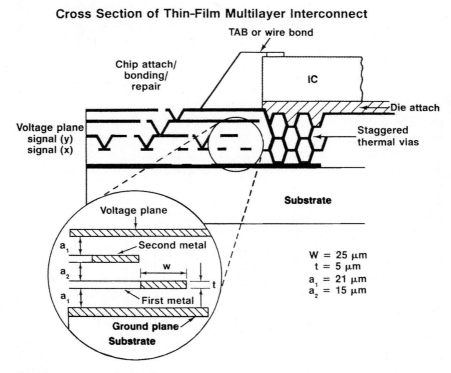

Figure 7.1. Honeywell TFML module.[3]

because of its high conductivity. Relatively thick (2 to 6 μm) photoresist layers are then deposited and imaged. The conductor materials are then etched using wet processes for aspect ratios of less than 0.5 or ion beam milling for higher aspect ratios.

The polyimide dielectric layers are either spin or spray coated, in multiple coatings with a cure following coating of the required thickness, usually two or three coats. The ability of polyimides to flow before curing enhances the process of planarizing the underlying conductor topology. Following the cure, the polyimide exhibits high thermal stability and high tensile strength and is chemically inert, which prevents degradation during the following process steps, which usually involve strong solvents and acids and high temperatures. The low dielectric constant of polyimide results in low-capacitance interconnects requiring lower power levels for driving signals between chips, high signal-propagation speeds, and low levels of crosstalk between adjacent conductor lines.

After coating the polyimide, a silica hard mask is deposited, and holes are formed in the hard mask using a reactive ion etching process. The holes are then filled with a conformal sputtered layer of Cr-Cu-Cr. Although the Honeywell process uses conformal vias, some processes use stacked or solid vias. This process is duplicated for all layers; usually five metal layers are common.

Other design options exist, as shown in Fig. 7.2, which is an illustra-

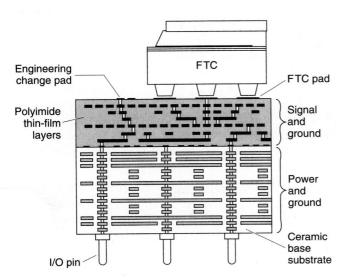

Figure 7.2. NEC's MCM-D module.[5]

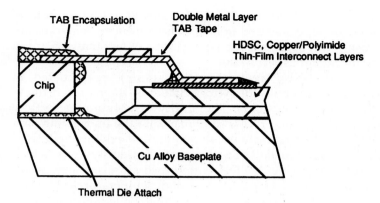

Figure 7.3. DEC's VAX 9000 MCM module.[5]

tion of NEC's technology for their SX-3 supercomputer. This MCM involves building up thin layers of interconnect on a cofired ceramic substrate; IC devices that are TAB bonded into individual micropackages are then solder connected to the thin-film structure. The substrate is 10 cm^2 and has five conductor layers, two ground mesh planes, orthogonal xy signal planes, and a top bonding layer. The thin-film interlayer dielectric is polyimide. The micropackages are referred to as "flipped TAB carriers" (FTCs).

Another technology, illustrated in Fig. 7.3, involves building up thin film layers (one structure for power and one for signal lines) on a temporary aluminum carrier substrate, removing the thin film layers from the carrier, and then laminating the layers together onto another metallic substrate. The chips are then TAB bonded onto the thin-film interconnection layers.

GE's MCM technology, termed the *HDI process,* is illustrated in Fig. 7.4. This completely different approach involves mounting chips into recessed slots in the ceramic substrate and depositing the interconnecting structure over the top. Vias are formed by laser ablation, and the interconnect pattern is defined by an interactive laser. A more complete description of this technology is given later in this chapter.

7.2 Materials[5]

As many material combinations exist as there are MCM-D technologies, with several options for each component to the MCM. The material components of a typical MCM-D include the dielectric, the conductor and surface metallization, the support substrate, the substrate, and

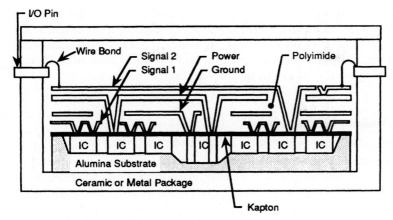

Figure 7.4. GE's HDI module.

also the outer protective enclosure. Prior to selecting the individual material components of the MCM, a determination must be made of the design and system requirements.

This section describes the characteristics and performance of organic dielectrics and effects on fabrication ability, the characteristics and performance of various metallizations, and the attributes of the various substrate materials used for MCM-D. In addition, the thermal performance is vastly affected by each choice of material and assembly technique, and requires consideration. Compatibility between the materials is a key to developing a high-yield, low-cost, and reliable MCM.

In general, closely matched coefficient of thermal expansion (CTE) materials should be used to minimize stress for enhanced reliability. High thermal conductivity materials are useful for getting heat to the next level of packaging. For weight saving, low-density materials are preferred. In the case of the substrate, additional considerations are ease of packaging, mechanical strength, and stability.

Materials with a low dielectric constant are best for interlayer dielectric; since propagation delay is proportional to the square root of the dielectric constant, this also reduces line capacitance. At a given dielectric constant, the dielectric thickness can be reduced to permit higher line density while maintaining the same aspect ratio. Other material-dependent properties which are also important are adhesion, process compatibility, stress, and dissipation factor.

Metals used in high-density interconnect must have both excellent electrical and thermal conductivity. High thermal conductivity is important to remove the substantial amount of heat found in high-density interconnects. Low electrical resistivity is essential in high-density systems because it minimizes the conductor's cross-sectional area for a given design requirement. Interlayer contact resistance, electromigration, and resistance to thermal and chemical degradation also must be considered in the selection of conductor materials.

7.2.1 Dielectric Materials[6]

The selection of a dielectric is often the key to the performance of an MCM system. The lowest dielectric constant material is needed to reduce crosstalk and propagation delay. Although the key attributes of a dielectric are dielectric constant, moisture absorption, adhesion, coefficient of thermal expansion, and Young's modulus, processibility, shrinkage, and planarization characteristics are also important.

The material should exhibit minimal moisture absorption and controllable release if the multilayer structure is to be manufacturable. It should be thermally stable to avoid any damage to the thin-film structure from outgassing during processing. It is important to exhibit good adhesion to the substrate, conductor metallization, and subsequent layers.

Presently, the most popular dielectric used in MCM-D modules is polyimide, which, in spite of its problems, remains the dielectric of choice. Other dielectric options, in addition to various polyimide formulations (some proprietary), are BCB, PPQ, SiO_2, polyquinoline, Teflon, and silica. A comparison of the properties of the various dielectrics is presented in Table 7.1.

Important characteristics of dielectric materials are the following:

- *Dielectric constant.*   Low to achieve the best propagation speed.

- *High resistivity and dielectric strength.*   Minimizes short circuits.

- *Low dissipation factor.*   Minimizes signal voltage attenuation.

- *Low moisture absorption.*   Reduces copper migration into polyimide, and reduces variation in dielectric constant.

- *High adhesion.*   Has acceptable adhesion to conductors, barrier metals, and base substrates to minimize delamination.

- *Coefficient of thermal expansion.*   Low enough to minimize stress in the multilayer assembly.

- *Processibility.*   Controllable deposition of film, which planarizes well, is free of pinholes, is cohesive, and is easily patterned to open via holes.

Table 7.1. A Comparison of Properties of Dielectrics for MCM-Ds[5]

Dielectric	Dielectric constant	TCE (ppm/°C)	% moisture absorption	Adhesion
Standard polyimide	3.4–3.8	35–50	1–3	Good
Low-stress polyimide	2.9–3.5	3–6	1–2	Fair
Acetylene-terminated polyimide	2.9	38	1–3	Good
Polyimide siloxane	2.8–3.4	6–15	0.8	Good/ excellent
Polyquinoline	2.5–2.8	6–8	0.3	Good
BCB	2.6	35–66	0.5	Fair
Teflon	2.1	—	—	Very poor
Silica	3.5–4.0	0.5	<0.1%	Excellent

SOURCE: TechSearch International, Inc.

7.2.1.1 Polymers.[7] Polymer dielectric materials are the most popular in use today. The main reasons for this are probably their low dielectric constant and the fact that polymers may be applied in a number of processes (by lamination or by spray or spin coating). Multiple layers may be deposited and patterned successfully using a number of different techniques.

A number of polymers are available, with a wide variety of materials available to suit particular applications. The most common are the *polyimides,* a term that is essentially interchangeable with polymer. As noted in Table 7.2, there are many different types of polymers, including fluorinated polyimide, low-stress polyimide, photosensitive polyimide, PPQ (polyphenylquinoxaline), and BCB (benzocyclobutane).

There are three distinct advantages to using polyimides in the manufacture of MCMs:

1. Polyimide materials are more process compliant than other inorganics. They have superior step coverage compared with those materials.

2. Thick dielectric films, such as polymers, are essential in reducing capacitance. Polyimide forms thick films easily; even multiple coat-

Table 7.2. Polymer Dielectric Material Properties[1]

Polymer name	Polymer type	Dielectric constant	Dissipation factor	CTE, 10^{-6}/°C	T_g, °C	Modulus, GPa	Tensile strength, MPa	Percent elongation	Moisture uptake, wt%
Amoco Ultradel 4212	Fluorinated polyimide	2.9	0.005	50	295	2.7			0.9
Amoco Ultradel 7501	Photosensitive polyimide	2.8	0.004	24	>400	3.4			3.4
Cemota IP 200	Polyphenylquinoxaline	2.7	0.0005	55	365	2.0	117	8–12	0.9
Dow BCB-13005	Benzocyclobutene	2.7	0.0008	65	>350	3.3*	68*	2.5	0.3
Du Pont PI-2545	Standard polyimide	3.5	0.002	20	>400	1.4	105	40	2–3
Du Pont PI-2555	Standard polyimide	3.3	0.002	40	>320	2.4	135	15	2–3
Du Pont PI-2610D/ 2611D	Low-stress polyimide	2.9	0.002	3(x − y)	>400	8.4	350	25	0.5
Du Pont PI-2732/33	Photosensitive polyimide	2.9		25	>400	6.0	192	8	1.5
Hitachi PIQ-13	Standard polyimide	3.4	0.002	45	>350	3.3	130	20	2.3
Hitachi PIQ-L100	Low-stress polyimide	3.2	0.002	3	410	11	380	22	1.3
National Starch EL5010	Preimidized polyimide	3.2	<0.002	34	214	2.8	150	7	1.3
National Starch EL5512	Fluorinated preimidized polyimide	2.8	<0.002	35	225	2.8	150	6	0.8
OCG Probimide 400	Preimidized photosensitive polyimide	3.0	0.003	37	357	2.9	147	56	2.0
OCG Probimide 500	Low-stress polyimide	2.9	0.003	6–7	400	11.6	444	28	0.7
Toray UR-3800	Photosensitive polyimide	3.2	0.002	40	280	(3.4)	140	11	1.1

*Values given are for flexural modulus and flexural strength, respectively.

ings are needed to do this. Many inorganic materials are prone to cracking, and the internal stress in these materials is too great to permit use of multiple layers. Polyimide materials may be applied onto various substrates in thick coatings without a cracking problem.

3. Polyimide has a low dielectric constant (typically 3.5), reducing the propagation delay. Also, it is possible to etch polyimide materials to form fine patterns, which further reduces propagation delay through the shorter wiring length that results.

Despite the advantages of polyimides, there are a number of disadvantages. One of the main problems is that in some cases they corrode copper when deposited from polyamic acid. To overcome this, deposition is made of chromium over nickel, meaning that each layer of copper is then composed of Cr-Ni-Cu-Ni-Cr, adding up to five layers of metallization. Therefore, line corrosion severely limits the use of copper directly over most polyimides.

Another problem is inadequate adhesion of copper to the polyimide, and some type of adhesion promotion is needed. Polyimide also absorbs water and suffers an increase in dielectric constant in doing so, increasing from a value of 3.5 for a standard, unmodified material to over 4 when absorbing water. This can cause considerable problems with impedance values.

The low-stress polyimides are formulated to produce films that have reduced CTE in the xy direction, most notable when used with another low-CTE material, silicon. Low-stress formulations also have an inherently lower dielectric constant and a lower percentage of water absorption than standard polyimides. The benefits of using a low-CTE material are most evident when the substrate is silicon, since warpage of the wafer is most evident during processing, especially when thick or multiple layers of the polymer are used. Owing to a highly oriented structure, the low-stress formulations characteristically have lower dielectric constants and lower water uptake absorption than normal polyimides.

A disadvantage is that low-stress polyimide does not adhere well to other materials, including itself. For this reason, processing steps must be taken when using this material to ensure adequate adhesion, normally surface modification steps.

The advantage of photosensitive polyimide is self-evident: It reduces the number of steps in processing to build multilayer structures, especially in the area of via processing. However, the incorporation of photosensitive chemistries into the polyimide chain has a negative effect on some of the mechanical properties of the resultant dielectric. Specifically, this is reduced moisture absorption and shrinkage during final cure, which can produce distorted features.

PPQ is another polymer with many desirable properties, including a low dielectric constant and dissipation factor, good mechanical properties, lower shrinkage, good adhesion, and no need of solvents for cure. On the negative side, however, it is only soluble in noxious solvents.

Benzocyclobutane, or BCB, while not by definition a polymer, has properties not unlike those of the preimidized polyimides. It has one of the lowest dielectric constants and loss factors of all the polyimides, similar to PPQ. It also has a lower moisture absorption than most of the polyimides. It adheres well to ceramic, copper, and aluminum. The most important advantage of this material, however, is its ability to produce a level surface even over previous layers with heavily patterned lines.

Preimidized polyimides have several advantages, including reduced reactivity to metals and the fact that no water is produced during cure. These low-molecular-weight materials, however, have a reduced modulus, elongation, and tensile strength, distinct disadvantages. Some of the disadvantages in the use of standard polyimides are their reactivity to metals, (particularly in their polyamic acid form), high stress formation, and high water absorption.

7.2.1.2 Silicon Dioxide Dielectrics.   The first dielectric to be used for multichip interconnection, silicon dioxide is easily deposited on silicon substrates and is available from all types of foundries. Deposited by a chemical vapor deposition (CVD) process in layers up to 15 μm thick, it is not the dielectric of choice for thin-film processes. It has a relatively high (3.9) dielectric constant, it is susceptible to pinholes, and it is not easily planarized, especially at the required low deposition temperatures. Another disadvantage is that it is difficult to deposit more than several microns of SiO_2. These films are chemically stable, do not absorb a significant amount of moisture in processing, and have adequate adhesion to most of the other materials used in fabricating thin-film structures.

7.2.2 Conductor Materials[8]

The conductor material system for MCM-D modules is comprised of the conductors, or primary interconnect conductors, various metals for adhesion and diffusion barriers, and metals for surface metallization. The most popular thin-film conductor metals are copper, aluminum, and gold. Barrier or adhesion "tie" layers may consist of nickel, palladium, titanium, titanium-tungsten, and chromium.

Table 7.3. Properties of Thin-Film Metals[6]

	Resistivity, $\mu\Omega \cdot cm$	Thermal conductivity, W/cm $\cdot$ K	TCE, ppm/K
Aluminum	2.67	2.38	23.5
Copper	1.69	3.97	17.0
Silver	1.63	4.25	19.1
Gold	2.20	3.16	14.1
Tungsten	5.4	1.74	4.5
Molybdenum	5.7	1.37	5.1
Nickel	6.9	0.89	13.3

7.2.2.1 Conductors. The major considerations in choosing a conductor for MCM-D fabrication are primarily low resistivity, low intrinsic stress, good corrosion immunity, good adhesion to adjacent dielectric layers, and good corrosion resistance. For systems requiring low resistivity, copper metallization is used. For some applications, aluminum is satisfactory. Aluminum has good adhesion to dielectrics and is easy to apply. Widely used in the semiconductor industry, there is a wide experience base using aluminum for this application. However, aluminum has a relatively low electrical conductivity, which limits its use for high-speed applications.

The excellent conductivity, low cost, and high thermal conductivity make copper an attractive material for conductor use. A drawback is its poor adhesion to the primary dielectric used, polyimide, and also the formation of oxides in this application, requiring the use of barrier and adhesion metal layers between it and most dielectrics.

Aluminum is certainly preferred for low-speed, low-cost operations, but copper is the most popular material and certainly the most used for high-speed applications. Properties of conductor metals are shown in Table 7.3.

7.2.2.2 Barrier Metals. The primary reason for using barrier metals is to prevent chemical interactions on metals or diffusion of metals and also to provide good adhesion between the conductor and the dielectric. Barrier or adhesion "tie" layers may consist of nickel, palladium, titanium, titanium-tungsten, and chromium. Most frequently used are titanium, nickel, and chromium. Barrier metals are deposited primarily by sputtering.

7.2.2.3 Surface Metallization. The primary purpose for surface metallization is for die attachment and lead bonding. It must therefore be compatible with these requirements, as well as maintain a good adhesion to the dielectric layer and exhibit good corrosion resistance. For these reasons, gold is the most popular material for this purpose. Gold is usually plated, electroless or electroplate, or sputtered. A barrier metal, usually nickel, is required. Although for wire bonding the gold may range in thickness up to 3 µin, for soldering, less than 1 µin is advisable because of the propensity for the formation of brittle tin-gold intermetallics in soldering.

7.3 Substrate Materials[3]

Certainly one advantage of the thin-film process is that it can be implemented on a wide variety of substrates, including silicon, ceramic, and metals. Substrate choice will be dictated by the system requirements and overall package design. The substrate serves as the supporting structure for the circuitry. It acts as a surface for depositing the conductive, dielectric, and resistive materials that form the passive circuit elements. The material most suitable for a particular application should be determined with consideration of the following properties of substrate materials:

- *Mechanical strength.* This is the ability to withstand mechanical shock. Young's modulus, tensile strength, flexural strength, and compressive strength are considered measures of mechanical strength.
- *Thermal conductivity.* The material must have good heat-conductive properties to take heat away from critical circuit components. High thermal conductivity is desired.
- *Electrical insulation.* The material should have good electrical insulating properties.
- *Refractory property* (if applicable). This is the ability of the material to withstand high temperatures. A high melting point is necessary for processes requiring heat treatment.
- *Chemical susceptibility.* This is the ability of the substrate to withstand exposure to processing chemicals.
- *Flatness.* The material should be flat or have a capability to be flattened for the subsequent process requirements.
- *Forming of conductors* (if applicable). This is the ability of the mate-

rial to be metallized successfully with thick-film, thin-film, or other metallization technique.

The ideal substrate will possess high thermal conductivity for high thermal dissipation, a high modulus of elasticity, and a coefficient of thermal expansion (CTE) close to that of polyimide, the dielectric of choice, typically 20 to 40 ppm/°C. Also available now are low-expansion polyimides, with coefficients of expansion in the range of 2 to 3 ppm/°C, to minimize the warpage due to thermal mismatch with polyimide.

A substrate CTE close to that of silicon (2.3 ppm/°C) is desirable for flip-chip bonding or the attachment of large dice. The material should be chemically inert to be resistant to wet etchants and the plasma processes characteristically used in fabrication. The processed surface should be smooth, flat, and free of defects, usually requiring grinding or polishing. Finally, the ideal substrate should be inexpensive, light weight, nontoxic, and available in or machinable to a variety of sizes and configurations.

The major choices for base substrate are multilayer ceramic packages, silicon, metals, and composites. Cofired (or multilayer ceramic) substrates appear to be the most popular, for a number of reasons, namely, the fact that customized wiring is possible in the ceramic base and that the package for the module is formed by the module.

Metal substrates have the advantage of low cost, higher ductility, high strength, excellent thermal conductivity, and the capacity for tailoring the CTE of the substrate to that of the silicon. Some designs use silicon for the substrate. Among the advantages are that it can be processed on an IC line, both active and passive devices can be incorporated, and it has similar thermal expansion properties as the silicon devices. Silicon, however, has a low modulus and a poor CTE match with polyimide, requiring a very thick substrate to prevent warpage.

7.3.1 Ceramic Substrates

Ceramics (particularly alumina) are widely used for substrates because they are stiff and have high mechanical strength. They are chemically inert, can contain multilayer interconnect patterns, and also can serve as the outside package. Some recently developed ceramics, such as silicon carbide and aluminum nitride, also have high thermal conductivity.

Alumina substrates are made of polycrystalline Al_2O_3 with small amounts of metal oxide glasses to achieve certain desirable physical properties. Alumina is commonly available in 96 or 99.6 percent forms, with the 99.6 percent form preferred when a low RMS surface finish is required. Alumina is the most popular substrate material for MCM-D modules because it is readily available in sizes ranging from tiny chips to large area substrates and in thickness ranging from 0.05 to 1.27 mm (0.002 to 0.05 in) or greater. It is characteristically flat or can be ground or machined so and is available in a variety of shapes and sizes. It is refractory, and the finished substrate can be drilled or cut with diamond tools or lasers.

Beryllia (polycrystalline BeO), with impurities required for physical properties, is used primarily in applications requiring rapid heat removal from the circuit. As with alumina, it is available in a large variety of sizes, thicknesses, shapes, and designs. Because of its toxic nature and high cost, beryllia is less widely used than alumina.

Aluminum nitride is the first of the CTE-matched materials to find widespread use as an MCM-D substrate. It has high bending strength (43 to 57 ksi), and high strength (21 ksi), making it stronger than silicon. A significant advantage of AlN is that it has a low dielectric constant and a CTE that is reasonably close to that of silicon. Drawbacks for the material are its lack of availability, coupled with limited industry experience in its use. Also a problem is the propensity for the material to decompose into hydrated aluminum oxide in the presence of heat and moisture.

Tradeoffs to consider when choosing a specific material for an MCM substrate are outlined in Table 7.4. Properties of substrate materials are found in Table 7.5.

7.3.2 Metal Substrates

The advantages of metal substrates are low cost, high modulus and strength, ductility higher than that of silicon or ceramic, good thermal conductivity, and the ability to be processed in large sizes. It is also possible to "tailor" the CTE of such substrates through the use of alloys. The popularity of metal substrates may be due to their high thermal conductivity and low cost. Metal substrates, since they must have insulating qualities, may either require an insulator under the first metal layer or may be a coated metal core material. Prior to coating, the metal may be inexpensively shaped or punched to suit process requirements. Although most metals vary in terms of roughness or flatness, they may be machined and/or polished to arrive at a surface suitable for thin-film conductors.

Copper is an excellent choice for substrate based on its superior thermal conductivity. It is also low in cost and easily machinable.

Table 7.4. Tradeoffs for Various Ceramic Substrate Materials[5]

Ceramic material	Advantages	Disadvantages
Alumina	Processing knowledge Ability to cofire Final package	High dielectric constant Poor thermal conductivity High TCE
Aluminum nitride	High thermal conductivity TCE close to silicon High modulus, strength Machinable grades	Process repeatability Reliable metallization Very high sintering temperature High dielectric constant
Glass-ceramics	Very low dielectric constant TCE close to silicon Low sintering temperature	Very poor thermal conductivity Brittleness
Mullite	Low dielectric constant TCE close to silicon	Poor thermal conductivity High sintering temperature

Silicon carbide	Very high thermal
	  conductivity
	TCE close to silicon
		Difficult to metallize
		High sintering
		  temperature
		High dielectric constant

Beryllia	High thermal conductivity	Processing toxicity

SOURCE: TechSearch International, Inc.

Table 7.5. Properties of Substrate Materials[6]

	TCE, ppm/K	Thermal conductivity, W/cm · K	Bending strength, kg/mm²
GaAs	6.86	0.46	—
Silicon	2.6	1.5	—
Alumina (96%)	7.7	0.2	33
Silicon carbide	2.8	2.7	45
Beryllia	4.7	2.36	20
Aluminum nitride	3.8	1.4	50
Aluminum	23.5	2.38	—
Copper	17.0	3.97	—

However, it has an unfavorable CTE match with that of silicon and is extremely reactive toward most metal etchants used in processing. The metal can be alloyed with other materials to solve the first problem and also can be coated with insulation to solve the second.

Aluminum is light weight, machinable, low in cost, and has high thermal conductivity. It has a similar problem to copper, however, in its poor CTE match with silicon and reaction to processing chemicals. It also has a lower modulus than ceramic and is not commonly used for MCM-D modules.

7.3.3 Diamond and Silicon Substrates

7.3.3.1 Diamond Substrates.[9] In many ways diamond is an almost perfect substrate material for MCM applications. It has an extremely high thermal conductivity, about $k = 2000$ W/m · °C in natur-

Table 7.6. Electronic Packaging Materials Comparison[9]

Material	Thermal conductivity, W/m · °C	Electrical insulator, Y/N?	Thermal expansion, ppm/°C
Diamond:			
Natural	2000	Y	0.8–1
CVD	500–1600	Y	1–1.5
Beryllia, BeO	223	Y	6.4
AlN	70–230	Y	3.3
Alumina, 99%	29	Y	6.3
GaAs	45	Semi	5.9
Silicon	149	N	2.6
Kovar (FeNiCo)	17	N	5.9
Molybdenum	146	N	5.1
Aluminum	237	N	23.8
Copper	396	N	16.8
Silver	428	N	19.6
Diamond-epoxy	8.7	Y	120
Silver-epoxy	5.8	N	120
Polyimide	0.2	Y	>50

al diamond, with values up to 60 to 80 percent of that measured in synthetic diamond. Table 7.6 compares the thermal conductivity , CTE, and electrical or insulating properties of diamond with those of other materials of potential MCM interest. Another advantage of diamond is its very high modulus, and it has a good CTE match with silicon. However, it is extremely expensive, and to be practical for MCM production, it would have to be more reasonable in price.

7.3.3.2 Silicon Substrates. One of the early choices for substrate material, silicon is cheap and readily available in a form suitable for IC processing equipment. The unique property of the CTE of silicon matching that of the IC chip device makes this a popular choice for substrate material. Silicon has a high thermal conductivity (6 to 8 times greater than that of alumina), which also makes it a good match for the IC die. It is easily polished, naturally flat and smooth, and dimensionally stable, allowing fine-line lithography.

High interconnection densities are achievable with a minimum number of metal layers. Active and passive devices can be fabricated on the silicon substrate. Silicon can be doped, which can make it a conductor with a desirable property: it can still have the coefficient of thermal expansion of the silicon chips to be mounted on it.

A significant disadvantage of silicon used for a substrate is its low coefficient of thermal expansion, resulting in considerable warpage when used with polyimide, the dielectric of choice. It also has a low modulus, resulting in the need for supporting structure when used in MCM-D fabrication. It is a brittle material and will certainly lose its dimensional properties when dropped. It is usually supported by or bonded to some other material to overcome this problem.

7.4 MCM-D Processing[8]

MCM-D processing can be characterized by series of repetitive process steps for depositing and defining conductor and dielectric layers and some method of via formation. This section will cover the discrete steps to be followed by some application examples of these processes.

7.4.1 Metallization Alternatives[10]

A number of metallization alternatives have been used for MCM-D module fabrication, and the most common approaches are characterized schematically in Fig. 7.5. Thin-film metals can be deposited by a

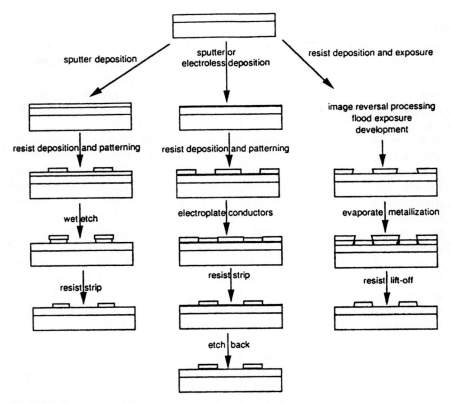

Figure 7.5. Generic MCM-D metallization options.[10]

variety of processes such as plating (electrolytic or electroless) or by
such vacuum-based methods as ion plating, vacuum, and sputtering.

In the sputter deposition process, metal is sputtered over the entire
panel and then patterned by use of photoresist. A wet etch defines the
pattern, and following stripping of the resist, the final pattern is formed.
Aluminum is the most widely used metal in this process. Also, high-resolution subtractive patterning of 2- to 4-μin-thick sputtered aluminum
produces feature sizes as small as 8 to 10 μin with good reproducibility.

Semiadditive copper electroplating is also used, as illustrated in
Fig. 7.5 (center). In this approach, a thin plating layer of material 500 to
1000 Å thick is deposited by sputtering or electroless copper plating.
The bulk of the conductor thickness is then built up through a normal
photoresist mask. Subsequent stripping of the resist layer followed by

etching of the remaining thin electroless metal layer leaves the isolated conductor layers. Known in the printed wiring industry as *panel plating,* this process results in a lower-cost approach for MCM-D metallization.

The third approach, called the *evaporation/lift-off approach,* owes its origins to semiconductor processing. In this additive approach, a thick photoresist layer is formed and imaged with the desired conductor pattern in order to achieve a retrograde sidewall profile. The desired copper-based conductor with appropriate required barrier metals is then sequentially deposited by evaporation onto the substrates. The carefully optimized photoresist profile together with the inherently directional nature of the evaporation processes results in a discontinuous metal deposition. By postevaporation dissolution of the photoresist layer in a suitable organic solvent or stripper, the metal that was on the photoresist layer is lifted, leaving the isolated metal lines on the surface of the dielectric layer.

A newer approach, *laser patterning,* is based on the use of lasers to define conductor lines directly on the dielectric. This process circumvents the use of masks and is normally controlled by a computer, resulting in economies of scale in processing. The two basic procedures for laser patterning are (1) using a laser to remove a catalytic metal followed by electroless deposition of the surface metal and (2) using a laser beam to expose a negative photoresist followed by metal etching to remove the unwanted conductor metal.

7.4.2 Vacuum Deposition and Sputtering

Vapor or vacuum deposition is one of the oldest known processes for thin-film deposition. Basically, it consists of heating metals or alloys by resistance or induction heating in a relatively high vacuum. Gold, aluminum, copper, and silver are vaporized by resistance heating at 800 to 1000°C in a vacuum of about 10^{-6} torr.

The argon atoms are accelerated and bombard the target with such great force that they rip off particles of the target material. In contrast to vapor deposition, sputtering is an electrophysical process in which atoms of inert gases (e.g., argon) are converted to positively charged ions through an applied potential of several thousand volts across closely spaced electrodes. Electrons are released to interact with other argon atoms to form a plasma.

The argon cations are very energetic and are attracted to the "target," or cathode, which is composed of the material to be deposited. The sputtered material deposits onto the substrate, which is placed on a stage and either grounded or rendered cathodic. Termed *direct sput-*

tering, this is only one version of many different methods used for the sputtering process.

A more universal approach is *radiofrequency sputtering*, which is not limited to only metals but also dielectrics, inorganic compounds, alloys, and some plastics. A third technique, *reactive sputtering*, features use of a reactive gas such as nitrogen or oxygen, which is introduced along with the argon. It reacts with the sputtered material as it deposits on the surface, generating a completely new compound. A comparison of vacuum deposition and sputtering is given in Table 7.7.

Table 7.7. Vacuum Evaporation versus Sputtering[8]

	Vacuum evaporation	Sputtering
Mechanism	Thermal energy	Momentum transfer
Deposition rate	Can be high (to 750,000 Å/min)	Low (20 to 100 Å/min) except for some metals (Cu = 10,000 Å/min)
Control of deposition	Sometimes difficult	Reproducible and easy to control
Coverage for complex shapes	Poor, line of sight	Good, but not non-uniform thickness
Coverage into small blind holes	Poor, line of sight	Poor
Metal deposition	Yes	Yes
Alloy deposition	Yes (flash evaporation)	Yes
Refractory metal deposition	Yes (by e-beam)	Yes
Plastics	No	Some
Inorganic compounds (oxides, nitrides)	Generally no	Yes
Energy of deposited species	Low (0.1 to 0.5 eV)	High (1 to >100 eV)
Adhesion to substrate	Good	Excellent

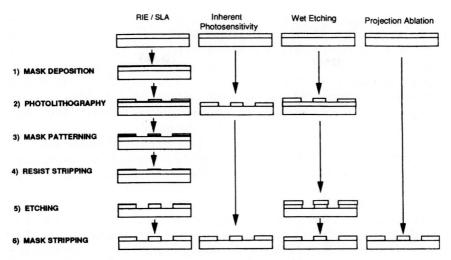

Figure 7.6. Generic MCM-D via-generation alternatives.[10]

7.4.3   Via Formation

Via formation is generally considered to be a significant contributor to the overall cost of MCM-D fabrication due to the large number of sequential steps required. In this way, it is similar to the conventual PCB fabrication, where hole formation is a serial process and a cost driver. Several unique via-generation processes are currently used for MCM-D fabrication. Figure 7.6 presents a schematic comparison of the most commonly used methods. Reactive ion etching (RIE) has been the most commonly used approach because of its common use in the manufacture of semiconductors. Although several alternative RIE masking methods have been used, thin metal masking layers are the most common. In this procedure, the mask is deposited and then defined by photolithography. The resist is then stripped, and the dielectric is etched by wet or dry etching methods.

Chemical or wet processing of dielectrics involves the use of aqueous or organic solvents to etch vias in MCM-D dielectric layers. These approaches have fallen into one of two major material/process categories, the inherently photosensitive dielectrics and the wet-etchable materials.

In wet etching, a relatively thin (1 to 5 μm thick), patterned photoresist layer serves as the template to define the sites of via etching in the dielectric layer. In the inherently photosensitive process, a negative-acting photosensitive dielectric material is used and is defined by conventional photolithography. It is then developed or stripped, resulting in the via.

Volatilization and removal of a dielectric material are also done by the use of a laser ablation procedure. Most laser ablation procedures use an eximer laser, which removes, in selected areas, dielectric by means of direct write, scanning, or projection technique. Direct write involves the use of a laser beam which is collated by an aperture that permits the removal of the dielectric material by individual vias. In scanning or projection ablation, the substrate is "flooded" with laser energy through a patterning mask, usually metal.

Projection ablation via-generation processes involve the use of a patterned, discrete dielectric ablation and a computer-controlled scanning or step and repeat eximer-based ablation tool. This type of process has been used for GE's HDI process, as well as for volume production of MCM substrates for IBM's ES9000 computer.

Several via metallization processes are used in fabrication of MCM-D modules, with sidewall metallization carried out simultaneously with the deposition of the next layer, resulting in electrical connection to the previous metal layer. Stair-stepped vias generally consume space and are a major problem in this technology. Stacked vias require a greater number of processing steps, and substrate planarization is maintained during the whole of the sequential substrate fabrication process. A number of different via filling approaches are used, including electroless nickel, via fill by evaporation/lift-off, and via postformation with subsequent dielectric deposition and lap back. A comparison of the stair-stepped and stacked via arrangements is given in Fig. 7.7.

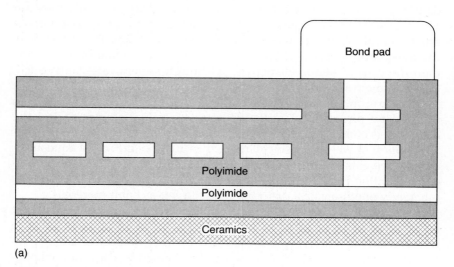

(a)

Figure 7.7. Stacked (a) and stair-stepped (b) vias.[2]

7.5 Design Considerations[1]

Many different design options exist for the MCM-D module, dictated by the particular interconnection technology employed. This makes it difficult to define typical design rules. It is certain that MCM-D design is process-driven and depends heavily on the process and material used. Normally, the system partitioning decides the total number of chips to be used for a module. The packing density of active elements in the MCM is most often determined by factors such as thermal density, routing density, and the type of chip-module interconnection and off-module interconnection to be used.

7.5.1 General Design Considerations

MCM-D presents the most interesting possibilities for digital systems designers. The use of additive processes adopted from the semiconductor industry can produce excellent circuit results. Well-defined design rules for MCM-D modules are highly dependent on the process used. This section will define typical design guidelines to develop the MCM-D substrate.

The MCM-D assembly is an electronic assembly incorporating a base substrate with one or more deposited dielectric and conductive circuit layers. The conductive layers supply both the conductive pat-

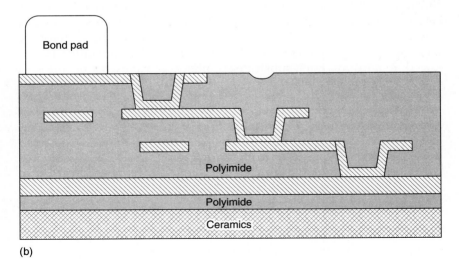

(b)

Figure 7.7 (*Continued*)

tern and the device interconnect features. Additionally, the materials and processes selected for the substrate will affect both device attachment and terminal technology. A wide range of choices in substrate materials, metal interconnects, and dielectric materials is used, and these choices will have a bearing on both operational limits and economic considerations. The design engineer must determine the actual requirements for the finished product prior to selecting the base material, dielectric, and process technology to be used.

Type D multichip modules (MCM-Ds) are produced by the deposition of thin-film circuitry on a variety of substrate materials. The thin-film elements are formed by sequentially evaporating or sputtering resistive or conductive materials from a source or target on a substrate in a vacuum chamber. In the evaporation process, the source materials are heated to their vapor-phase temperatures and then allowed to condense onto the substrate (see Sec. 7.4.1).

These processes are subtractive, in that materials are put down on the total substrate and then subtractively removed by photolithographic methods. In general, the resistive material is under all conductor patterns and is exposed by etching the conductor to form the resistive elements.

7.5.2 Layout

MCM design begins with system partitioning and the selection of a particular process technology. System partitioning is determined by considering the nature of the electronic system. Once partitioned, circuit performance, cost, weight, production volume, environmental conditions, and other factors determine selection of the technology. Each technology determines a set of design rules that must be followed. In addition, each substrate supplier will have a set of rules and concerns that needs consideration by the designer in order to complete a cost-effective, reliable layout. Typical rules include

- Trace widths
- Trace clearances
- Via sizes and shapes
- Pad sizes and shapes
- Via stacking rules
- Component-attachment methods
- Maximum/minimum trace lengths

Table 7.8. Electrical Characteristics of Thin-Film–Deposited Conductors[1]

Resistance per 25 mm (1 in)		
Line width, mm (in)	Typical	Maximum
0.13 (0.005)	2.00 Ω	4.00 Ω
0.25 (0.010)	1.00 Ω	2.00 Ω
0.38 (0.015)	0.67 Ω	1.33 Ω
0.51 (0.020)	0.50 Ω	1.00 Ω

Current Rating 25 mm (1 in)	
Line width, mm (in)	Current
0.13 (0.005)	300 ma
0.25 (0.010)	600 ma
0.38 (0.015)	900 ma
0.51 (0.020)	1200 ma

Capacitance Between Adjacent Conductors	
0.13 mm (0.005 in) apart	<1 pF per 25 mm (1 in)

Material
Electroplated gold 0.001 to 0.005 mm (40–200 µin)
Over titanium 0.00015 to 0.0003 mm (6–12 µin)
Over tantalum nitride 0.00005 mm (2 µin)
Over alumina substrate 0.64 mm (0.025 in)

Resistivity	
Gold plating thickness	Ohms square
0.0018 mm (70 µin)	0.015 to 0.020
0.0025 (100 µin)	0.010
0.0036 mm (144 µin)	0.006 to 0.009

Temperature Coefficient of Resistance
40 ppm/°C

7.5.3   Conductor Pattern

Conductors for MCM-D modules may take a variety of shapes, from single conductor traces to conductor planes. In general, electrical design requirements dictate conductor definition with accompanying close dimensional control. Conductor widths, lengths, and spacings determine specific electrical characteristics. The conductor must be kept as thin as possible in order to use design equations and maintain dimensional control yet must be thick enough to minimize "skin effect" losses. Ground connection should be made by use of through holes or edge metallization. Typical electrical characteristics of thin-film conductors are listed in Table 7.8.

7.5.4   Conductor Routing

The length of a conductor between any two lands should be held to a minimum. However, conductors should run in straight xy directions to aid computerized documentation for mechanized or automated layouts. Conductor junctions, the corners of mounting lands, and conductor-resistor patterns should be designed with right-angled turns. Table 7.9 and Fig. 7.8 present guidelines for the layout of thin-film conductors and lands.

7.5.4.1   Land Pattern.   Table 7.10 and Fig. 7.9 provide guidelines for the dimensioning and spacing of lands for active and passive components. Layouts should be prepared with the exit bonding on the substrate in alignment with the metallized areas or pins in the module package. When space allows, probe lands should be provided for troubleshooting and for use for resistor-trimming purposes, in which case they should be placed as close as possible to resistor terminators.

7.5.5   MCM-D Applications

7.5.5.1   General Electric High-Density Interconnect (HDI) Approach.[11,12]   High-density interconnect is a novel approach for the interconnection of high-performance IC chips in an ultradense configuration. It departs from the conventional methods in that chips are mounted in the substrate, the interconnection layer is deposited over the top of the chips, and interconnection to the chips is made in this fashion. Advantages can be summarized as follows: The overlay layer makes the entire chip area available for interconnect lines, thermal management is more efficient because dies are in direct contact with the substrate, via and line formation are under computer control, the interconnect has

Table 7.9. Dimensional Constraints for Thin-Film Conductors and Lands[1]

Conductor and pad sizes and spacing	Minimum dimension, mm (in)	Nominal dimension, mm (in)	Maximum dimension, mm (in)	Figure 7.8 item
Conductor width	0.06 (0.0025)	0.25 (0.010)	None	1
Conductor to edge of substrate	0.25 (0.010)	0.32 (0.0125)	None	2
Conductor-to-conductor spacing	0.06 (0.0025)	0.13 (0.005)	None	3
Conductor-to-resistor spacing (for resistors without laser trim tabs and tolerance <20%) (only required on side to be trimmed)	0.13 (0.005)	0.19 (0.0075)	None	4
Conductor-to-resistor spacing (trim side, for resistors with laser trim tabs)	0.06 (0.0025)	0.13 (0.005)	None	5
Exit bonding pads (width)	0.25 (0.010)	0.32 (0.0125)	None	6
Exit bonding pads (length)	0.25 (0.010)	0.32 (0.0125)	None	7
Wire bonding pads (width and length, one wire)	0.13 (0.005)	0.25 (0.010) in direction of wire	None	8
Wire bonding pads (width and length, two wires on same pad)	0.25 (0.010)	0.32 (0.0125)	None	9

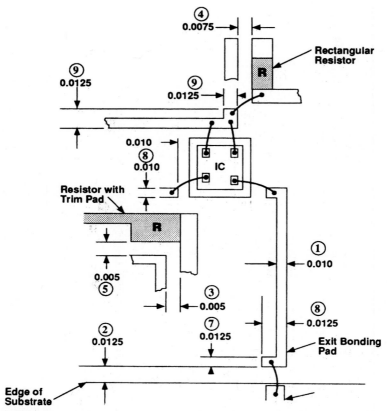

Figure 7.8. Nominal thin-film conductor and land dimensions (see Table 7.9).

very high density, and no patterning mask is required. Figure 7.10 shows a schematic of the HDI module construction.

The HDI fabrication process is as described in the following nine steps (see Fig. 7.11):

1. Small cavities are milled into the ceramic substrate blanks. Module I/O fingers, power and ground distribution busses, and chip-back bias metals are then deposited, patterned, and etched away, creating the module foundation.

2. IC chips and surface-mount capacitors and resistors are bonded to the ceramic.

3. A thin sheet of kapton is laminated to the entire substrate surface.

Table 7.10. Chip-Mounting Lands[1]

Pad size and spacing	Minimum dimension, mm (in)	Nominal dimension, mm (in)	Maximum dimension, mm (in)	Figure 7.9 item
Semiconductor chip-to-chip spacing	(1)	(1)	None	1
Semiconductor chip mounting pad (width and length beyond chip)	0.25 (0.010)	0.32 (0.0125)	None	2
Passive chip-to-bonding pad wiring distance beyond chip (width or length)	0.76 (0.030)	0.82 (0.325)	2.54 (0.100)	3
Passive chip mounting pad (beyond chip width)	0.13 (0.005)	0.19 (0.0075)	None	4
Passive chip mounting pad (beyond chip end)	0.38 (0.015)	0.43 (0.017)	None	5
Passive chip-to-conductor overlap	0.25 (0.010)	0.32 (0.0125)	None	6
Passive chip-to-wire bonding pad spacing	1.02 (0.040)	1.27 (0.050)	None	7
Inductor lead mounting pad (width and length)	1.02 (0.040)	1.27 (0.050)	None	8
Inductor body-to-wire bonding pad	0.13 (0.005)	0.19 (0.0075)	None	10
Passive chip end-to-end spacing	1.02 (0.040)	1.27 (0.050)	None	9

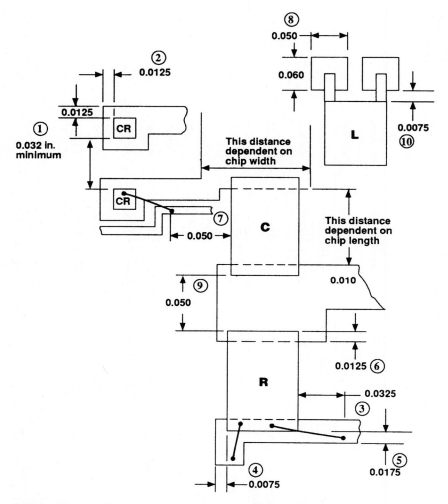

Figure 7.9. Nominal dimensions for chip-mounting lands (see Table 7.10).[1]

4. An image scanner locates the I/O pads on each chip, and a laser is used to bore a hole "via" through the kapton.

5. Titanium and copper metals are deposited using sputter and electroplating processes.

6. Rasterized trace and coverpad data are adapted and exposed. Unwanted metal is etched to form the conductor pattern.

7. A new layer of dielectric is applied.

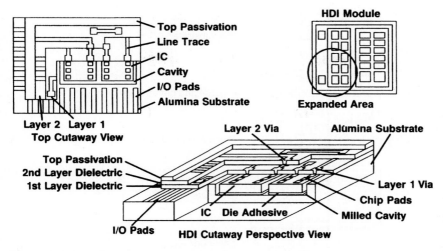

Figure 7.10. Schematic cross section of an HDI MCM.[11]

8. To complete the interconnect in a multilayered structure, the process is repeated from step 4.

9. When all layers are complete, a passivation layer is applied to form a seal from outside contamination.

HDI process parameters are outlined in Table 7.11.

7.5.5.2 Polycon High-Density MCM.[16]

Termed the *high-density multilayer interconnect* (HDMI), this landmark design is characteristic of the MCM-D interconnect systems. In this approach, a thin-film interconnect is formed over a silicon substrate, and the dielectric used is BCB (bisbenzocyclobutene). The silicon is used to capitalize on the perfect CTE match with the silicon IC chip and with the flatness and dimensional stability of the silicon. The basic polycon process flow is shown in Fig. 7.12. The process consists of conventional definition of metal layers by sputtered metal (aluminum), photoresist patterning, and etch, followed by a coating of the BCB polymer, and etching of vias in the polymer by reactive ion etch following photolithographic definition of the via pattern. This process is repeated for successive layers, followed by a final step in preparation of bonding pads.

The basic HMDI line structure and conformal via structure are shown in Fig. 7.13. Structures are typically fabricated with 2.5-μm conductors, 10 to 25 μm wide. Via diameters are typically equal to the conductor line widths. The dielectric thickness is 8 μm. A stair-

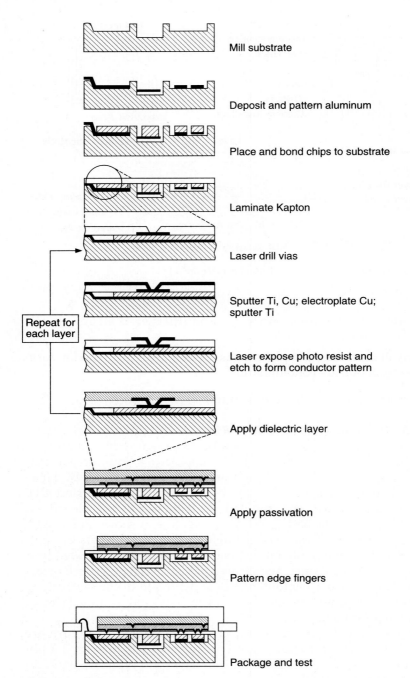

Mill substrate

Deposit and pattern aluminum

Place and bond chips to substrate

Laminate Kapton

Laser drill vias

Sputter Ti, Cu; electroplate Cu; sputter Ti

Laser expose photo resist and etch to form conductor pattern

Apply dielectric layer

Apply passivation

Pattern edge fingers

Package and test

Repeat for each layer

Figure 7.11. HDI process flow.[12]

Table 7.11. HDI Process Parameters[11]

Property	Value
Dielectric thickness	
Layer 1	25–30 µm
Layers 2, 3, 4	10–30 µm
Line width	25 µm
Line spacing	25 µm
Via bottom	10–30 µm
Conductor thickness	2–5 µm
Chip-to-chip spacing	≥100 µm
Thermal conductance through chip, substrate, and chip-to-substrate bonding layer	~ 1°C/W
Die shear	>30 lb for 1 cm^2 chip
Dielectric properties	
Dielectric withstand	>1 kV
Dielectric constant	about 3
Interconnect capacitance	0.7–1 pF/cm

case via structure is used, assisted by the superior planarization properties of BCB.

7.5.5.3 DEC VAX 9000. DEC's MCM technology for the VAX 9000 computer involves building up thin-film layers (individual layers for ground and power and for signal lines) on an aluminum substrate, removing the thin-film layers from the temporary carrier, and then laminating the layers together onto a another metallic substrate. The basic architecture of this module, illustrated in Fig. 7.3, consists of two separate thin-film structures mounted on a copper-alloy substrate and interconnected to a silicon die, also mounted on the substrate. Briefly, the process consists of the fabrication of a power core and a signal core, both thin-film structures. The power core and signal core processes are similar in many ways to IC processes, for the power core is fabricated by using a 6-in aluminum wafer which is coated with polyimide, then coated with sputtered Cr-Cu, and electroplated with a thin layer of copper. The first power layer is then defined using conventional photolithographic methods and is etched to define the first power plane.

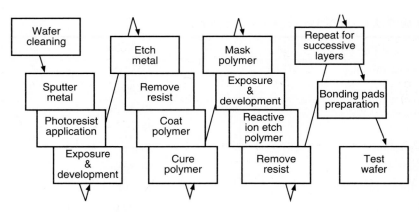

Figure 7.12. Polycon HDMI process flow.[13]

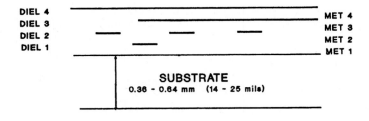

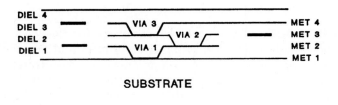

Figure 7.13. Basic polycon HDMI structure.[13]

This process is then repeated three more times and followed by a top polyimide coating layer.

The signal core is fabricated in a similar manner, using a 6-in aluminum wafer as a starting substrate and spin coating polyimide in multiple coatings to the necessary thickness. A layer of Cr-Cu-Cu is sputtered on, followed by more polyimide, and then etched to define the metal reference plane. More polyimide is then spun on and cured, more Cr-Cu is sputtered on, and a pattern for the first signal line is defined, followed by electroplating to form the signal lines. Thicker resist is then spun on to form the via structure, vias being formed by wet chemical processing. This process is continued for a maximum of three metal layers to the final polyimide layer deposition and via etch.

7.5.5.4 AT&T Polyhic MCM.   The AT&T Polyhic MCM is manufactured using multiple layers of photodefinable dielectric and thin-film conductors on a ceramic substrate. A schematic cross section of

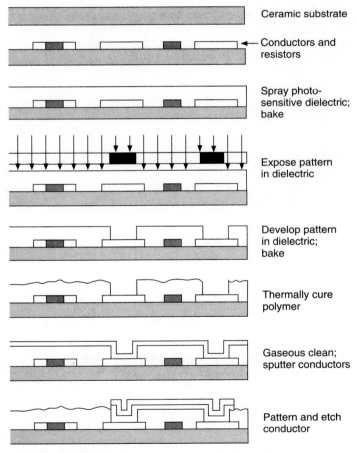

Ceramic substrate

Conductors and resistors

Spray photo-sensitive dielectric; bake

Expose pattern in dielectric

Develop pattern in dielectric; bake

Thermally cure polymer

Gaseous clean; sputter conductors

Pattern and etch conductor

Figure 7.14. Polyhic fabrication process.[14]

Figure 7.15. Polyhic MCM.[14]

the polyhic fabrication process is illustrated in Fig. 7.14. The baseline for the Polyhic MCM is a 99 percent alumina substrate, with conductors and resistors deposited. Photoresist is sprayed on this substrate, and the pattern is exposed to form the vias. The vias are etched through a chemical vapor deposition (CVD) oxide layer used as an etch mask, the etching done by a reactive ion process. Via diameter is 4 to 6 mils. The 2-μm-thick copper conductors are electroplated onto a sputter deposited Ti-Cu or Ti-Cr-Cu adhesion layer. Typical line widths and spaces are 2 to 4 mils. Typically, two layers of copper interconnect are used. An example of a typical Polyhic MCM is shown in Fig. 7.15.

References

1. Guidelines for Multichip Module Technology Utilization." Institute for Interconnecting and Packaging Electronic Circuits, IPC-MC-790, 1992.

2. John W. Balde, Interconnect Decision Consulting, "Overview of Multichip Technology," private correspondence.

3. Thomas J. Moravec and Ronald Jensen, Honeywell Solid State Electronics Center, and Sharon A. Coogan and Jack W. Steubs, Honeywell Space and Strategic Systems, "Multichip Modules for Todays VLSI Circuits," *Electronic Packaging and Production,* November 1990, pp. 48–53.

4. R. Wayne Johnson, Alabama Microelectronics and Technology Center, "Thin Film Multichip Modules: An Overview," *Proceedings, NEPCON,* 1989, pp. 655–672.

5. Mary Wesling Hartnett and E. Jan Vardeman, TechSearch International, Inc., "Worldwide MCM Status and Trends: Material Choices," *Proceedings, NEPCON West,* 1991, pp. 1111–1120.

6. Steven Poon, J. Tony Pan, Tsing-Chow Wang, and Brad Nelson, MCC, "High Density Multilevel Copper-Polyimide Interconnects," *Proceedings, NEPCON West,* 1989, pp. 426–448.

7. Gretchen M. Adema, Michele J. Berry, and Iwona Turlik, MCC, "Dielectric Materials for Use in Thin Film Multichip Modules," *Electronic Packaging and Production,* February 1992, pp. 72–76.

8. James J. Licari, Hughes Aircraft, "Hybrid Thin Film Processing Enters a New Era," *Electronic Packaging and Production,* September 1989, pp. 56–63.

9. Richard C. Eden, Norden Company, "Applicability of Diamond Substrates to Multi-Chip Modules," *Proceedings, ISHM,* 1991, pp. 363–367.

10. T. G. Tessier, Motorola, and P. E. Garrou, Dow Chemical, "Overview of MCM Technologies: MCM-D," *Proceedings, ISHM,* 1992, pp. 235–244.

11. L. M. Levinson, C. W. Eichelberger, R. J. Wojnarowski, and R. O. Carlson, GE Corporate Research and Development, "High-Density Interconnects using Laser Lithography," *Proceedings, NEPCON West,* 1989, pp. 1319–1327.

12. Jim Sabatini, GE, "MCM Design Using High Density Packaging," *Surface Mount Technology,* March 1992, pp. 18–19.

13. John Reche, Polycon, Philip Garrou, Joseph Carr, and Paul Townsend, Dow Chemical, "High Density Multichip Module Fabrication," *The International Journal for Hybrid Microelectronics,* Vol. 13, No. 4, December 1990, pp. 91–98.

14. Melissa Katz, AT&T, "Critical Application Roles for Polyhics," *Printed Circuit Design,* September 1990, pp. 32–34.

8

Laminated-Dielectric Multichip Modules (MCM-L)

Certainly one of the oldest of the multichip module (MCM) technologies, MCM-L involves the use of printed wiring boards as the interconnection substrate. Modules built based on this technology were given the common industry designator COB (chip-on-board), and MCM-L is an extension of this technology. Although other interconnection methods, such as flip chip and TAB bonding, are also practical for MCM-L modules, the usual technique was to wire bond the die to the printed wiring board. The interconnection density of this method was extremely low when compared with other MCM technologies, giving advantage to the other more densely packaged methods, MCM-C and MCM-D.

8.1 MCM-L Characteristics[1,2]

8.1.1 Comparison with Other Technologies

A complete description of the three MCM technologies was presented in Chap. 1, but a short review of the different techniques is appropriate considering the many divergent uses and capabilities of the substrate structures. MCM technologies are characterized by a wide diversity of design, material, and structural options.

MCM-L modules consist of substrates fabricated using typical printed wiring board materials and processes. This group includes both reinforced (woven and unwoven) and unreinforced dielectric materials, such as epoxies and polyimides, with copper conductors formed using both subtractive and additive methods. The conductive layers are laminated together, at times sequentially, and drilled and metallized using both electroless and electroplated copper. The MCM-L approach is a low-cost option for MCM technology. Applications requiring roughly 50 to 150 cm/cm^2 of interconnection density and 100 to 200 MHz of performance can be met using this technology.

MCM-C modules cover substrates typically made from thick-film ceramic (TFC), high-temperature cofired ceramic (HTCC), and low-temperature cofired ceramic (LTCC) technologies. Not unlike PC boards, this technology is not new. Recently, low-temperature cofired processes and materials have been incorporated using glass-ceramic dielectric materials with low coefficients of thermal expansion (CTE) and low dielectric constants and more compatible with low-resistivity conductive materials, making them more process-oriented. The optimal glass-ceramic slurry is cast into a green sheet using a doctor blade method, and via holes are formed by punching. Conductive pastes containing low-resistivity metals such as gold, copper, and gold-palladium are patterned using a thick-film screen printing technique to form the conductor and via patterns. The patterned green substrates are then laminated, cut, and fired to form the multilayer substrate.

The MCM-D is made by a process much like the one used to manufacture integrated circuits, except that the substrate is large enough to contain several bare dice. The base substrate is usually silicon or ceramic, with conductors ranging in width between 1 μm and 1 mil. The thin-film elements are formed by sequentially depositing by evaporation or sputtering resistive and conductive materials from a source or target on the substrate. Vias are formed by laser ablation. The conductive layers are separated by laminated or deposited dielectric layers, usually materials such as silicon dioxide of polymers. MCM-D is projected to be the low-cost alternative for applications requiring high interconnection densities in the range of 200 to 400 cm/cm^2 and beyond.

8.1.2 Advantages and Disadvantages

The advantages of MCM-L over MCM-C (ceramic-dielectric multichip modules) and MCM-D (deposited-dielectric multichip modules) are its faster time to market, lower substrate cost, and overall lower cost (see Table 8.1). Since it is primarily a printed wiring board, another significant advantage is its multisource capability and attendant risk reduction. Controlled impedance can be designed into the structure, as with any critical circuitry. Laminate technology is well established, and manufacturing costs are amortized by the volume manufacturing of conventional printed wiring boards. Also, it is possible to place chips on both sides of the substrate, a distinct density advantage.

The use of copper as the conductor is another advantage, since the high conductivity of this material for signal routing and power distribution makes it the best material for electrical performance. The conductors on the other two types of MCMs have higher dc resistance and are lossy, while on the MCM-L, copper conductors of any required thickness and cross section over a controlled dielectric thickness can be provided, accommodating different characteristic impedances.

A primary shortcoming of the MCM-L is certainly the high coefficient of thermal expansion (CTE) of the substrate. This limits the size of the IC chips to be used and places a burden on the type of die-connection technique used, especially in the short-lead methods such as flip chip and short wire bonding. Another problem is the limitation in board density caused by the requirement to drill completely through the board to interconnect layers, limiting the space required to run signal lines. Improvements for high-density MCM-L modules are available, including use of blind and buried vias, finer lines and spaces, smaller vias, and landless holes. Laminates are poor heat conductors, and this makes it difficult to extract heat from small, powerful chips.

Table 8.1. MCM Cost Comparison[1]

MCM type	Material	Cost ratio
MCM-L	BT laminates	1
MCM-C	Cofired alumina	1.5–2
MCM-D	Thin-film alumina	2–3
MCM-D	Silicon substrate	7–10

Based on a 4 × 4 in substrate with 10 metal layers and a run of 10,000.

However, heavy copper planes and heat vias or embedded metal plates can alleviate this problem.

8.2 MCM-L Process Considerations[1,3,4]

The process for the manufacture of MCM-Ls is essentially identical with that used for highly dense multilayer boards. Common areas where MCM-L module requirements will differ include fine-line pattern definition, etching, selective plating, additive plating, special materials requirements, and other features directed toward the particular density requirements of the MCM-L technology.

Five standard types of processes are used in the manufacture of MCM-L, or printed wiring board, substrates:

- Photoresist application to substrate core layers, imaging, and development
- Etching of copper foil on inner layers
- Lamination of inner layers with B-stage (adhesive) dielectric layers
- Drilling of holes through single layers for buried and blind vias, through partial laminate sections (sublaminates) for buried or blind vias, or through the entire laminate for plated through holes (PTH)
- Plating of drilled holes to accomplish the through-hole or interlayer electrical connection, as well as finish plating of the surface layers for etch resist or for surface feature definition

For the sake of organizing the explanation of the fabrication of

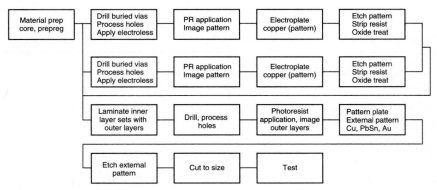

Figure 8.1. MCM-L substrate process flow.

MCM-L modules, it is convenient to summarize the processes as shown in Fig. 8.1. These process all have a number of steps which are further described below. More complete descriptions of process steps may be found in references 4 and 10.

8.2.1 Internal-Layer Patterning

One of the most critical process steps in the manufacture of printed wiring boards is image transfer, or *patterning*, since it is the step at which the design or artwork is injected into the manufacturing cycle. Prior to the processing of the inner layers, the copper surfaces are cleaned by mechanical abrasion or chemically by etching. This step, called *A treatment*, is an oxidation step, which actually increases the surface area of the copper and enhances adhesion in the subsequent lamination of the inner layers. An etch-resist material is then applied, either by screening or by use of a photoresist.

Screening, a process borrowed from the graphic arts industry, provides a method for selectively transferring resist material to the foil surface through the open, or "clear," areas of the screen. However, because of the density requirements of MCM-L technology, screening is rarely used. For this reason, photoresist is used most commonly, and photoresists are available in either the liquid or dry-film form. Liquid resists are applied by spraying, roller coating, or curtain coating.

Often, liquid resists provide finer pattern definition than the solid-film photoresists, and for this purpose, they are applied by means of electrostatic spray or electrophoric or plating methods. Dry-film resists are laminated to the copper foil surface in a hot roller press. Because of the availability of thicker films (1.0 to 2.5 mils), which withstand the hot, harsh plating solutions, dry-film resists are superior for plated circuits, which are used for outer-layer processing.

Following application of the photoresist, the pattern is exposed using appropriate artwork, the resist is developed, and the pattern is etched. Following removal of the photoresist, the surface of the copper is processed chemically to form an oxide to assist in adhesion for the subsequent lamination.

8.2.2 Etching

One of the major steps in the chemical processing of subtractive printed boards is etching, or removal of copper, to achieve the desired circuit patterns. Etching is also incorporated into the preparation of surfaces by microetching (minimal metal removal) during inner-layer preparation.

The most common etching systems are based on cupric chloride, hydrogen peroxide–sulfuric acid, and alkaline ammonia. Other systems include ferric chloride, chromic sulfuric acids, and persulfates. Alkaline etchants, with their high production capacity and good economics, are the most important etchants used for fine-line etching.

Etching technologies and equipment used today have evolved from four basic methods: immersion, bubble, splash (paddle), and spray etching. The latter is used most commonly, since it is fast, well suited to high production, and capable of fine line definition. Control of the process is important. During etching, since the depth of etch proceeds vertically, the sidewalls tend to etch sideways and produce an undercut action, known as *etch factor*. Conventional etch factors of 0.3 to 0.5 will not suffice for fine-line conductors. To overcome this, new anisotropic etchants are being used, as well as additive plating, to preserve line-width tolerances.

8.2.3 Buried and Blind Via Generation[2,5]

In standard multilayer technology, the drilled holes extend entirely through the board thickness and are plated to interconnect the buried layers, forming the plated through holes (PTHs). Illustrated in Fig. 8.2, blind and buried vias are a method for increasing the density of the MCM-L by not forming a hole in layers where there is no interconnection to the hole, thereby taking up valuable "real estate." By designing the substrate with blind and buried vias, many variations in signal processing are possible. Standard multilayer boards incorporate holes that are formed through the entire multilayer board to provide electrical interconnection. However, most high-density MCM-L modules are fabricated with interconnections that do not span the entire board structure.

A *buried via* can be described as a plated through hole connecting two or more layers of a multilayer board, buried inside the board structure but not coming to the surface of the board. The main advantage of the buried via construction is that it provides an internal path to an adjacent signal plane. When the connecting via goes between an internal layer and only one of the outside layers the via is referred to as a *blind via*.

As noted in Fig. 8.2, two via holes can be stacked over one another in the *xy* direction, whereas in the conventional multilayer board, only one could be used in this location. When an area is saved from being used for a via hole, that area is available for routing signal lines. This

Plated vias

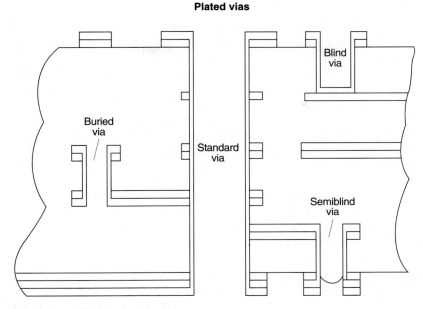

Figure 8.2. Blind and buried vias.[5]

construction also allows smaller via holes because it is drilled and plated in a thin piece of laminate, resulting in an aspect ratio of 1:5 or higher. When the aspect ratio is very low for these holes, they are easily plated.

When smaller holes are used, smaller pads (or lands) can be used, which then permits even more room for signal lines. Blind vias, in comparison, are plated vias that connect from the surface to an internal layer by a hole that does not pass entirely through the board.

Blind vias are fabricated in several ways. For instance, a laser or mechanical drill can create a hole down to the level of the interconnect point required. Interconnection is then accomplished through the same process and concurrently with the formation of the board's regular plated through holes. Alternatively, a drilled core can be wet processed in the same manner as a buried layer, except that the top layer is not etched until the outer-layer circuit features are also ready for etching. These vias are sometimes referred to as *semiblind* or *semiburied* vias. As in the buried via construction, blind vias can be stacked on top of one another, and they can be made smaller, leaving more room for signal lines.

8.2.4 Lamination

Multilayer-board (MLB) lamination is a process roughly identical to that used for the original manufacture of the printed wiring substrate material. In "laying up," or assembling, the stack of sheets to be laminated, sheets of fully cured circuit layers are placed alternatively with adhesive over registration pins. The adhesive is known as *prepreg* or *B-stage dielectric*. Similar to the circuit-layer material, the prepreg is partially cured and has higher resin content and low flow characteristics to ensure good encapsulation of all circuit features. Circuit registration is critical to the entire process in any printed wiring facility. Each layer of the MLB must be located as accurately as possible in relation to all other layers.

The purpose of vacuum lamination is to remove air, moisture, and residual solvents which can produce bubbles in the bond line and voids in the laminate. At the same time, a further improvement can be realized by lowering temperatures, pressures, and lamination time, at the same time reducing the amount of misregistration from movement of the layers with respect to each other. Lower pressures are possible, since less resin flow is needed to remove air bubbles.

Good bonding or lamination practice is important because the myriad of other processing steps—chemicals, hot solder, etc.—may cause delamination without proper lamination procedure. Typical bonding materials reach the optimal cure in about 40 min at temperatures ranging from 180 to 335°F. The lamination cycle is highly dependent on the design of the laminates, dimensional control required, and the polymer system used in the substrate and prepreg materials.

8.2.5 Drilling[4]

Drilling and subsequent hole cleaning are extremely critical in the fabrication of a PTH, since they provide the interconnect between individual layers. Holes may extend through the entire substrate or, in the case of buried vias, only through adjacent layers in the internal portion of the multilayer substrate.

Drill hole size and quality are essential to the reliability of the MCM-L, since smaller size relates to higher density, and good-quality holes make for more reliable plating and interconnection. The seven basic variables in the drilling process are the drilling machine, stacking and pinning, drilling parameters, drill bits, entry and backup materials, and laminate materials. The first six factors are controlled and determined directly by the drilling operation. The last, laminate materials (including construction and condition), is controlled by design.

Drills for making holes in printed circuit boards are made of tungsten carbide. This is due to interrelated factors, including cost, handling properties, wear, and machinability. The design of a drill is equally important to the materials used. Design and wear of the drill determine its ability to remove material, drilling temperature, tendency to create burrs and smears, and smoothness of the hole wall, all related to hole quality.

High-speed multispindle drills are used for MLB drilling, driven off a CAD database that is coordinated with the design software used to create the board artwork. In the interest of reducing costs, stack drilling is also done, but rarely with MLBs. In many cases, stack drilling is a source of drill errors.

It is important to maintain the proper drill speed and feed, determined by the drill size and material drilled. Entry and backup materials are used to serve as drill guides, to prevent drill breakage caused by drill wander, and to cool the drill. Entry materials also prevent damage to the stackup due to the drill pressure foot. Entry materials are usually composites of aluminum-clad fiberboard.

Backup materials are used to prevent burrs in drilling, to cool the drill, and to prevent hole wall smearing and drill breakage. Phenolic or hardboard are commonly used as drill backup, but vented aluminum material is also popular.

Following drilling, it is essential to clean the holes to ensure good plating in the holes. During drilling, a number of defects are introduced which can affect hole quality. The heat produced by friction during drilling can cause the resin to smear over the surface of the drilled copper, effectively insulating that surface from the barrel of the plated hole. To remove this material, or "desmear," the board is cleaned chemically (usually with sulfuric acid or fluorosulfonic acid) or subjected to a plasma cleaning cycle.

8.2.6 Plating[4,6]

The most critical plating use is in the plated through hole, where it acts as an interconnecting link between the various circuit layers. Plating is also used in the additive method for building up circuitry, and lastly, it is used as an etch resist, where protective solder is plated over the entire circuit pattern and in the holes to protect them during the final etch. The process starts with treatment of the holes to permit plating and to promote adhesion. This is done by the chemical reduction of copper.

The board is sensitized, or made conductive, usually by tin and palladium formulations, by sorbing the sensitizer at polar sites. This deposit is then reduced in place to a thin metal film. Intermediate flash plating is used in the plating bath to prevent dissolution of the film in the plating bath or adhesion failure from plating stresses. The board is then usually electroplated.

Electroplating, or electrodeposition, consists mainly of the deposit of metal on a conductive surface (normally the cathode) from a suitable electrolyte. The plating is produced by the reduction of the metal ion in solution through electrons supplied to the cathode from an external dc source. The plating thickness obtained is proportional to the current density and the plating time. With thickness constant, plating time may be decreased by increasing current density, solution temperature, concentration, or the amount of agitation. Physical characteristics of the copper, such as grain structure and ductility, are affected by these processing parameters.

There are three common plating baths used in manufacturing printed wiring boards: pyrophosphate, fluoroborate, and sulfate. The pyrophosphate bath has good throwing power and provides a very ductile deposit, but is high in cost and sensitivity to contamination. Fluoroborate baths produce copper of medium ductility and have a high cost and very high sensitivity to contamination. The low-cost sulfate, or acid, bath has low sensitivity to contamination, is low in cost, and produces copper of medium ductility. The primary requisite for copper plating in PTH formation is ductility, since the reliability of the plated through hole during temperature cycling is determined by this. For this reason, the pyrophosphate bath is favored for high-density plating of MCM-L products, although some of the new composition sulfate baths have approached the ductility of deposited copper found in the pyrophosphate bath.

Panel plating involves copper plating of the entire surface area and the drilled holes prior to conductor pattern definition and etching. *Pattern plating* provides only the copper-defined circuit pattern and holes, which are subsequently overplated with etch-resistant metal. A pictorial description of these two methods appears in Fig. 8.3. Pattern plating, although requiring up to six fewer steps than panel plating, is more sensitive to plating current and has a tendency to contaminate the bath with organic resist material. It is, however, easier on the environment, since it results in less etching of copper and provides better tolerance control on conductor line width. On the other hand, panel-plated boards require longer etching time and introduce a control problem in line width and spacing, since both the plating and etching tolerances must be considered.

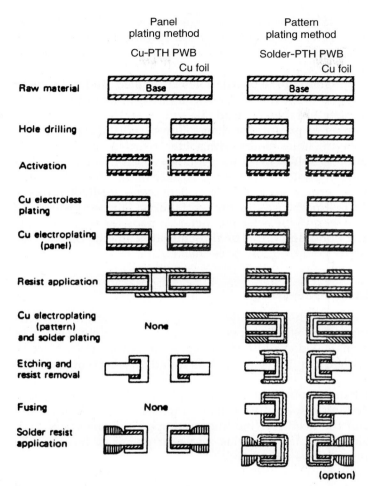

Figure 8.3. Pattern versus panel plating. (*Courtesy of DuPont, Inc.*)

8.2.7 Surface-Layer Processing

Final or outer-layer processing of the MCM-L structure involves the plating through of through hole connections as well as the special plating required for the attachment of surface-mount devices. This requirement highlights a similarity of MCM-L boards with those of printed wiring board (PWB) surface mount, where plating is required for attachment of surface-mount devices, in addition to that required as an etch-resistant metal to protect the holes. In normal PWBs, copper pads on the surface of the boards are tin-lead plated to permit mass reflow of surface-mount devices or soldering of through hole devices by wave soldering.

Following lamination of the board, holes are drilled, and photoresist is applied, imaged with the outer-layer pattern, and developed. Plating with copper and then tin-lead takes place on the surface and in the holes. Stripping of photoresist then follows, and the exposed copper is etched, leaving holes plated with solder, which is reflowed.

The application of solder mask may follow, which involves application and imaging of photoresist over the surface of the board, exposing the solder pads. Termed *solder mask over bare copper* (SMOBC), this is necessary on fine-line boards to prevent shorts. Further processing may be required to provide selective metal on pads for wire bonding, tape automated bonding (TAB), or flip-chip attachment. Usually the metals applied are gold over low-stress nickel.

8.2.8 Additive Processing[7]

Subtractive processing (discussed above) involves the definition of circuits by etching or removing copper. A completely different method of circuit definition, called *additive processing,* is finding increased use in highly dense circuit requirements such as found in processing MCM-L products.

The unique benefits offered by additive plating are an advantage in MCM-L processing, especially with the increased use of blind and buried vias and the need for fine lines and spaces. Boards with predictable circuit shapes, landless vias, and near-planar surfaces can be created through additive processing.

The fully additive process, in its simplest terms, involves drilling an unclad laminate using a permanent resist to define the circuit image and using full-build electroless copper to create the circuitry, as seen in Fig. 8.4. A more complete description of the process may be found in Fig. 8.5.

Specifically, a catalyzed, unclad, glass-epoxy substrate is coated with a special adhesive, dried to both sides, and drilled. A dry-film photoresist is then roll laminated to the panel, imaged, and developed. That portion of the resist is polymerized and becomes a permanent part of the panel; the remainder is washed away in the development process. The resist is then completely polymerized by curing with additional ultraviolet (UV) energy and a thermal bake. With the circuit channels formed, the panel is processed through an electroless plating to deposit copper in these channels. With this process, there is no

Additive Process

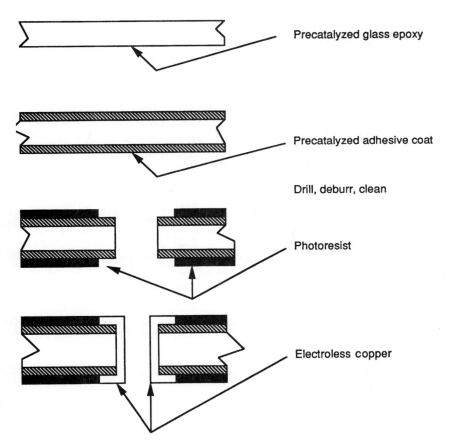

Precatalyzed glass epoxy

Precatalyzed adhesive coat

Drill, deburr, clean

Photoresist

Electroless copper

Figure 8.4. Steps in the additive process.[7]

resist stripping step, no etching, and no solder stripping step. A variation of the additive process, which uses normal laminate and requires a catalyzation step, is also shown in Fig. 8.5.

This process requires about half the steps required for subtractive processing and has a number of advantages over the subtractive process which relate to the needs for high-density circuits found in MCM-L PWBs. There is no line loss due to overetching. A near-planar

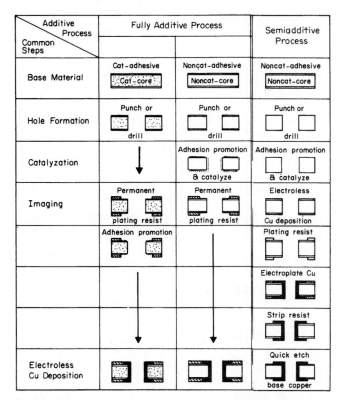

Figure 8.5. Simplified illustration of the additive process.

surface is formed by this process, making surface mounting of IC chips easier and also simplifying the subsequent application of solder resist to the surface.

The semiadditive process starts the same as the additive process, but after the initial sensitizing of the material, the circuit pattern and hole walls are built up using standard electroplating processes. After the registered printing of a plating-resist pattern to both sides of the board, copper is electroplated to the desired thickness on exposed areas. Resist is removed, unwanted electroless copper is "flash etched" off, and excess adhesive is removed with appropriate solvents. The last step is the curing of the adhesive by subjecting it to a heat and pressure cycle.

8.3 Material Considerations[3,8]

Materials used in the fabrication of MCM-L modules are essentially similar to those used in conventional PWB design. The basic material for PWBs is a composite of reinforcing material and a continuous-dielectric polymer-reinforced plastic, conductor material, and finishing materials. The substrate material is normally glass-epoxy, although other materials are used. The substrate material is a rigid glass-epoxy, while the prepreg, or adhesive, material is a semicured, or B-stage material. Typical conductor material used for power, ground, and signal layers is copper. Finishing materials used on the outer layers of the MCM-L substrate for component and die attachment are tin-lead and gold.

8.3.1 Substrate Materials

The overall mechanical structure of a typical PWB is composed of the reinforcing fiber, woven or nonwoven, the resin, and the copper conductors. The dielectric layers range in thickness from 0.004 to 0.030 in; copper ranges in thickness from 0.0008 to 0.028 in. Two types of substrate material are used in the manufacture of typical multilayer boards, the core material, or *C stage*, and the adhesive material, or B stage.

Significant requirements for a substrate material for MCM-L modules include

- A dielectric constant below 2.5 at gigahertz frequencies
- A T_g greater than 180°C to permit component repair and allow for reduced drilling smear
- A 3 to 5 ppm/°C CTE (The reinforcement and resin ratios could then be tailored to accommodate the higher percentage of copper present in a given PWB.)
- Low loss tangent, less than 0.1 percent
- Moisture absorption values less than 0.01 percent
- The same thermal dissipation characteristics as copper
- Low xy plane CTE
- Low z-axis CTE
- Strong interlaminate and surface bonds
- Good processibility, e.g., drilling and machining ease

The most popular laminates for MCM-L are still the FR-4(GF) class of

Table 8.2. Properties of Selected Laminate Materials for SMT[8]

Material	T_g, °C	CTE xy, z, ppm/°C		Thermal conductivity, W/m·K	Weight ratio	Dielectric constant, 1 MHz	Moisture absorption, %	Cost ratio
Glass/FR-4	25	14	189	0.18	1	4.8	0.1	1
Glass/polyimide	160–240	13	60	0.35	1	4.5	0.4	2–3
Glass/PTFE	75	24	261	0.26	1	2.3	1.0	15
Kevlar/Quatrex	185	6	90	0.16	0.7	3.9	0.9	3–7
Kevlar/polyimide	180–200	6	83	0.12	0.7	3.6	1.5	4–8
Quartz/polyimide	160–240	6	34	0.13	1.1	4.0	0.6	14
Cu/In/Cu-glass/polyimide	160–240	6	60	75	1.6	4.5	0.4	3–5

materials, However, higher-performance materials are now available, including polyimide (GI), multifunctional epoxies (FR-5), bismaleimide-triazine (BT), and other engineered resin systems. Polyimides have emerged as the most significant material in the high-performance area.

Table 8.2 summarizes some important properties of the more popular MLB dielectric materials. Weight control and thickness, as well as CTE control, are critical in selecting the appropriate reinforcement material for MCM-Ls exposed to thermal cycling. The laminate also must fulfill many requirements; e.g., it should permit easy drilling of small-diameter holes and provide dimensional stability 10 times that of standard E-glass.

8.3.1.1 Reinforcement Material. Reinforcements in laminates are materials embedded in or coated with a chosen resin to provide rigidity, dimensional stability, and strength of the laminate. While different materials have been used as reinforcements, woven glass cloth is the most common. The most significant reinforcement materials available for MCM-L PWBs include Kevlar aramid fibers, epoxy-glass, quartz, or graphite. Many of these reinforcements are available in woven, nonwoven and film-tape forms.

The growing problem of laminate dimensional stability is a direct result of the miniaturization of electronics packaging, as evinced by the use of MCMs. As grid layout, feature size of lines and spaces, and hole/via sizes decrease, laminate materials can develop dimensional stability problems. Using nonwoven reinforcement material and applying the copper metallization by additive or vapor deposition constitute one way of reducing dimensional instability.

8.3.1.2 Resin Material. The principal reasons for departing from the use of standard FR-4 epoxy-glass dielectric are to increase the glass transition temperature (T_g), reduce the thermal expansion of the module, and attain a lower dielectric constant. A higher T_g is recommended whenever the assembly temperatures will exceed the substrate's glass transition temperature. The ideal resin systems for high-performance laminate applications have T_g values over 180°C. High T_g values minimize a laminate's z-axis expansion during vapor phase or IR soldering and during most thermal cycling conditions. A number of high-T_g materials are available from laminate manufacturers, as noted in Table 8.3.

8.3.2 Conductors

The choice of conductors is typically confined to copper. The copper thicknesses used today are commonly 1 oz (0.0014 in) and ½ oz (0.0007

Table 8.3. Properties of Selected Resin Compositions[8]

Material	T_g, °C	Dielectric constant, 1 MHz	Flammability UL-94 rating	MLB processibility
FR-4 epoxy	120–125	4.0–4.5	V-0	Good
Tetrafunctional FR-4	130–135	4.0–4.5	V-0	Good
Polyimide/epoxy	220–260	3.3–3.5	N/R	Fair
Epoxy/polyimide	185–220	3.5	V-0/V-1	Fair
Quatrex 5010	185	3.9	V-0	Good
PTFE	75	2.1	V-0	Fair
Cyanate ester	230–250	2.8–3.1	V-0	N/A

in). The MCM-L, however, will require thickness of $\frac{1}{4}$ and $\frac{1}{8}$ oz (0.00035 and 0.00018 in). Most copper foil used in multilayers is made by an electroplating process in which the copper is plated from a solution onto a polished drum and then peeled off as a foil. The side against the drum is smooth; the other side is relatively rough, resulting in a better bond to prepreg resin systems. To increase this bond, the copper is oxidized or plated with a proprietary metal composition on one or both sides.

The copper foil is also formed by rolling. The rolled copper is by far the most ductile, but for reasons of economy, the electrodeposited foil is used most commonly. The electrical conductivity of all coppers is similar, but ductility, as mentioned above, can vary.

The CTE values of the copper foil and of the PWB to which the copper is adhered are different, and this necessitates a high copper peel strength. In addition, the line widths used in MCM-L are smaller than those used in conventional PWBs, and the dissimilar CTE values could result in a break of the conductor path. The peel strength of copper at room temperature for epoxy and modified-epoxy resins is usually adequate, but it is not adequate for polyimide and modified-polyimide resins.

To improve the copper-to-polyimide peel strength, it is necessary to perform an oxide treatment, referred to as *A treatment*. Because the conductor line widths will be narrow, the copper cladding must be chosen so that the surface to which the resin adheres will be rough and have considerable asperities, or roughness. Such cladding is called *high-profile material*.

The copper conductor patterns are formed most commonly by photoimaging and etching. It is becoming more common, however, to use an additive method to form conductors, usually with an electroless deposition process. Often the ductility and elongation are greater than those exhibited by rolled foils. Additive processing can produce finer, thicker lines with straighter sidewalls than usually possible with subtractive processing.

8.4 Design Considerations[9,10]

Well-defined design rules exist for PWBs, since this is certainly a mature technology. Requirements for MCM-L printed wiring may differ based on the extreme density requirements dictated by the MCM-L module. When comparing the design rules for normal PWBs and MCM-Ls, the conductor lines and spaces, number of dielectric layers, via sizes, and grid spacings are the areas of difference. The number of layers is typically less, and the conductor lines and spaces are reduced in size.

MCM-L substrate design should reference the latest version of IPC-D-275, a general guide for PWB design and related technology. IPC-MC-790 also should be referenced for general guidelines pertaining to MCM design.

8.4.1 Design Layout

The *printed wiring layout* is defined as a sketch that depicts the printed wiring substrate, the physical size and location of all components, and the routing of conductors that serve to interconnect the electronic parts. The layout is usually prepared in sufficient detail to permit the generation of documentation and artwork.

The layout generation process should include a formal design review of layout details by as many affected disciplines as possible, including fabrication, assembly, and testing. Their approval will ensure that these design-related factors are considered.

The success of an MCM design depends on many interrelated considerations. From an end-product use standpoint, the impact on the design by the following typical parameters should be considered:

- Equipment environmental conditions, such as ambient temperature, heat generated by the components, ventilation
- Materials selection

- Testing/fault location requirements that may affect chip placement, conductor routing, chip pad sizes and locations, etc.

- Process allowances such as etch factor compensation for conductor widths, spacing, land fabrication, etc.

8.4.2 Schematic/Logic Diagram

The initial schematic/logic diagram designates the electrical functions and interconnectivity to be provided by the substrate and its assembly. The schematic should define, when applicable, critical circuit layout areas, shielding requirements, grounding and power-distribution requirements, the allocation of test points, and any preassigned I/O pad locations. Schematic information may be generated as hard copy or computer data.

8.4.3 Electrical Design Considerations

The important electrical considerations in PWB design are primarily the conductor material and configuration, geometry of the conductors, and insulating substrate properties. The critical electrical parameters of the insulating substrate in dc and low-frequency ac applications are insulation resistance, arc tracking resistance, and flashover strength. In high-frequency and microwave applications, the important considerations are capacitance, dielectric constant, and dissipation factor. In all applications, the current-carrying capacity of the printed conductor is important.

8.4.3.1 Resistance. Current-carrying capacity of conductors is rarely a problem, but the ohmic resistance may be a factor when conductive paths are long or where voltage regulation is critical. To minimize resistive loss, the conductor should be low in resistivity with short signal lines and a large cross-sectional area. The resistance may be calculated from the expression

$$R = 0.000227W$$

where R is the resistance per linear inch, in ohms, and W is the width of the line, in inches, based on 99.5 percent minimum purity copper 0.0027 in thick.

8.4.3.2 Capacitance. Capacitance may be of considerable importance, especially at high frequencies. Low capacitance is of importance to reduce the power required to charge a circuit and also to minimize the RC delay interval. The basic capacitance equation is

$$C \,(\text{pF/in}) = W \,(10^{-3}\,\text{in}) \times E^r / \text{dielectric separation} \,(10^{-3}\,\text{in}) \times 4.45$$

where C is capacitance, W is conductor width, and E^r is dielectric constant. The capacitive coupling between conductors may be minimized by limiting the lengths of conductors running in the same vertical plane.

8.4.3.3   Transmission Lines.   Signal routing on PWBs is sometimes done randomly with little regard for electrical considerations. This is adequate as long as electrical energy is confined to the flow or charges in the conductor without regard for its wave property. At higher frequencies, the design rules change, and the signal is propagated in waves between conductors. At low frequencies, a signal path on a printed circuit board may be represented as a capacitance in parallel with a resistance. When frequency is increased, however, the signal paths must be regarded as transmission lines; the electrical and dielectric properties of the printed circuit board material take on increased importance, and greater care must be taken with the design and termination of the circuit.

Failure to match the transmission-line impedance with the impedance at the end of the line will result in part of the signal being reflected back to the source, which could cause false triggering of the device. Reflections result in line ringing, which is a serious problem in high-speed circuitry. Transmission-line discontinuities are affected by package type, circuitry layout, and connections. Care must be taken to give priority to the high-speed signal layout paths to minimize discontinuities, which will, in turn, reduce line ringing.

8.4.3.4   Velocity of Propagation.   The two parameters of transmission-line conductors of most importance in designing circuitry are the velocity of propagation and characteristic impedance. The velocity of propagation is influenced by the effective dielectric constant of the transmission-line configuration being used. In the case of the microstrip, both the insulating substrate material and the air surrounding the conductor must be considered, while with the stripline type, only the insulating substrate material's dielectric constant is used.

8.4.3.5   Characteristic Impedance.   Another parameter of concern in transmission-line design is characteristic impedance, which is the single most important electrical parameter in determining the performance of high-speed designs. Mismatch of impedance can result in signal reflections, distortions, and crosstalk. The characteristic impedance of the line

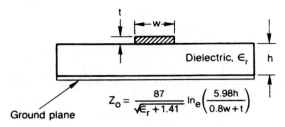

Figure 8.6. Microstrip transmission line.[10]

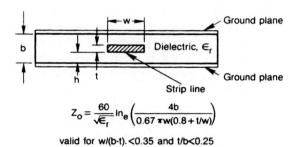

valid for $w/(b-t) < 0.35$ and $t/b < 0.25$

Figure 8.7. Stripline transmission line.[10]

is determined by the physical characteristics of the line, such as capacitance and inductance.

Two basic printed wiring configurations are used to implement designs in which characteristic impedance and other critical electrical parameters are important. These are microstrip and stripline. The *microstrip configuration* (Fig. 8.6) consists of a conductor separated from the ground plane by a dielectric, which is usually glass-epoxy. *Stripline* (Fig. 8.7) consists of conductors surrounded by two ground planes. The electrical characteristics of these two printed wiring configurations are a complex function of the board material's dielectric constant, the dielectric thickness, the conductor width, and the conductor thickness.

8.4.3.6 Electrical Clearance. Spacings between conductors on individual layers should be maximized wherever possible. Minimum conductor spacing must be determined to preclude voltage breakdown or flashover between adjacent conductors. The spacing is variable and depends on several factors: the peak voltage difference between adjacent conductors, atmospheric pressure, use of conformal coating, and capacitive coupling parameters.

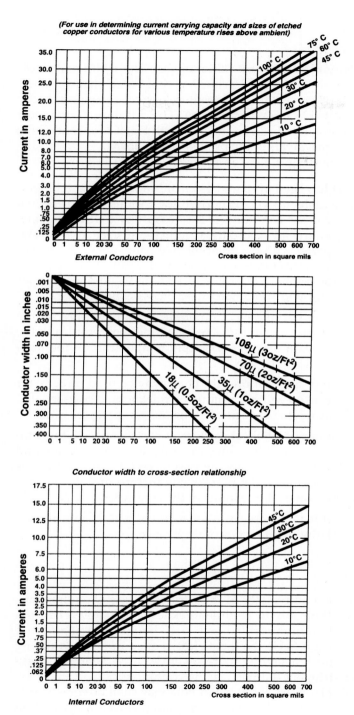

External Conductors

Cross section in square mils

Conductor width to cross-section relationship

108μ (3oz/Ft²)
70μ (2oz/Ft²)
18μ (0.5oz/Ft²)
35μ (1oz/Ft²)

Internal Conductors

Cross section in square mils

Figure 8.8. Conductor width and thickness.[10]

8.4.3.7 Conductor Width and Thickness. The width and thickness of conductors on the finished printed wiring board shall be determined on the basis of the signal characteristics, current-carrying capacity required, and allowable temperature rise. The minimum conductor width and thickness should be in accordance with Fig. 8.8 for conductors on external and internal layers of the printed circuit board.

Notes to accompany Fig. 8.8 are as follows:

- The design chart has been prepared as an aid in estimating temperature rises (above ambient) versus current for various cross-sectional areas of etched copper conductors. It is assumed that for normal design, conditions prevail where the conductor surface area is relatively small compared with the adjacent free panel area. The curves as presented include a nominal 10 percent derating (on a current basis) to allow for normal variations in etching techniques, copper thickness, conductor width estimates, and cross-sectional area.

- For general use, the permissible temperature rise is defined as the difference between the maximum safe operating temperature of the laminate and the maximum safe operating temperature in the location where the board will be used.

- For single-conductor applications, the chart may be used directly for determining conductor widths, conductor thickness, cross-sectional area, and current-carrying capacity for various temperature rises.

- For groups of similar parallel conductors, if closely spaced, the temperature rise may be found by using an equivalent cross section and an equivalent current. The equivalent cross section is equal to the sum of the cross sections of the parallel conductors, and the equivalent current is the sum of the currents in the conductors.

- The final conductor thickness in the design chart does not include conductor overplating with metals other than copper.

8.4.4 Holes[11]

In order to meet the requirements of the various classes of equipments, the plated through hole size to module thickness ratio should be from 1:3 to 1:5, and the minimum drilled hole size should be in accordance with Table 8.4, which reflects the three classes of equipment assuming that each class requires a slightly more severe environment, thus having to meet more stringent thermal cycling conditions.

The drilled hole size used for through hole vias shall be represented on the master drawing as the maximum plated-through dimension

Table 8.4. Minimum Drilled Hole Size for Plated Through Hole Vias[9]

Board thickness (in)	Class 1 (in)	Class 2 (in)	Class 3 (in)
<1.0 mm (0.040)	Level C 0.15 mm (0.006)	Level C 0.2 mm (0.008)	Level C 0.25 mm (0.010)
1.0–1.6 mm (0.040–0.063)	Level C 0.2 mm (0.008)	Level C 0.25 mm (0.010)	Level B 0.3 mm (0.012)
1.6–2.0 mm (0.063–0.080)	Level C 0.3 mm (0.012)	Level B 0.4 mm (0.016)	Level B 0.5 mm (0.020)
>2.0 mm (0.080)	Level B 0.4 mm (0.016)	Level A 0.5 mm 0.020)	Level A 0.6 mm (0.024)

Note: If copper in hole is greater than 0.03 mm (0.0012 in), hole size can be reduced by one class.

Table 8.5. Minimum Drilled Hole Size for Buried Vias[9]

Board thickness (in)	Class 1 (in)	Class 2 (in)	Class 3 (in)
<0.25 mm (0.010)	0.1 mm (0.004)	0.1 mm (0.004)	0.15 mm (0.006)
0.25–0.5 mm (0.010–0.020)	0.15 mm (0.006)	0.15 mm (0.006)	0.20 mm (0.008)
>0.5 mm (0.020)	0.15 mm (0.006)	0.2 mm (0.008)	0.25 mm (0.010)

that assumes that the hole contains a minimum plating thickness. No minimum plating thickness is specified, since there are no leads in the through hole and it could theoretically be plated shut.

The requirements for the minimum hole size of buried vias should be in accordance with Table 8.5. The minimum drilled hole size for blind vias should be in accordance with Table 8.6.

8.4.5 Mechanical Design

Mechanical properties of substrate materials that often have an important bearing on the MCM are water absorption, coefficient of thermal

Table 8.6. Minimum Drilled Hole Size for Blind Vias[9]

Board thickness (in)	Class 1 (in)	Class 2 (in)	Class 3 (in)
<0.10 mm (0.004)	0.1 mm (0.004)	0.1 mm (0.004)	0.20 mm (0.008)
0.10–0.25 mm (0.004–0.010)	0.15 mm (0.006)	0.2 mm (0.008)	0.3 mm (0.12)
>0.25 mm (0.010)	0.2 mm (0.008)	0.3 mm (0.012)	0.4 mm (0.016)

expansion, thermal rating, flexural strength, tensile strength, shear strength, and hardness. Properties of popular printed wiring materials are covered in Sec. 8.3.1.

Although warp and twist of an etched printed wiring can be attributable to the fabrication process, conductor pattern configuration, or unbalanced layup, they are more frequently induced during the manufacture of the copper-clad laminate. The larger problem for small MCM substrates is flatness, which is critical for component mounting. The designer can help minimize the effects in two ways. First, the direction of conductors should be such that bending stresses released in the etched copper foil on one side of the board are opposed by a similar pattern on the other side. Additionally, the layup of the board should symmetrically distribute large copper planes, such as ground and power, and produce a balanced design.

8.5 Assembled MCM-L Applications[2,3]

8.5.1 Attachment Methods

The three basic methods for attaching bare integrated circuits to the MCM-L substrate are tape automated bonding, (TAB), wire bonding, and flip-chip bonding (Fig. 8.9). In many cases, the type of die available determines the MCM technology used, since the die may only be suitable for one of these attachment methods. Both wire bonding and TAB are perimeter connection techniques.

8.5.1.1 Tape Automated Bonding (TAB). The options for tape automated bonding depend on the metallurgy of the TAB lead and the

Three chip attachment methods for MCM-L

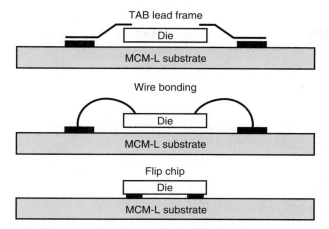

Figure 8.9. MCM-L chip-attachment methods.[2]

substrate material. Three bonding techniques are used: solder reflow, single-point gold-gold bonding, and conductive adhesive. The options are determined by the metallurgy of the TAB lead, the substrate material tolerance of the TAB lead, and reliability goals. TAB has some advantages to consider. An integrated circuit destined for TAB attach may be tested following outer lead bonding but prior to mounting on the substrate. This is important in view of the problem of acquiring "known good" die for commitment to the MCM. Bare dice or dice intended for chip-on-board (COB) cannot be tested on-line prior to assembly.

The TAB package is the easiest of the three methods mentioned to rework, facilitating servicing or prototyping. The need for gold on the substrate is eliminated if TAB is used, an obvious cost saving. Outer-lead bonding is done with hot gas or hot bar soldering. TAB leads also can be soldered individually using laser or focused IR.

8.5.1.2 Wire Bonding. Wire bonding, on the other hand, requires installation of the die on the substrate with adhesive prior to wire bonding. Otherwise known as *chip-on-board*, it is widely used for MCM-L substrates. With these types of modules, the dice are many times tested and burned in on the module. The three basic types of wire bonding used in MCM-L are thermocompression, ultrasonic, and thermosonic. Thermocompression is one of the most commonly used bonding processes. The principle here is to join two metals using heat and pressure.

Ultrasonic bonding employs a rapid scrubbing or wiping motion in addition to pressure in order to achieve the molecular bond. It is an extremely flexible process, and both gold and aluminum wire can be used. Thermosonic wire bonding combines ultrasonic energy with the basic elements of thermocompression wire bonding. This technique relies on the vibrations created by the ultrasonic action to scrub the bond area to remove any oxide layers and also to create heat for bonding. Thermosonic bonding is used for polymeric boards, since it does not expose the board to extreme temperatures.

Each wire must be attached individually, and gold plating is required on the substrate mounting pads. Wire-bonded dice are removable and repairable, but automated repair equipment is not normally available, making wire-bonded modules of higher cost and better performance than the other types.

8.5.1.3 Flip Chip. Flip chip is an attachment method in which the die is inverted and placed face down on the substrate's matching pads. This also requires special processing of the IC chip, since it must be "bumped," or fabricated with solder dots to accommodate the soldering

Figure 8.10. SPARC processor module.[3]

of the chip. The assembly is then reflowed. This method has the advantage of eliminating one level of interconnect which is required in both TAB and wire bonding. The most famous flip-chip attachment is based on the IBM C4 technology, wherein PbSn solder balls are deposited on die I/O pads. A disadvantage is that the component mounting pads on the substrate are of extremely high density, providing a difficult build for PWB manufacturers. Even using advance PWB manufacturing processes, it is not always practical to provide fan-out for the signals from the ball contact pads without the use of a high number of vias and wiring planes.

8.5.2   MCM-L Applications

Figure 8.10 illustrates an MCM-L product for a dual SPARC processor built by Ross Technologies, Inc. A substrate composed of polyimide with six metal layers, it houses 10 chips, fastened by TAB and hot bar soldered, and encapsulated with silicone. The high-power dice, for heat-sinking reasons, are attached directly to the aluminum backplane.

Figure 8.11. Litronics Industries module.[3]

Another polyimide-glass substrate MCM-L is illustrated in Fig. 8.11. This high-density module is made by Litronics Industries, Inc., and has over 1000 nets, with approximately 1000 vias, not counting buried vias. The module houses 4 processor dice, 32 static RAMs, several small logic dice, and a number of passive components or glue circuits. Gold-plated TAB tape and single-point OLB were used for assembly. The substrate was laid out using three internal signal planes, consisting of 0.003-in lines and spaces and buried 0.008-in-diameter vias.

Figure 8.12 shows a Motorola MCM-L design containing a 64,000-gate CMOS array chip and two static RAM chips. The chips are set in recessed cavities to protect the wire bonds. The MCM 6264 is of a seven-layer construction. Layers 1, 4, and 7 are signal layers, layers 2 and 6 are power and ground, and layer 3 is the 150-µm copper lead frame. The latter becomes an efficient heat spreader because the chips are bonded directly to its surface.

A developmental substrate from Motorola is shown in Fig. 8.13. This substrate, made from bismaleimide-triazine-glass, has three internal metal layers. It connects a processor chip, three FSRAMs (fast-static RAMS), six chip resistors, and seven chip capacitors. The

Figure 8.12. Motorola MCM 6264 module.[3]

substrate has a routed cavity for the processor, and thermal vias are used for three SRAMS. The lead frame has a full-area heat spreader and is soldered and adhesively attached to the back of the substrate. The dice are all gold wire ball–bonded, and the passives and dice are die bonded with silver epoxy. The electrical design features an embedded microstrip format with a characteristic impedance of 60 Ω at 40-MHz operation.

Shown in Fig. 8.14 is a high-density MCM-L from MCC which interconnects three fine-pitch TAB dice (0.008 and 0.004 in OLB) in the center of the substrate. TAB and gold wire ball–bonded memory dice are mounted on the left and right sides. The module has eight metal layers, 0.010-in vias, 0.003-in lines and spaces, and contains gold and solder plating to accommodate the TAB and wire bonding.

Figure 8.13. Prototype MCM-L module. (*Courtesy of Motorola, Inc.*)

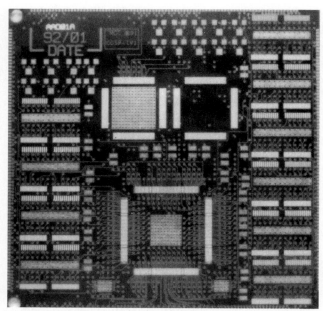

Figure 8.14. High-density MCM-L for TAB and wire bonding. (*Courtesy of MCC.*)

References

1. Howard Markstein, EP&P, "MCM-L Offers Easiest Path to Higher Performance," *Electronic Packaging and Production,* January 1993, pp. 68–71.

2. John A. Biancini, Supernova, "MCM-L: A Dynamic Evolution to the Multilayer PCB," *Electronic Packaging and Production,* May 1992, pp. 34–37.

3. Leo M. Higgins III, Motorola, "Material, Manufacturing, and Assembly Considerations for Laminate Substrate-Based Multichip Modules (MCM-L)," *Proceedings, ISHM,* 1992, pp. 216–224.

4. Clyde F. Coombs, *Handbook of Printed Circuits,* 3d ed. New York: McGraw-Hill, 1988.

5. Joseph Fjelstad, J. C. Fjelstad and Associates, and O. Leigh Mueller, Printed Circuit Builders, "Designing Manufacturable COB Circuits," *Electronic Packaging and Production,* February 1991, pp. 74–77.

6. Randy E. Haslow, Cray Research, "Cleaning and Plating of Sub-9 Mil Holes," *PC Fab,* February 1989, pp. 78–90.

7. Roger H. Landolt, E. I. DuPont de Nemours, "Additive and Surface Mount: Complementary Technologies," *Surface Mount Technology,* October 1990, pp. 25–26.

8. Lyle R. Wallig, E. I. DuPont de Nemours, "Coming Soon: The Ideal Laminate," *Circuits Manufacturing*, January 1988, pp. 33–35.

9. "Guidelines for Multichip Module Technology Utilization," Institute for Interconnecting and Packaging Electronic Circuits, IPC-MC-790, 1992.

10. Gerald L. Ginsberg, *Printed Circuits Handbook*. New York: McGraw-Hill, 1990.

11. George Messner, AMP-AKZO Corp., "Laminate Technology for Multichip Modules," *Electronic Packaging and Production*, October 1992, pp. 32–34.

9

Supplementary Interconnection Devices

The trend toward designing more functionality into multichip modules (MCMs) increases both the number of components placed on an MCM substrate and the power needed to drive these components.[1] The advantages of high-density characteristics in the use of MCMs cause significant problems in the interconnection of these modules. The basic connection of the integrated circuit (IC) chip in its package is the first-level, or level 1, connection.

Second level, or level 2, connections are the connections that join the MCM to the interconnecting substrate, either a hybrid or, more commonly, a printed wiring board (PWB). Although the level 2 connections serve primarily to provide electrical connection between the MCM and the interconnecting plane, they also serve other purposes, such as physical support for the module, and they also help to retain the module in the assembly. Some connectors also serve to remove heat from the module.

Serving as a critical interface between the MCM and the remainder of the electronic system demands thoughtful choice in selecting the method of connection. The performance of the system can be seriously affected by the connector used. The connector should be an integral part of the system, with the ideal connector serving as a truly invisible part of the system. It should be reliable, cost-effective, and complement, not deteriorate, the performance of the system in which it is used. In terms of electrical signals, the connector should be essentially invisible; i.e., signals passing through the connection should not be reduced, distorted, or reflected.

Current pin-in socket technology can accommodate design and production of high-density connectors with a pitch of 0.050 in, permitting design of standard interconnects with up to 20 lines per inch along the side of an MCM. This translates to less than 160 pin sites available for interconnect use. Future requirements for MCM interconnects mandate many more than this, with interconnect requirements of 90 or more I/O lines per inch, requiring a pitch of 0.020 in or less between lines, with expected densities reaching to 100 I/Os per linear inch. For this reason, the connector should be capable of providing a large number of contacts typical of current MCMs, ranging from 100 to over 8000 in some cases.

The high speeds found in current equipment, ranging up to 50 MHz and beyond, also place a requirement on the interconnect, making the design even more challenging. High speeds make short, impedance-matched interconnect lengths very desirable, particularly for bus structures where significant variations in signal path length may cause timing problems. High frequencies also give reason to expect matching impedances of interconnects, shielding of signal lines, and the need to provide isolation between lines to reduce crosstalk and noise generation within the interconnection.

The need to provide for efficient and reliable mating/demating of the MCM and the interconnect plane is another requirement of increasing importance. Other than the permanent soldered interconnection, MCM mating/demating schemes should allow for variations in planarity and thickness of the MCM substrate, as well as potentially high heat removal requirements, to be most effective. Furthermore, the insertion and withdrawal force should be as low as possible to circumvent the large forces which would be required for large lead count devices.

9.1 Connection Alternatives[2–4]

The selection of second-level connection alternatives can be categorized in three ways: by package configuration or geometry, by type of leads, and by the connection method, i.e., permanent or separable. The geometry choices are the patterns needed to disburse the connections, namely, edge array and area array. Lead types are either leaded or leadless. The connection method presents many variations, since permanent connections may be soldered or wire bonded, and the separable types rely on a large number of options, including lead/pin-in socket, elastomeric, through hole mount, and surface mount.

Figure 9.1. Area-array package.

Area-array packages (Fig. 9.1) feature contacts over the entire area of the package in a square or rectangular array. The interconnection medium has an identical, matching pattern. Due to the geometry, the area-array package provides an option on the spacing between contacts and also provides the maximum density of contacts for a package. Unfortunately, since the contacts are obscured, they are virtually uninspectable, a problem especially with soldered connections.

Figure 9.2 illustrates a typical edge-array package, in this case a dual in-line package with leads along two sides. However, edge-array packages may have leads along only one side or also two, three, or four sides, as illustrated in Fig. 9.3. Although this configuration, a plastic quad flat pack (PQFP) offers the most flexibility in connection methods, all visually inspectable, because of the geometry, it is most restrictive in the number of leads available for I/O, dictated by the allowable contact spacing.

Leadless or leaded devices are found in both the area-array and edge-array configurations. The leads are either pins or formed flat leads, which may be either surface mounted or used in a through hole mode. The formed leads may be used with single-row, or, more rarely, double-row geometry. Figure 9.4 illustrates a typical leadless package, in this case a type C chip carrier.

In addition to the edge-array configuration, as shown in Fig. 9.4, leadless packages are also configured in the area-array mode; with

Figure 9.2. Edge-array package.

Figure 9.3. Leaded MCM package.

Figure 9.4. Leadless MCM package.

pads or lands only, these are called *land-grid array* (LGA) devices. Packages with pins are usually soldered through a hole or plugged into separable connectors. Pinned packages are found most commonly in the *pin-grid array* (PGA) form.

Connection methods for attaching MCMs to printed wiring boards (PWBs) or other interconnection planes fall into two categories, permanent and separable. As the name implies, *permanent connections* use either a metallic bond, solder, welding, wire bonding, or, in some cases, a conductive adhesive.

Permanent connections offer a reliability advantage, but with the disadvantage of lack of maintainability. In this case, the MCM becomes a more or less permanent part of the assembly and may require special methods for removal and replacement. Often the removal of large lead devices from PWBs results in damage to the board, such as lifted pads or damaged PWBs, essentially making the module a throwaway. Other permanent connection types are used commonly. One is the "leads last" method, or wire bonding. Another is the use of a flexible ribbon which is attached to the MCM and to the PWB.

Soldering is perhaps the most important of all the permanent attachment methods and one that is quite familiar to packaging engineers. In the case of PGAs, the pins are soldered into a PWB plated through hole. Soldering of leaded and leadless devices on the surface of the board has the additional advantage of accommodating both sides of the PWB, vastly increasing the density of packaging.

Separable connections create an electrical connection by mechanical means, by the use of a metallic element. Characteristically, all separable connections require two elements, a male and a female, or a plug and a socket element.

Separable connections fall into two major categories, the pin and socket type and the type using some sort of interposer or intermediate contact material. In the pin and socket type, the pin is the male member and fits into some sort of gap or hole in the socket. Variations on this are the low-insertion-force (LIF) and zero-insertion-force (ZIF) sockets, which are used in the case of high-pin-count connections.

9.2 Connector Choice Issues

The ideal electrical connection for MCMs should be capable of providing a large number of connections characteristic of MCMs, where individual I/Os can number up to 8000 per module. The connector should be easily processed, cost-effective, and fit in with the system requirements, including mechanical and thermal performance. Electrically, the connection should be virtually invisible, or pass signals with as little impact as possible in terms of crosstalk, attenuation, or stage delay.

9.2.1 Electrical Performance[1]

A number of electrical characteristics of connectors need to be considered in selecting a connector system for MCMs.

9.2.1.1 Crosstalk. *Crosstalk* is the mutual inductance and capacitance between different electric signal paths. This contributes to unwanted electrical coupling, referred to as *crosstalk noise*. With the closeness of the conductors and higher signal speeds, the coupling of signals into adjacent conductor lines becomes greater and introduces noise and false signals into systems. If not controlled through proper design, this can cause system failure in digital circuitry by the sudden and erratic appearance of false data in a circuit.

Crosstalk decreases as the distance between two lines (or contacts) decreases and increases as the signal frequency increases. Crosstalk can be reduced by making sure that lines operating at high frequency are spaced an allowable distance apart or are shielded in some manner. In many cases, power and ground planes are used to shield the signal lines to reduce coupling. For contacts, this can be done by introducing shielding fundamentals into the selection of the contact interconnection system.

9.2.1.2 Characteristic Impedance. The characteristic impedance of a line is determined by the physical aspects of the line, such as capacitance and inductance. The capacitance and inductance of the lines bear on the high-speed performance of the circuit. The characteristic impedance of the printed circuit board interacts with the impedance of the system components to cause load and driver delays. The load-point delay is proportional to the product of the characteristic impedance and the load capacitance.

These factors, plus other delay factors which react in opposite directions with characteristic impedance, can contribute to false switching signals in critically timed or high-speed systems unless the printed circuit board characteristic impedance is optimized to both the load capacitance and the driver output impedance. Basic physics dictates that maintaining a constant characteristic impedance along a signal path provides maximum energy transfer with minimal attenuation. For this reason, controlled-impedance PWBs are used increasingly in high-speed applications. Interconnections, which represent an important link in the system, must be impedance matched in high-speed systems.

9.2.1.3 Propagation Delay. This is the time it takes for a signal to propagate across a printed circuit board and between any parts of the system, including connections. This becomes important when system frequency increases, since it can make the connector smaller. Other major effects include gate delays of the circuits and propagation delay through cables, connectors, and modules. The net effect of these phenomena determines the ultimate speed of a computer system.

Disparities in delay between lines is a cause of signal *skewing*. Normally, the system design calls for balanced connections to equalize skew. Propagation delay may not be a factor for other than high frequencies, since normally the distance through an MCM connection tends to be short.

9.2.2 Solder or Separable Connection[2,5]

The method for attaching the MCM to the PWB or interconnecting plane can be direct and permanent or by using a socket or separable connection, making it removable. The choice must be determined by evaluating such things as electrical performance, maintainability, reliability, and costs—both component and total system costs.

Permanent connections involve some type of metallic bond to make the electrical (and mechanical) connection to the PWB. This can be accomplished in a number of ways, usually by soldering or by the use of wire bonding to attach the MCM to the board. The use of this permanent connection makes the MCM a permanent part of the assembly, requiring special attention in removal and replacement. Soldering of MCMs is done through holes, by placing pins in holes in the PWB and soldering, or by using leaded or leadless components where components can be mounted on the surface of the PWB. This permits MCMs to be soldered to both sides of the PWB.

Separable connections are not permanent and allow the removal or reconnection of MCMs. They permit the electrical connection to be made by mechanical means in a number of ways. The most common is the use of a male-female arrangement—a pin and socket or blade and tuning fork connector. Another popular method of separable connection is the interposer, specifically used for surface-mount applications. This device is made up of a flexible structure that conducts current only in the z axis when mounted between two surfaces with opposing contact pad patterns. Compressive force ensures reliable contact. Since there are no pins involved, interposer connectors can be used for mounting MCMs to both sides of a PWB. Interposer connectors use either an elastomeric material with conductors interspersed for the active element or metal springs or "fuzz buttons" in appropriate holders for connectors.

9.2.3 Material and Mechanical Considerations[4,6,7]

Conductor material is important for mechanical as well as electrical and environmental reasons. The bulk resistivity characteristics are important to provide the best conductor available for the application. High-conductivity materials minimize the voltage drop across a connector. Contact materials are fabricated from any one of several alloys depending on the design and type of contact. Normal materials used for contacts are high-performance alloys such as phosphor-bronze (Cu-Sn-P), the nickel-silvers (Cu-Zn-Ni), and the beryllium-coppers (Cu-Be and Cu-Be-Co).

Brass, a good electrical conductor, deforms easily under flexing and does not have good spring properties. Phosphor-bronze is harder than brass and retains its resiliency. It provides good reliability in most connectors, where mating and unmating cycles are relatively low or in connectors with nominal contact flexure. Beryllium-copper is superior to brass or phosphor-bronze in mechanical properties. After annealed beryllium-copper is formed and hardened, it retains its shape and is most resistant to mechanical fatigue. It is also good for high-temperature applications. Table 9.1 gives electrical and mechanical properties of metals commonly used in connectors.

Plating is important for connectors, especially if low normal force is employed. Contact platings may be classified as either noble (gold, rhodium, palladium, and platinum) or nonnoble (tin, tin-lead, or nickel). Gold is the commonly used noble metal; tin and tin-lead are the most commonly used nonnoble metals. Nickel, copper, and silver are used as underplates with top coatings of gold and/or other noble metals.

Metallic oxides generally have high resistances, and they should be considered when choosing a contact plating. The major reason for using gold as a contact plating is its superior oxidation resistance. However, gold-plated contacts may be contaminated by diffusion of base metals to the surface and subsequent oxidation. Another source of contamination is the porosity of the gold, which will always increase as repeated matings of the connector wear away the gold, leaving increasing areas of base metal.

Nonnoble metals will always have some oxide film on their surfaces. Electrical conductivity of such contacts depends on penetrating the oxide film to establish clean metal-to-metal contacts. Such penetration can occur in two ways: First, the oxide film can be punctured by the electric field, which occurs when two surfaces are in close contact, provided the open-circuit voltage is adequate. Although the exact value of this voltage depends on the nature and thickness of the oxide, it is at least 50 mV in most situations. Second, low-energy circuits—often called *dry circuits*—with less than 50 mV of open-circuit voltage may not provide sufficient potential to penetrate oxides electrically. In such cases, the contact must be designed either with gold plating thick enough to remain oxide-free or with base metal platings with contacts designed so that the oxide films are penetrated mechanically.

Obtaining the lowest possible and practical level of combined resistance in a connector depends on the kind of metal used in the connector, the surface finish, and the contact pressure. When two conductors are joined, true areas of contact occur only at minute points of asperity spread over the two interface surfaces. These are called *A spots.* The

Table 9.1. Properties of Typical Contact Metals[4]

	Alloy 172,* beryllium-copper†	Alloy 510, grade A phos. bronze	Alloy 638	Alloy 725	Alloy 762, nickel-silver
Nominal composition	Cu 98.1 Be 1.9	Cu 94.81 Sn 5.0 P 0.19	Cu 95.0 Al 2.8 Si 1.8 Co 0.4	Cu 88.2 Ni 9.5 Sn 2.3	Cu 59.25 Zn 28.75 Ni 12.0
Electrical conductivity					
Percent IACS at 68°F Megmho-CM at 20°C	22% (0.128)	15% (0.087)	10% (0.058)	11% (0.064)	9% (0.050)
Thermal conductivity					
BTU/ft²/ft/h/°F at 68°F Cal/cm²/cm/s/°C at 20°C	62–75 (0.26–31)	40 (0.164)	23 (0.097)	31 (0.130)	24 (0.100)
Density					
lb/in³ at 68°F gm/cm³ at 20°C	0.298 (8.26)	0.320 (8.86)	0.299 (8.29)	0.321 (8.89)	0.314 (8.70)
Modulus of elasticity					
10^6 lb/in² 10^6 kg/mm²	18.5 (13.0)	16.0 (11.2)	16.7 (11.7)	19.0 (13.5)	18.0 (12.7)
Yield strength, 0.2% offset					
Annealed,‡					
ksi kg/mm²	at 155 (109)	22 (15)	58–67 (41–47)	25 (18)	29 (20)

Half hard					
ksi	½HT 175	47–68	76–89	57–73	58–82
kg/mm²	(123)	(33–48)	(53–63)	(40–51)	(41–58)
Hard					
ksi	HT 180	74–88	91–103	74–79	82–97
kg/mm²	(127)	(52–62)	(64–72)	(52–56)	(58–68)
Spring					
ksi	N.A.	92–108	100–112	78–93	101–110
kg/mm²		(65–76)	(70–79)	(55–65)	(71–77)
Extra spring					
ksi	N.A.	98–110	107 min.	89–102	102 min.
kg/mm²		(69–77)	(75 min.)	(63–72)	(72 min.)
Relative cost index	1.00	3.80	1.44	1.44	1.33

*Copper Development Association.

†All property data for beryllium-copper is for material after age hardening heat treatment.

‡At 0.02 mm grain size except in the case of alloy 638 which is in the standard annealed condition.

number and location of the A spots depend on the shape and finish quality of the two contact members.

The total area of true contact is small, often as little as 0.01 of the apparent contact total force. The A spots are affected by electrical and plastic deformations that flatten the asperities and create enough area to support the applied load. The spots are under high unit pressure, constant and equal to the flow pressure of the materials involved in the contact. The A spots are enlarged in area, and additional A spots are created when contact force is applied. Even when the contact load is as high as several pounds, the true contact area remains a very small fraction of the apparent surface in contact.

Contact theory states that natural surface irregularities of contact materials prevent intimate contact of mating surfaces—except for A spots. An increase in contact pressure or a reduction in material hardness will increase the intimacy of the contact. Wiping action will burnish the high spots. Prow formation or metal buildup upon mating also will increase the intimacy of contact, as well as break through the insulating films and oxides on the contact surfaces.

Wipe is defined as the relative translation under load of two contact surfaces. Through the action of sliding one surface relative to another, a *plowing* action occurs that helps to break up or fracture surface oxides and contaminants and remove them. Wipe is normally built into the design of separable connectors.

9.3 Connection Types and Applications[1,5]

9.3.1 Soldered Direct Attachment

Soldering is the most reliable but most permanent method for attachment of a module to an interconnection plane. It is used with all types of MCMs, peripheral leaded and leadless, PGA, and LGA. The soldered connection may be either through hole or surface mount.

Historically, soldering has been the assembly method of choice due to the fact that all connections are made simultaneously, a cost and reliability advantage. Additionally, these connections can be made at the same time that other components are soldered.

Eliminating the cost of a socket and any mechanical hold-down devices, soldering produces definite assembly cost savings. The reliability of the soldered component is enhanced over the pluggable type, since there is only one interconnection—the soldered type requires only one connection, contrasted with the two junctions required for most pluggable connections. Any increase in the number of connections in a system decreases the reliability of the system.

Soldering presents a design compromise both for the interconnection plane and for the MCM. Certainly the MCM and constituent parts must withstand the high soldering temperatures required—less in the case of through hole mount than with surface mount. The interconnection plane must be designed to accommodate the footprint of the package to be soldered—plated through holes of the right size for through hole mount and correct pad footprint for surface mount.

For surface-mount applications, soldering is done in a variety of ways, depending on the type of package used. For peripheral-array packages, hot bar soldering, infrared oven, conduction-reflow belt soldering, or vapor-phase soldering is used. Area-array MCMs, such as PGAs and LGAs, are soldered by either infrared oven or vapor-phase methods. Most surface-mount packages require the deposition of solder on the PCB—either by heavy plating or, more often, by screening solder paste onto the PCB.

For through hole applications, such as PGAs, wave soldering is used. This traditional PWB assembly method employs the use of pumped solder waves, with the PCB passing over the solder wave. Flux is used to clean the surfaces and to ensure good wetting. A conveyor belt is employed to pass the board through the solder. Wave soldering is rarely used for surface-mount applications.

Vapor-phase, or condensation, soldering requires that parts be placed on screened solder paste and passed through a chamber with a condensing vapor, usually at 250°C. As the vapor condenses on the parts, the part leads are heated and solder reflowed. Infrared soldering employs an oven enclosure with parts passed through on a conveyor or belt. Either focused or unfocused infrared energy produces heat to reflow the solder. Conduction-reflow belt soldering conducts the necessary heat required through the PCB by a series of heated platens located under a continuously moving belt.

The use of soldering requires that some attention be given to the finishes of the constituent parts to be soldered. Pads or leads need to be plated with tin-lead to accommodate the soldering process. The solder, or tin-lead, is usually a composition of 62 percent Sn, 36 percent Pb, and 2 percent Ag. Gold leads should be avoided because of the possible formation of a brittle tin-gold intermetallic which affects the reliability of the joint.

The standard procedure for ensuring the reliability of the solder joint is visual inspection. This is possible with peripheral lead devices, but area-array MCMs, either through hole or surface mount, present an inspection problem owing to the limited visibility of this type of connection method. Soldering requires that some attention be given to the problem of stresses on the solder joint. The junction should be able to absorb the stresses caused by mechanical vibration and the differential thermal expansion between the component and the interconnection plane. A coefficient of thermal expansion (CTE) of the MCM closely matching that of the board is desirable. An alternative is the use of flexible leads, either J leads or gull wing leads for leaded devices and for leadless devices, controlled-expansion substrates or a close CTE match.

9.3.2 Wire Bond Direct Attachment[4]

Not commonly used, this interconnection technique is a takeoff on traditional chip wire interconnection techniques (see Chap. 4). In this case, the peripheral pads on the MCM are wire bonded to corresponding pads on the PCB or interconnecting substrate. In most cases, the MCM is fastened to the substrate with some type of adhesive. Automated wire bonding equipment can be used to perform the wire bonding.

This is a reliable, well-known technique that incorporates a built-in pull test after bonding. The leads are also visually inspectable, unfortunately, though, at the expense of electrical characteristics, since the long leads required can increase inductance and resistivity. Also, some protection is needed over the assembly to prevent damage to the exposed wire bonds.

9.3.3 Leads Last/Chip-on-Board

In some cases it is desirable to connect the MCM die directly to the interconnecting substrate by means of wire bonding. This method is usually employed to eliminate packages in normal IC packaging and to provide the maximum packaging density, but in the case of MCMs, it is a convenient way to mount chips directly to the interconnecting substrate. In this way, one connection level is eliminated.

The three basic bare-die termination techniques or derivatives thereof, i.e., wire bonding, tape automated bonding (TAB), and flip-chip (controlled-collapse) soldering, have been used, in some cases for more than 20 years, in semiconductor packages and hybrid microcircuit assemblies. These three methods are adequately described in Chap. 4. Selection of the method of connecting the chip to the substrate is the primary decision in the physical design of the MCM. The termination technique must be compatible with other parts of the module.

These applications usually require some type of encapsulant, since there is no package involved. The bare die needs to be protected from grease, dirt, contaminants, and moisture. An epoxy material, silicone, or some type of gel is used to encapsulate the chip or assembly. The encapsulant provides minimal protection but is not a true hermetic seal.

9.3.4 Separable Connections[8]

Traditionally, sockets have been used in electronic equipment to provide some flexibility in the design of the PCB and to allow for removal and replacement of parts or modules without the need for desoldering and resoldering. Sockets are also useful for testing modules before committing them to the interconnect substrate.

The particular geometry of the contact used for the connector is largely a matter of choice by the particular company supplying the connector. The contact serves not only as the electrical connection between the PCB and the MCM but in some cases also as the mechanical retention mechanism. Configuration of the contact includes the traditional pin and socket type, the leaf spring, and other variations such as the twist pin and brush contact. The mechanical action required by the contact arrangement is to provide adequate normal force on the mating member to provide minimal contact resistance.

Sockets for MCMs are categorized as either peripheral-array termination or area-array termination. Socket selection is determined primarily by the particular system packaging approach used or by such other elements as cost, producibility, reliability, etc. Most sockets used for MCM termination are updated versions of traditional IC sockets.

System design considerations enter into the choice between area-array sockets and peripheral-array arrangements. The former certainly have the advantage in terms of providing a maximum number of I/Os, but at the expense of inspectability. The peripheral-array configuration provides the least area for contacts but facilitates easy inspection of the contact termination.

9.3.4.1 Leaded Sockets for MCM Modules[4,9,10]

Peripheral-Array (Quad Flat Pack) Sockets. Figure 9.5 shows a typical leaded socket for quad flat pack (QFP) MCMs. This socket uses a clamp arrangement which establishes contact on the leads by pressing them between the socket contacts. Normal force is provided by the clamping arrangement. This connector does not provide a wiping action, so contacts must be gold plated. The sockets are commonly available and

Figure 9.5. Quad flat pack (QFP) socket for peripheral MCMs. (*Courtesy of AMP.*)

reasonably priced to adapt to surface mount (SM) needs. Although low profile, the connector shown is for through hole mount to a PWB on a 0.075 × 0.100 in grid. A disadvantage of this type connector is that it uses larger holes in the PWB for pin mounting, reducing routing space for conductors.

Surface-mount connectors do not require through holes for mounting, allowing for easier routing of the PWB. Surface-mount versions of this connector are offered, with a footprint matching the device. This type has the advantage of allowing mounting of the MCMs on both sides of the PWB.

Area-Array (LIF, ZIF) Sockets.[4,11] The connection of large numbers of pins such as found in PGAs can be addressed only with the use of LIF and ZIF connectors. ZIF sockets use a camming action to hold the contacts open during insertion, and then the cams serve to close the contacts during operation. A typical ZIF connector is illustrated in Fig. 9.6. Another version of ZIF sockets use a beta-phase material to make contact by using a thermally responsive alloy as the contact element, with an electric heater to actuate the contact element to provide clamping force

Figure 9.6. ZIF PGA socket. (*Courtesy of AMP.*)

on the mating pin or to clamp the substrate tightly to the motherboard. This class of specialized connector appears to offer the impedance matching, wiping, and ZIF required for MCMs. LIF connectors operate on a different principle, mostly by staggering the depth of contacts to lower contact insertion force.

These PGA sockets, commonly available commercially, feature high-pin-count versions with grids of up to 30 × 30 (900) positions. The main disadvantage of these connectors, common with most through hole mount connectors, is that the mounting method utilizes critical board area, reducing routing space and PWB density capability. The electrical problems presented are typical of those found with long leads—high inductance and stage-delay problems in some applications.

Flexible Circuit Contact for VAX.[12] A leadless MCM socket, developed for leadless MCM packages for the VAX 9000 computer, is illustrated in Fig. 9.7. The connector is composed of three main components: the MCM, heat sink, and flexible circuit interconnection. Four flexible circuit

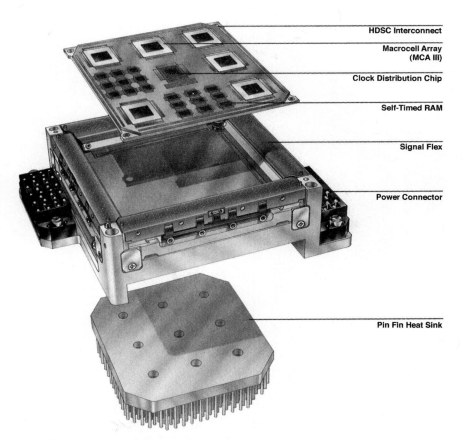

HDSC Interconnect

Macrocell Array
(MCA III)

Clock Distribution Chip

Self-Timed RAM

Signal Flex

Power Connector

Pin Fin Heat Sink

Figure 9.7. VAX 9000 multichip unit.[12]

interconnection assemblies are bonded at the outer periphery of the
HDSC, or MCM. Each flexible circuit is shaped into an S bend, while an
elastomer is assembled and housed within a cavity in the flex frame, as
shown in Fig. 9.8. Mounting of the MCM on the PWB is performed using
four bolts located in the corner of the aluminum housing. This results in
compression of the elastomer, generating the necessary pressure distribution on the connector contact array. The connector provides a total of 268
contacts covering a footprint area of 2 in^2.

The 6- to 12-mil-diameter raised contact features, often termed
"bumps," are solid copper plated over with nickel and gold. The
"bumps" may be modeled as truncated cones. Each of the gold "bumps"

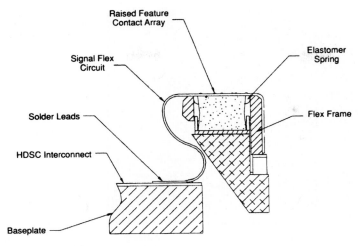

Figure 9.8. Cross-sectional view of connector assembly.[12]

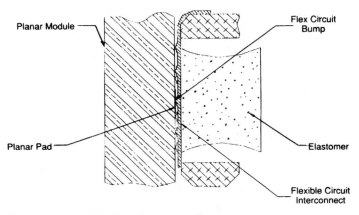

Figure 9.9. Detail of contact array.[12]

mates to a flat, gold-plated pad on the planar module. A cross section of the connector mated to a planar board is shown in Fig. 9.9. The orientation shown is similar to its vertical operating direction onto a planar module. Force on each "bump" is generated by compressing the elastomer, which occurs as an MCM is mated to the planar module. Initiation of compression engages a ramp cam action on the aluminum housing, causing a wiping action across the flat, plated pads on the planar module.

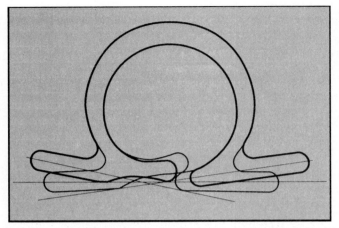

Figure 9.10. AMP Micro-Interposer contact. (*Courtesy of AMP.*[14])

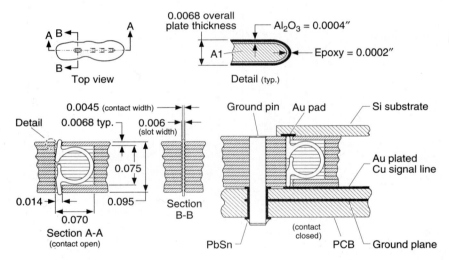

Figure 9.11. Micro-Interposer connector structure. (*Courtesy of AMP.*[14])

9.3.4.2 Sockets for Leadless MCM Modules

Interposer by AMP.[13,14,15] The AMP Micro-Interposer contact, illustrated in Fig. 9.10, forms the basis for a number of connectors for both peripheral- and area-array sockets. This contact is shown in both the free and compressed states. The contacts in the free state are oriented approximately 19 degrees with respect to the axis that develops after closure. The basic contact, as illustrated, is 0.090 in high, stamped from 0.0045-in-thick BeCu, which is gold over nickel plated. These contacts are placed in

Figure 9.12. Micro-Interposer and Ampflat sockets. (*Courtesy of AMP.*[14])

cavities constructed of aluminum sheets of 0.0068 in thickness each, which are anodized and impregnated with epoxy or Teflon. This stack, as shown, contains contacts placed inside cavities; one such cavity is shown on the left-hand side of the illustration. The contact legs project through the upper and lower plates which enclose the cavity.

The height of this projection on both sides, typically 0.023 in, is the portion of the contact which activates closure of the "omega" when assembled. During this closure, a wipe occurs which is necessary to obtain a good, low-resistance electrical contact between the MCM pad and the substrate. Also, when closed, the contacts are shunted together, giving a low-inductance, low-capacitance contact. The contact is rated at 100 g contact force with a wipe of at least 0.0025 in. An example of the use of this contact is shown in Figs. 9.11 and 9.12.

A recent development by AMP is the Ampflat connector. In this design, the contacts are fabricated from an etched sheet of beryllium-copper which is laminated between two pieces of prepunched Kapton. After lamination, the contacts are formed and then separated from each other, and the compressed contact array is only 0.0009 in high, making this suitable for low-profile applications. The contacts must be gold plated, however, because of the low compression force available. The socket array is on a 0.050-in grid. Figure 9.12 illustrates a connector using this contact.

Cinch Fuzz Button. Another type of interposer connector utilizing a resilient metal button is the Cinch Cin:apse connector, manufactured by Cinch Corp. The connector element is composed of "fuzz buttons," which are made by twisting gold plated wire into contacting elements. The fuzz buttons are placed in preformed holes in a plastic holder which forms the connector body. Illustrated in Fig. 9.13, this connector is also called a *button board connector* and is also an LIF connector.

TRW Button Board.[13] The TRW button board connector, made by TRW Company, is another interposer connector utilizing a fuzz button concept for the connector element. Figure 9.14 shows a typical contact, a wadded wire cylinder made from 0.002-in-diameter gold-plated silver-copper wire. The contact structures are variations of simply supported beams, cantilevered beams, and columns. The small diameter of wire produces a small contact area, giving high contact pressure and low contact resistance.

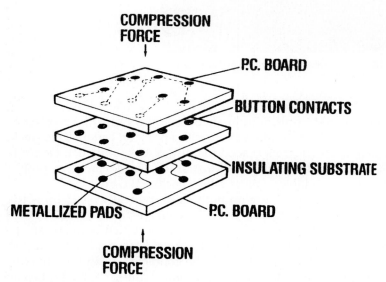

Figure 9.13. Cinch button board connector. (*Courtesy of Cinch Connector Co.*)

Figure 9.14. Button board inter-connect contacts.[13]

In a typical application, the buttons protrude above and below the button board 0.007 to 0.010 in. The wire is pressed into the hole with a spring constant that is directly proportional to the density of the wire in the hole. The button board allows direct board-to-board, MCM-to-board contact, reducing interconnect conductor lengths and propagation delays. Such connectors also provide a very low resistance (less than 1 mΩ) contact network that greatly diminishes system-generated noise and bypass capacitance requirements. The contact can be made and remade without loss of performance. A typical button board connector is illustrated in Fig. 9.15.

9.3.4.3 Elastomeric Connectors.[8,16-18] Elastomeric connectors are produced in a number of forms and consist of an electrically conductive material within a flexible polymer, usually silicone rubber. The elas-

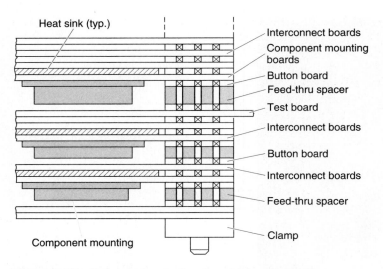

Figure 9.15. Connectorless button board interconnect.[13]

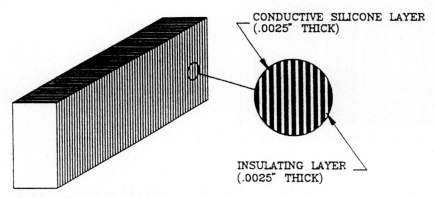

Figure 9.16. Layered elastomer element.

tomeric element is essentially a form of interposer. These connectors are used for either peripheral- or area-array MCMs.

The two elastomeric elements that are most common are the layered conductors and the metal in elastomer elements. The layered elastomeric element (LEE) is composed of alternating layers of nonconductive elastomer and silver or other conductive material, as shown in Fig. 9.16. The layers are very thin, and the pitch of the conductors is typically 0.005 in. These layered elastomeric connectors provide redundant contacts; i.e., several conductive elastomeric layers contact each device pad in any position. This eliminates the need for precise positioning of the LEE while ensuring positive contact between mating pads and isolation between adjacent pads. Resistances of 0.030 to 0.100 Ω are typical.

Many different conductor materials are used, including carbon fibers or particles, silver, and nickel. Carbon-filled elastomeric connectors are most widely specified because of their lower cost compared with metallized designs and because they meet most performance specifications requiring low current. Higher-current applications require that the connector offer a lower resistance. For example, a change from carbon particles to carbon fibers will increase electrical conductivity by about 10 percent.

Although carbon-filled elastomeric connectors are applicable to current in the milliamp range, metal-filled and metallized designs are good for currents approaching 1 A and over. The 0.040- to 0.500-Ω resistance of silver LEEs allows their use in a much broader range of applications. For example, a silver LEE 0.050 in wide on a 0.030-in-wide component pad has a current-carrying capacity of 0.3 A and a resistance of about 0.100 Ω. These designs are more applicable where high-speed signals are involved, such as in MCMs.

The metal-on-elastomer element produced by Elastomeric Technologies is known as the matrix MOE (MM) and is shown in Fig. 9.17. In this connector, the thin gold or nickel ribbons span the silicone rubber body. Conventional connectors rely on the shape and the material of the contact to provide the force necessary to maintain contact as well as conduct the flow of electrons, requiring the conductor to be designed so that temperature, creep, vibration, etc. will not affect the function of the connector throughout its life.

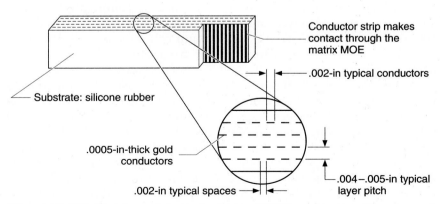

Figure 9.17. Matrix metal-on-elastomer (MOE) connector. (*Courtesy of Elastomeric Technologies, Inc.*)

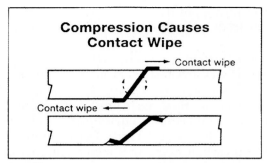

Figure 9.18. Isocon contact. (*Courtesy of Rogers Corp.*[18])

   In contrast, the matrix MOE connector relies almost entirely on silicone rubber to apply the contact force. Accordingly, the conductors of the matrix MOE need only be large enough to carry the current required for the application, making them very small and able to conduct in a direct path from one electrical substrate to another. The matrix also can be customized to match a specific pad pattern pitch. This type of construction lends itself to forming a pad-grid array socket for MCM use.

   The wrap-type designs are another version of the MOE connector. Fine-line metallizations are formed on either a thin silicone membrane or a flexible circuit, which is wrapped over a silicone core. Trace widths are usually 2 to 4 mils. Other z-axis conductive elastomers are available in the form of thin anisotropic material. Conduction through the material takes place only when the sheet is compressed and the conductive fillers, such as carbon or metal particles, are forced into contact. The filler also can be formed into columns at a specific pitch such as found in the ECPI (elastomeric conductive polymer interconnection) material developed by AT&T Bell Laboratories.

   Another type of elastomeric connector is the Isocon produced by Rogers Corporation, which emulates a conventional elastomeric connector but features a conductive element that consists of metal S-shaped pins as contacts embedded in a silicon rubber formulation (Fig. 9.18). When compressed, the pins provide a wiping action on the contact pads, a feature not present with conventional elastomeric connectors. For MCM interconnection, the connector is sandwiched between the bottom of the MCM substrate and the top of the PWB (Fig. 9.19). As the connector is compressed, each conductor rotates about its midpoint, wiping each end on the contact pads to be interconnected. The compres-

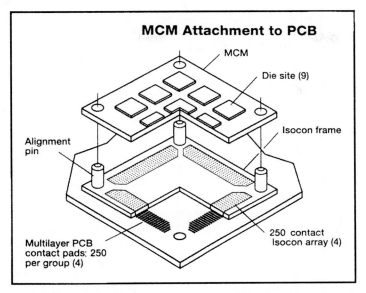

Figure 9.19. Isocon connector. (*Courtesy of Rogers Corp.*[18])

sion of the microcellular silicone insulator creates and maintains the contact force, with the conductors themselves remaining rigid during rotation, thereby transforming the compressive force of the silicone into contact force.

Connector holders or sockets are needed to locate substrates before pressure is applied to the assembly. The socket body has four functions: It must (1) hold the elastomeric elements in place between the mated substrate pads, (2) position the electronic package so that the pads are aligned with the substrate pads, (3) apply the force necessary to establish and maintain reliable contact, and (4) control the element deflection during clamping. The clamping force is most often applied by plastic or metal clips on the holder side or by means of screws, rivets, adhesives, or other devices. Figure 9.19 illustrates an MCM socket using elastomeric elements for connection to the substrate.

Elastomeric connectors are believed to be highly reliable and even have been approved by the military. The main reason for this is the simplicity of the connector and the redundant nature of the connection. The layers, or contacts, which are much narrower than the substrate pads, form the connection. Another advantage of these connectors is their low profile and high contact density. Virtual immunity from shock and vibration, high temperature tolerance, and ease of installation are also in their favor. Disadvantages include the absence, or minimum, of wiping action, poor film-penetration ability, and the need for high compressive pressure to ensure a good connection.

9.4 Summary

In many ways, the MCM represents an extension of the connection needs currently seen in the highly dense packaging technology in use today. Dense packaging, larger component size, higher-speed performance, and large I/O counts are some of the driving needs for connectors for MCMs. The connector must be capable of meeting system needs, be mechanically capable, yet provide the best electrical match for system requirements. In many ways, these needs are not compatible or consistent. The long mechanical path required by some connectors may degradate electrical performance of the system. The choice of connectors varies widely from permanent connections to many different types of separable connectors, with wide varieties of specialized sockets, including LIF and ZIF sockets. Many cost and performance options must be considered. Many different types of connections are available, and the choices involve tradeoffs in cost, system needs, and performance. It is important to consider these choices seriously.

Certainly smaller packaging is needed to meet the trend toward providing the best connector for the need. Many new reasons are developing to get away from through hole mount connectors, which use vital routing space in the PWB. Use of the LGA is one attempt to do this. LGAs have no pins or leads to be damaged, and the shorter connection length offered by these devices is consistent with the needs seen in the smaller and smaller packaging currently in use and planned. As speeds increase, we also may see a need to use novel forms of signal transmission, such as optical networks, this in turn producing a need for suitable large-pin-count connectors for this application. Fiberoptic connectors are now available, but not in the large I/O format required for MCM applications. Many different types of connectors are being developed in response to customer demand, and the growing need for larger pin-out packages. A multitude of new packages has been developed, many of them off-shore, to meet these packaging needs. Many of these are now in use and represent an opportunity for connector manufacturers to provide connectors for these new applications.

References

1. Chris Schreiber, Hughes Interconnect Systems, "Looking for the Best Interconnect," *Electronic Engineering Times,* June 15, 1992, pp. 46–49.
2. Ernest Meyer, *Computer Design,* "Fine-Pitch Technology Shrinks System Size, Boosts Performance," *Computer Design,* November 1 1989, pp. 71–76.
3. Michael F. Laub, AMP, "Leaded Multichip Module Connector," AMP Publication P-336-92.
4. Gerald L. Ginsberg, *Electronic Equipment Packaging Technology.* New York: Van Nostrand Reinhold, 1992.
5. Gerald L. Ginsberg, *Surface Mount and Related Technologies.* New York: Marcel Dekker, 1989.
6. Robert Mroczkowski, AMP, "Connectors: Choosing the Right Contact Materials," AMP.
7. W. R. Lambert, J. P. Mitchell, and J. A. Suchin, AT&T Bell Laboratories, "Use of Anisotropically Conductive Elastomers in High Density Separable Connectors," AT&T Bell Laboratories.
8. Howard W. Markstein, EP&P, "Applications Widen for Elastomeric Connectors," *Electronic Packaging and Production,* May 1992, pp. 30–32.
9. Ernie Hartland, DuPont, "Attachment and Design Considerations for Surface Mount Connectors," *Electronics Packaging and Production,* March 1992, pp. 74–78.
10. Michael Kirkman, Augat, "Compression Mount Connectors," *Connection Technology,* June 1992, pp. 18–20.
11. Hal Kent, Beta Phase, Inc., "Multi-Chip Module Connectors and Sockets: High Density and High Speed," *Proceedings, IEPS,* 1991, pp. 726–749.
12. Louis Palmieri, Digital Equipment Corporation, "Performance Characterization of VAX 9000 Flexible Circuit Interconnect," *Proceedings, IEPS,* 1991, pp. 726–740.
13. Paula R. Hurt, TRW, "Advanced High Speed Packaging and Interconnect Developments," *Proceedings, IEPS,* 1991, pp. 774–780.
14. Dimitry Grabbe, AMP, "MCM Design and Interconnection Techniques," *Connection Technology,* June 1991, pp. 18–21.
15. Dimitry Grabbe, AMP, and Henri Merkelo, University of Illinois, "High Density Electronic Connector for High Speed Digital Applications," *AMP Journal of Technology,* Vol. 1, November 1991, pp. 80–90.
16. Leonard S. Buchoff, Elastomeric Technologies, Inc., "Elastomeric Sockets for Chip Carriers and MCM's," *Proceedings, 42nd Electronic Components Conference,* May 1992, pp. 316–320.
17. Leonard S. Buchoff, PCK Elastomerics, "Surface Mounting of Components with Elastomeric Connectors," ElectriOnics, June 1982, pp. 13–15.
18. M. E. St. Lawrence and S. S. Simpson, Rogers Corporation, "A High Density LGA Connector for MCMs," *Connection Technology,* June 1991, pp. 26–29.

10
Thermal Design Considerations

The introduction of multichip modules (MCMs) into the electronics packaging community has brought new meaning to thermal management techniques, in that the allowable heat to be tolerated on the module is significantly less than that for single-chip modules.[1,2] This is so because MCMs generate more heat, are spaced closer together, and present more difficult problems in thermal management owing to the wide variety of materials used in the system and the varying coefficients of thermal expansion (CTEs) involved. MCMs offer circuit designers many benefits—increased densities, greater operating speeds, and greater functionality and performance. Certainly one of the tradeoffs for the benefits gathered is the effect of higher temperatures on MCMs and the effect on circuit reliability. High-density designs produce a high heat flux, which drives temperatures to levels that can cause increased failures.

MCMs interconnect arrays of integrated circuits (ICs) and passive devices with as many as 20,000 interconnections on the top and bottom of the substrate. They also can incorporate thermal management features such as thermal vias on a structure ranging from 2 to 30 layers with input/output (I/O) counts from hundreds to thousands. Assuming normal chip I/O connectivity, an MCM can pack four ICs in the same space normally occupied by one IC in single-chip modules. As noted in Table 10.1, computer manufacturers are successfully packing tremendous amounts of circuitry and power into small volumes. The needed heat removal requires a variety of thermal management techniques as well as planning in the thermal design of the package.

Table 10.1. MCM Thermal Characteristics[3]

Company	No. of chips	No. of I/O	Area, in	Chip area fraction	Cooling method	Total watts dissipation	Heat flux, W/cm^3
Mitsubishi/HTCM	9	624	2.6 × 2.6	13	Airflow	36	0.83
Hitachi/RAM	6	108	1.7 × 1.7	06	Airflow	6	0.8
Honeywell/SLIC	110	240	3.2 × 3.2	18	Liquid	60	0.9
Honeywell/MP	110	420	3.2 × 3.2	18	Airflow	72	1.1
NEC/SX	36	2177	4.9 × 4.9	15	Liquid	250	1.6
IBM/4381	36	882	2.5 × 2.5	19	Impinge	90	2.2
IBM/3090 TCM	100	1800	5.9 × 5.9	10	Liquid	500	2.2
NTT	25	900	3.3 × 4.1	18	Liquid	377	4.2

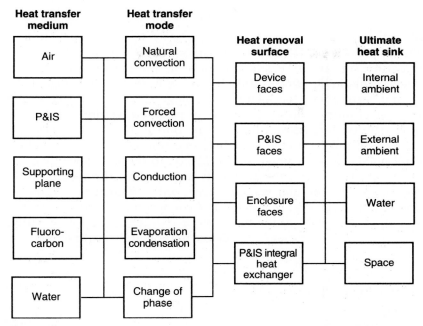

Figure 10.1. Thermal management cooling options.[3]

Reliability is closely related to thermal performance, and the primary failure mode in electronics is thermally induced. Materials also present a problem, in that the typical MCM designs introduce unsymmetrical stresses in the packaging setup. The thermal management of electronic equipment embraces all the natural and artificial processes and technologies that can be used to remove and transport heat from individual components in a controlled manner to the ultimate heat sink (see Fig. 10.1). A primary objective of thermal management for MCMs is to ensure that all circuit components, especially the ICs, are maintained within their functional temperature limits. The functional temperature limits establish the ambient or component package (case) temperature range within which electronic circuits can be expected to meet their performance goals. The temperature of the integrated circuit junction, however, must be maintained within its intended and allowable temperature range.

10.1 Thermal Management Overview[4]

Multichip modules (MCMs) offer considerable reduction in both interconnection signal delay and microelectronic packaging volume. However, this integration results in higher heat flux densities at the first- and second-level packaging technologies. Thermal management of microelectronic devices is required for proper operation and acceptable reliability. In addition to thermal control, the microelectronics engineer also must provide for interconnection wiring between chips and terminals for attachment of the MCMs to the next level of interconnect wiring. For applications that remove heat through the substrate, the use of thermal vias interferes with efficient heat removal and short wiring paths. The method of connection for the signals and power from the MCM to the next-level package (e.g., printed wiring boards, or PWB) can present a challenge for adequate heat removal.

10.2 Basic Thermal Management Considerations[3,5]

The dissipation of heat generated within electronic equipment is the result of the interaction between three modes of heat transfer, namely, conduction, convection, and radiation. Conduction, or radiation cooling, is heat removal by conduction with a cold plate or by radiation from a radiative surface. Convection can be natural, when no fluid circulators are used to move the fluid in the system, whereas forced convection employs a fluid circulator (pump, fan, etc.) to move the fluid. In addition, in the case of military or space electronics, liquid immersion or ebullition cooling may be used. Liquid immersion, as the name implies, involves immersion of the component in a liquid. In ebullition, the fluid boils at the component surface. Figure 10.2 presents a general comparison of these cooling modes. As is often the case, these modes not only act simultaneously but also affect each other. Efficient management of heat in electronic assemblies demands that some attempt be made to maximize the natural interaction of these modes of heat transfer.

10.2.1 Thermal Conduction

The first and primary mode of heat transfer to be encountered is *conduction*, which is germane to all materials in varying degrees. The con-

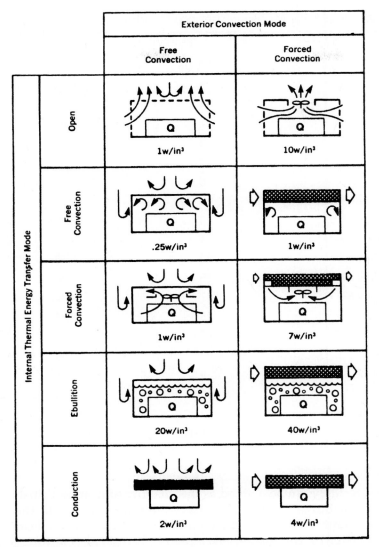

Figure 10.2. Thermal control methods.

duction of heat through a material is directly proportional to the thermal conductivity (*K*) of the material used (see Table 10.2), the cross-sectional area of the heat flow path, and the temperature differential across the material. The conduction is inversely proportional to the length of the path or thickness of the material.

Table 10.2. Heat Sink Material Thermal Conductivities[3]

Material	K (Btu/h/ft^2/°F/ft)	K (W/in · C)
Still air	0.016	0.0007
Alumina (99.5%)	16	0.70
Beryllia (99.5%)	14	5.00
Silver	42	10.6
Diamond	64	16.0
Gold	72	7.57
Epoxy	0.114	0.005
"Thermally conductive" epoxy	0.45	0.02
Aluminum alloy 1100	28	5.63
Aluminum alloy 3003	11	4.88
Aluminum alloy 5052	80	3.52
Aluminum alloy 6061	99	4.36
Aluminum alloy 6063	11	4.88
Copper alloy 110	26	9.94
Beryllium copper 172	62–75	2.7–3.3
Brass alloy 360	67	2.95
Stainless steel 321	9.3	0.41
Stainless steel 430	15.1	0.66
Steel, low carbon C1040	27	1.19
Titanium	1–11.5	0.2–0.5

Thermal conductivity can be defined as the quantity of heat (in British thermal units, or Btu's) conducted across a unit area normal to the heat path for a unit temperature gradient in the direction of the heat flow. Heat transfer by conduction takes place when there is a difference in temperature between two points in the same body or where two different bodies at different temperatures are in contact. Heat can be explained on the basis of motion of the molecules and atoms of the substance. Heat transfer by conduction therefore can be conceived of as a transfer of energy of molecular vibration from hotter and more rapidly vibrating molecules to the adjacent, less rapidly vibrating molecules. Conduction is the only mode of heat transfer that can occur within the confines of an opaque solid.

The conduction heat transfer through a solid is defined by the Fourier cooling law, that is,

$$Q = KA/L\,(T_h - T_c)$$

where Q is the heat flow in units of power (watts), K is the thermal conductivity of the material, L is the length of the heat path (or thickness of the material), A is the cross-sectional area, and T_h and T_c are the temperatures on the opposite sides of the block.

10.2.2   Thermal Convection

Convection, the second mode of heat transfer, is the exchange of heat between a surface and a fluid due completely to the intermingling of the fluid immediately adjacent to the surface with the remainder of the fluid. The rate of heat flow by convection from a body to a fluid is a function of the surface area of the body, the temperature differential, the velocity of the fluid, and properties of the fluid.

Convection can be subdivided into two types depending on the mechanics of the mixing or agitating process. *Forced convection* takes place where the flow of fluid is mechanically forced by an outside agent such as a pump or blower. *Free* or *natural convection* applies where the mechanical agitation is due to fluid density differences between the fluid and the limiting surface and the main body of fluid. In convection, heat flow is directly proportional both to the area A of the surface normal to the heat flow path and to the temperature differential between the heat source and the receiver media. Convection heat flow may be calculated by Newton's cooling law, that is,

$$Q = hS(T_s - T_f)$$

where Q is the heat flow in units of power (watts), S is the surface normal to the heat flow, and T_s and T_f are temperatures of the surface and fluid, respectively. Heat transfer by forced convection can be as much as 10 times more efficient than that by natural convection (see Fig. 10.2).

10.2.3   Thermal Radiation

Thermal radiation is the third mode of heat transfer. *Thermal radiation* is the transfer of heat by electromagnetic radiation, primarily in the infrared wavelengths. It is the only means of heat transfer between bodies that are separated by a complete vacuum, such as would take

Table 10.3. Natural Emissivity of Various Surfaces[3]

Material and finish	Emissivity
Aluminum sheet—polished	0.040
Aluminum sheet—rough	0.055
Anodized aluminum—color	0.80
Brass—commercial	0.040
Copper—commercial	0.030
Copper—machined	0.072
Steel—rolled sheet	0.55
Steel—oxidized	0.657
Nickel plate—dull finish	0.11
Silver	0.022
Tin	0.043
Oil paints—any color	0.92–0.96
Lacquer—any color	0.80–0.95

place in space environments. Thermal radiation does not require a medium, such as air, for energy transfer. The rate of heat flow by radiation is a function of the surface of the hot (i.e., heat-dissipating) body with respect to its emissivity (Table 10.3), its effective surface area, and the differential of the fourth power of their absolute temperatures.

The *emissivity* is a derating factor for surfaces that are not black bodies. It is defined as the ratio of emissive power of a given body to that of a black body with an emissivity of 1. The magnitude of radiation heat transfer is a function of the temperature difference.

10.2.4 Package Thermal Resistance[6]

A common figure of merit used for the comparison of different thermal designs of microelectronic packaging technologies is the junction-to-ambient thermal resistance, that is,

$$\theta_{ja} = (T_j - T_a)/q_c$$

where θ_{ja} = junction-ambient thermal resistance
T_j = junction temperature

T_a = ambient temperature
q_c = component power dissipation

This metric is often misleading, because no single parameter can adequately describe three-dimensional heat flow, which is a function of many parameters, such as geometry, flux source and placement, package orientation, next-level package attachment, efficiency of the heat sink, and method of chip connection. The junction-to-ambient thermal resistance may be considered to be the sum of two series resistances, the junction-to-case and the case-to-ambient thermal resistance. These also may be interpreted as the internal and external resistances. The junction-to-case, or internal-package, resistance θ_{jc} is primarily the conduction of heat from the die to the package external case. The case-to-ambient, or external-package, resistance θ_{ca} is primarily a measure of removal of heat from the package exterior surface by convection. The final temperature which the chip junction will reach is not only a product of θ_{ja} and chip power, but rather of the inlet air temperature plus the temperature rise of the coolant within the system.

A problem with using the concept of thermal resistance lies in the fact that it is good for single-chip packages but becomes deficient in cases where designs differ or in the case of MCMs, which have numbers of chips, sometimes at different powers. Despite these shortcomings, the concept of thermal resistance is worthwhile for understanding various cooling techniques and the thermal impact of different materials. The concept plays an important role in determining the all-important magnitude of junction temperature. A reduction of thermal resistances, either internal or external, has a beneficial impact on thermal management of the MCM.

10.2.5 Component-Level Thermal Analysis[3]

Heat generated within an MCM package is basically transported by thermal conduction to the external surfaces of the package and then is transferred to an external heat sink by conduction or to cooling fluids, usually air, by a convection process. Although complex analytical and numerical methods are often required to simulate these processes, a convenient way to characterize the results and to calculate the thermal features of the module is by means of internal and external thermal resistance. The idea of thermal resistance is an electrical analogy and is tied in with restricting the flow of heat through a medium (see Fig. 10.3). Voltage is similar to temperature, and current is similar to heat flow. The internal thermal resistances represent the temperature

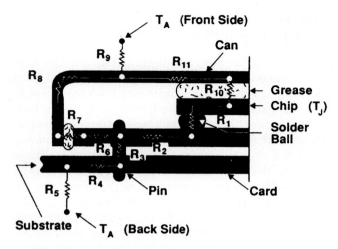

Figure 10.3. Cross section of an air-cooled MCM.[3]

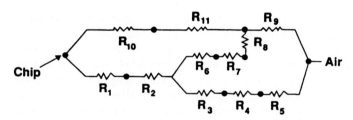

Figure 10.4. Thermal analogue of a typical air-cooled MCM.[3]

rise per unit of power dissipation that will occur within the MCM package; the external resistances represent the temperature rise per unit of power dissipation that will occur between the external surfaces of the package and the next level of cooling. For an air-cooled component, a parallel resistive circuit (Fig. 10.4) can be used to represent the combination of these parameters. This circuit can be used to find out acceptable values of internal and external resistance for given values of power dissipation and junction temperature, or vice versa.

The primary parameters that determine junction temperature are coolant or heat sink temperature, internal thermal resistance, external thermal resistance, and the amount of power being dissipated. The magnitude of the internal resistances, on the other hand, depends on the materials used in the package, the package geometry, chip-attachment method, and method of assembly. These factors are strongly dependent on the package manufacturer and are usually defined by the junction-to-case parameter. The resistances that are external to the component are then the only parameters that the packaging engineer can control.

10.3 MCM Thermal Management Types

While electrical performance advantages are possible with MCMs, thermal management of MCMs continues to be a challenge because of their construction and higher packaging density. MCMs usually have higher power outputs than single-chip modules and are combined with other components on circuit boards or backplanes with potentially high power requirements. This has led to a challenge for the MCM designer to customize the thermal design of the MCM system, forcing a move toward designing a cooling arrangement for individual chips on the substrate. The task involves integrating this scheme into the system and the overall cabinet. For high-performance systems such as seen in MCM design, thermal management must be a critical part of the design cycle and not the usual afterthought.

The first decision in thermal management of MCMs is to determine in which direction to remove the heat. The mainframe and supercomputer manufacturers have in part opted not to remove the heat through the substrate. In these constructions, the chips are mounted inverted, and the heat is removed from the chip backside with pistons or a conductive cap such as a "top hat." This is the more expensive approach but always yields lower temperature rises for a given power level. If the thermal path is through the substrate, metal thermal vias are fabricated into the interconnecting layers to make up for the poor thermal conductivity of the substrate dielectric. In some cases, thermal cutouts or wells are made in the dielectric layers, and the chips are mounted directly onto the high thermal conductivity substrate.

10.3.1 MCM Thermal Control Options[4,7]

In designing an MCM, the primary requirement is the needed electrical performance of the module. The system for cooling the module is known after the chip set and electrical functionality are determined. High-performance modules are usually cooled by conduction to a cold plate located above the substrate which makes integral contact with

**Fujitsu VP2000
above substrate cooling design**

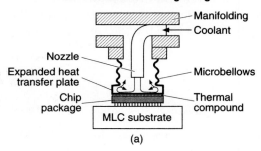

(a)

**Hitachi RAM module
through substrate cooling design**

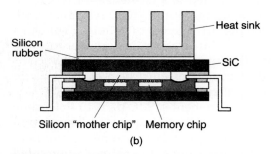

(b)

Figure 10.5. Above-substrate (*a*) and through-substrate (*b*) cooling for MCMs.[4]

the chips. Alternatives to cooling the chip from above the substrate are direct immersion and through-substrate cooling. Immersion cooling is used in some commercial products but not widely because of expense and reliability concerns.

Through-substrate cooling schemes, however, are less widely used in commercial products but find widespread application in military and avionics applications. Excluding systems where the fluid comes into direct contact with the chip, there are then two possible cooling geometries: *above-substrate cooling*, where the primary heat dissipation surface is above the chip and is attached mechanically to the radiating heat sink, and *through-substrate cooling*, whether the substrate is used to conduct the heat to a cold plate or heat exchanger at its back surface or edges. Figure 10.5 presents an example of each.

10.3.1.1 Above-Substrate Cooling. Also referred to as *chip-backside cooling,* above-substrate cooling is often used to accommodate other factors, such as the use of flip-chip bonding, the need for a PWB or multilayer ceramic board with a large number of layers, the need to make electrical connections from the substrate area to the next level of packaging, or the use of very high power ICs. The primary problem with above-substrate cooling is how to make contact with the chips in a reliable and thermally efficient manner.

Since MCMs may use up to 150 chips, compliant, conformable contacts are needed. The contact must be compliant to prevent damage to the chip as a result of the large thermal expansion differences between the substrate and the cold-plate structures. It must be conformal to accommodate the surface height variations, surface tilt, and roughness of the contacting surfaces. Tolerances produced by the chip-to-board electrical bonding technology used can produce significant thermal resistance, since height variations of 1 to 10 mils and surface tilt of 1 to 3 mils/cm are common. Thermal grease is sometimes used, but this also increases the thermal resistance.

The thermal contact must be predictable and reliable over the product's lifetime. Additionally, the cold plate must be removable periodically to allow servicing of the substrate or chips. For this reason, above-substrate systems usually require one contacting mechanism per chip, and for a large number of chips, this can affect the cost and manufacturability of the unit.

The main advantage of this method is that it decouples the thermal design from most substrate-level decisions and is not linked to assembly or fabrication tolerances. It has greater potential as a more capable cooling scheme, since there is only one interface along a short thermal path to the heat exchanger. A disadvantage is the difficulty in making the connection to the chips thermally reliable and repeatable; another is the expense of this heat sink assembly. An example of above-substrate cooling is given in Fig. 10.5.

10.3.1.2 Through-Substrate Cooling. In through-substrate cooling, heat is conducted through the substrate and interconnect to a cold plate or heat exchanger attached to the back of the substrate. The main heat dissipation surface, or cold plate, is beneath the chip. The heat-transfer path is through the substrate, by means of thermal vias or thermal cutouts. Clearly, this method is greatly affected by many choices of how to fabricate the module. The chip-to-substrate bonding technology has a significant impact on the thermal efficiency of the chip or chip-package connection to the substrate.

Three possible alternatives are tape automated bonding (TAB), flip-chip bonding, and chip carriers with solder pads. The next portion of the thermal path is the substrate or interconnect. The three alternatives are PWBs, ceramic substrates, and high-density thin-film substrates. Thin-film technology and multilayer ceramic technology are well suited to this method, while PWBs are not often used because of the low-conductivity material employed and the low interconnect density achievable with PWBs.

Advantages of this method are that many high-thermal-conductivity materials are available for substrate fabrication and that it avoids the high cost of top heat sinks, pistons, etc. A disadvantage is that this method limits routing density, in that thermal vias may be required. Also, the substrate processing requirements and heat resistivity of the substrate material limit the feasible size of the cooling channels that can be incorporated within the substrate. It is more compact and more efficient than the other methods and permits probing and testing of the system under operating conditions, however.

Through-substrate cooling is less common than the above-substrate alternative in commercial systems. Conduction through PWBs to conduction cores, however, is common practice in avionics packages. This division occurs because avionics packages generally have been less complex and require lower power than commercial packages used in mainframes and supercomputers. An example of through-substrate cooling is given in Fig. 10.5.

10.3.1.3 Thermal Cutouts.[8] Many options exist for removing heat from the chips on an MCM, the goal being to transfer heat to the bottom of the substrate or heat sink. High heat loads can be accommodated through thermal cutouts in the substrate or routing layers. At the expense of providing increased heat transfer, the penalty is a loss of signal routing area.

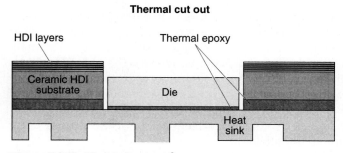

Figure 10.6. Thermal cutout.[8]

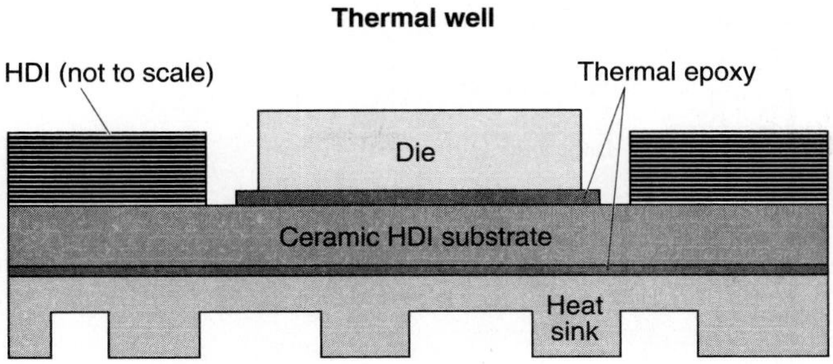

Thermal well

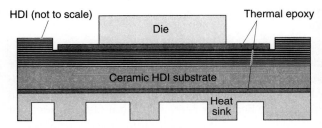

Figure 10.7. Thermal well.[8]

Partial thermal well

Figure 10.8. Partial thermal well.[8]

Figure 10.6 shows a typical thermal cutout, where the substrate and signal layers are removed to permit the chips to rest directly on the heat sink. This method maximizes heat transfer but takes over signal routing area and complicates assembly. In Fig. 10.7, only the signal layers are cut out, and the chip rests directly on the substrate. The dielectric, such as polyimide/metallization layers, is thin enough to provide good heat removal, and the method has less impact on wire bonding or TAB attachment than the cutout scheme shown in Fig. 10.6.

The signal layers also can be removed partially, as in Fig. 10.8, in a partial thermal well, with a moderate gain in heat transfer but with minimal impact on routing density. Figure 10.9 shows a method of processing the substrate to eliminate a layer of polyimide to provide a first-layer metallization that is a ground plane and also a thermal plane. In this case, eliminating the initial layer of polyimide dielectric increases heat transfer to the substrate.

Without planarizing layer

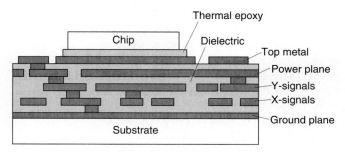

Figure 10.9. Substrate without planarizing layer.[8]

10.3.2 Auxiliary Cooling Methods for MCMs

10.3.2.1 Fin Heat Sinks.[9,10] A good heat sink tends to minimize temperature gradients and maximize surface area per unit volume consistent with the cooling technique employed. Heat generated from a component at one point on the heat sink is readily conducted throughout the heat sink to the exposed convection- or radiation-cooled surfaces (see Fig. 10.10).

Heat sink materials are selected for their good thermal conduction (see Table 10.2), their ability to perform as extended surfaces, and their ease of fabrication. Aluminum is the most widely used heat sink material for electronic packaging applications. This is due to its relative ease of fabrication and relatively light weight, which make it an excellent material for forming long individual fins. It is also less than half the cost of copper in a raw material size that conducts the same amount of heat. Although aluminum is very machinable, it is difficult to join by soldering or brazing. Copper is an excellent thermal conductor and finds many applications where high conductivity is required. Steel is used in high-pressure applications and other areas where high strength is needed.

The shape of the heat sink can have a significant impact on the efficiency of heat transfer through it. The smaller the temperature drop across the heat sink, the more efficient it is. Thus the shape of the conduction path in the material and its thermal efficiency significantly affect the performance of the heat sink. A large cross section in contact with the source of heat aids in heat flow.

The shape of the heat sink exposes the maximal surface area that is

Figure 10.10. Typical high-power dissipation heat sinks.

consistent with the mode of cooling used. Natural convection cooling imposes limitations on heat sink fin spacing. Close spacing of fins can impair the natural convection of air through them. Conversely, the use of forced convection allows the fins to be spaced closely together. Some heat sinks employ fins at right angles to each other to minimize heat reflection between fins, while other geometries promote cooling fluid turbulence and spacial arrangements to permit airflow from any direction.

10.3.2.2 Heat Pipes.[11] *Heat pipes* are devices that move thermal energy from one location to another by evaporation of an appropriate liquid. A heat pipe is a closed container with a capillary wick structure and a small amount of vaporizable fluid. It uses a vaporization-condensation cycle whereby the capillary wick pumps the condensate to the evaporator (heat source) and the working fluid removes the heat. Liquid vaporization at the heated segment of the pipe increases the pressure of the liquid-vapor interface. This, in turn, results in an increase in capillary pressure at the evaporation end, causing the liquid to be pumped through the wick. The vapor-pressure drop between the evaporator and the condenser is very small.

Two types of heat pipe are used for the thermal management of MCMs. One is based on the use of a vapor chamber; the other uses an embedded substrate. The vapor chamber heat pipe is constructed as a frame structure with the wick and face sheet skins joined together to form a single vacuum-tight enclosure. The embedded heat pipe assembly, on the other hand, uses multiple small, flat heat pipes that are sandwiched together in a frame. Both configurations have a number of advantages and disadvantages depending on system requirements. Thus the packaging engineer must choose the best configuration for the particular application.

Among the specific advantages that accrue to heat pipes is the significant improvement found with heat pipes when compared with solid aluminum heat exchangers. It is also found that heat pipes provide a simple and maintainable thermal interface between the module and chassis sidewalls. There are limitations, however, in the use of heat pipes for module cooling. Except for specialized cases, they may not be cost-effective, and they occupy considerable space. Limitations exist on the attainable heat-transfer rates based on the nucleate vaporizing in the wick structure, capillary pumping limitations, and a sensitivity regarding changing orientation of the pipe in portable applications.

10.3.2.3 Thermoelectric Devices.[3,12] Although thermoelectric cooling is not widely used in electronic devices, some packaging designers are turning to the use of solid-state thermoelectric heat pump modules for unique thermal "hot spot" management applications. Thermoelectric cooling is based on a principle discovered by Peltier in 1834. Peltier found that if two different metals are connected at two locations, and if the two locations are subjected to different temperatures, then an electric current will flow through the loop. Reversing this process (the *Peltier effect*), a thermoelectric heat pump can be created by inputting a current so that a temperature differential is maintained between two solid-state device junctions.

Thermoelectric modules for electronic applications are made using bismuth telluride doped to create the semiconductor (*N*- and *P*-type) elements. The modules, connected in series electrically and in parallel thermally, are integrated into modular devices or MCMs. The modules are packaged between ceramic plates with a high mechanical strength in compression for optimal electrical insulation and thermal conduction. In a typical application, the hot side of the thermoelectric heat pump is attached to a heat sink or other heat-transfer element. The cold side is mated to the component to be cooled. When a direct current is applied, electrons pass from a low energy level in the P-type material to a higher energy level in the N-type material. This causes heat to be removed from the cold-side ceramic plate.

Single thermoelectric modules are able to achieve temperature differences of up to 65°C and can pump tens of watts of heat. Greater differential can be achieved by stacking one module on top of another, a process known as *staggering* or *cascading.* This principle has specific advantages in applications where precise temperature control or low temperatures are required.

10.4 Thermal Analysis

The thermal analysis of an MCM design should be performed as early as possible in the overall equipment packaging process. The first and best opportunity is during the conceptual stage, when it is possible to estimate component operating temperatures. This is also the best time to uncover severe problems, if any, with the thermal management approach followed. The duration of the design stage and the associated development costs can be minimized if these analyses are done at the beginning stages of the system conceptualization.

10.4.1 Thermal Design Tools

A number of tools exist for engineers to analyze the thermal management aspects of MCMs. The tools are general in nature and are not problem-oriented, and they may be categorized as manual or analytical, numerical or CAD, and finally, thermal testing or experimental.

The manual, or "hand," calculation is the primary and most important method for defining the problem. The manual, or analytical, solution is the first approach to the solution and generally does not lend itself to analysis of electronic packages, since, in its most useful form, it describes a homogeneous material with uniform properties. The somewhat "ideal" boundary conditions assumed for the closed analytical solution do not generally apply.

10.4.1.1 Manual and Numerical Methods.[13] Between the closed analytical solutions and the simplified conduction correlations there is a wide range of numerical methods of analysis. Generally, these numerical methods involve subdividing the actual configurations into many small but finite subvolumes, typically called *nodes.* Both the thermal

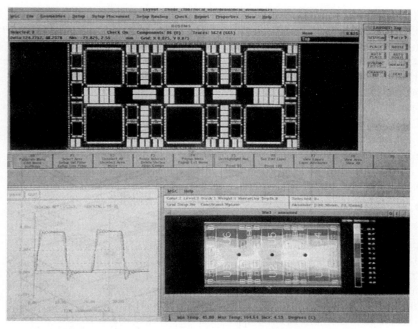

Figure 10.11. Prototype data memory.[13]

properties and temperature are assumed to be uniform throughout the subvolume.

It is further assumed that the heat transfer through each face of the subvolume is one-dimensional and can be calculated using a simple form of Fourier's conduction equation or appropriately modified convection or radiation equations. By noting that, for steady-state analysis, the sum of the heat entering a control volume must equal the sum of the heat leaving the control volume, a simultaneous array can be derived consisting of one equation and one unknown per control volume. Several approaches exist for approximating boundary conditions, heat dissipation, and transient conditions. This entire class of techniques is referred to as the *finite-difference method* or *finite-element method.*

To illustrate the finite-element method, the following example is presented. The assembly shown in Fig. 10.11 is a large prototype data memory. It houses 82 devices, of which 6 are 0.410 × 0.410 in VLSI memory devices of 5.0 W each. Total power for the MCM is 36 W. The substrate is made up of seven layers, including two signal layers and two 15-μin aluminum power and ground planes. The cooling method

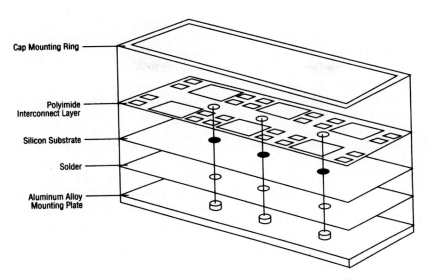

Cap Mounting Ring

Polyimide
Interconnect Layer

Silicon Substrate

Solder

Aluminum Alloy
Mounting Plate

Figure 10.12. Exploded view of data memory MCM assembly.[13]

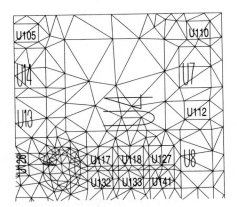

Figure 10.13. Finite-element analysis
mesh of MCM thermal patterns.[13]

is via thermal conduction through the substrate to the mounting plate
(Fig. 10.12).

The thermal analysis tool uses triangular elements to represent
design geometries. Triangular elements are appropriate because they
enable accurate representation of complex geometries such as holes
and curved substrates and modules. The thermal analysis tool auto-

matically places element boundaries onto geometric boundaries and refines mesh elements to an aspect ratio of 3:1 or better. Figure 10.13 shows the resulting mesh. Areas of increased complexity (e.g., many small components) may exhibit higher thermal gradients and therefore need a finer mesh to accurately define the finite-element model. The thermal tool's mesh generator automatically increases mesh density in areas of increased complexity. The mesh generator is geometry-based, not adaptive.

The first thermal analysis is done assuming that thermal vias are used. Heat dissipates only from the substrate through the cap mounting ring to the cap (see Fig. 10.12), the cap acting as a cold plate and keeping a constant temperature of 30°C. The thermal analysis is repeated using 169 thermal vias under each of the six VLSI devices. Results indicate that these vias have little impact on the junction temperatures. The reason is that the relatively low lateral thermal conductivity and long thermal path do not permit significant heat transfer to the edges of the substrate.

10.4.1.2 Thermal Testing. Although there is reason to rely on thermal or experimental testing as opposed to numerical or analytical methods for thermal analysis, such testing is normally so expensive and time-consuming that it is avoided. Experimental testing is often used when boundary conditions are not clearly defined or when there is a question of understanding the problem. Very soon after the beginning of the analytical portion of a thermal design effort, thermal testing should begin. First, there will be development tests, which are conducted in support of data to be used in the design of a specific component or subsystem. These tests will typically start with individual component thermal resistance tests where published data are not available or do not fit the configuration. As soon as hardware is fabricated and the design becomes finalized, more extensive testing of the MCM subassembly is done. Testing in this phase involves extensive instrumentation of temperatures, pressures, flow rates, etc. The intent is to ensure that numerical or analytical techniques are correct. Results are compared with predictions—and a final estimate of unit thermal performance is obtained.

10.5 Applications[14]

A review of some applications of various industry cooling techniques may serve to highlight their important thermal management features. References 4, 5, and 7 supply an excellent overview of this subject

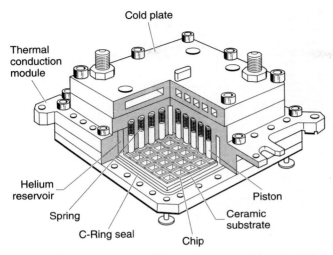

Figure 10.14. IBM thermal conduction module (TCM).[14]

and a guide to the following descriptions of these industry techniques.

10.5.1 IBM TCM Module

One of the most famous and earliest implementations of a large MCM was the thermal conduction module (TCM) shown in Fig. 10.14. The TCM relies on conduction to aluminum pistons which contact each chip. Piston heads are spherically shaped to promote contact at the center of each chip regardless of chip tilt. Each piston is spring loaded to ensure that it contacts the chip.

The first TCMs were used in the IBM 3081 processor and satisfied a design requirement for a chip T_j of 85°C by achieving an actual temperature of 69°C. The processor contained a 90 × 90 mm multilayer ceramic substrate designed to connect more than 100 semiconductor chips. Each logic chip contained 704 circuits, for a maximum of 45,000 circuits per module. Because of the high packaging density achieved, heat fluxes of 20 and 4 W/cm² were achieved at the chip and module levels, respectively.

As can be seen in Fig. 10.15, the heat flow path from an individual chip to the cooling water is comprised of a series of thermal resistances. Two of the resistances in the path, R_{c-p} and R_{p-h}, are influenced by the conductivity of the medium in the spaces between chip and pis-

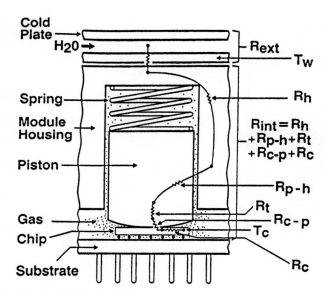

Figure 10.15. Thermal conduction path, IBM TCM.[14]

ton and piston and housing. It was calculated that temperature drops due to thermal conduction across air in the gaps would be too high to satisfy cooling requirements. An interface medium with a higher thermal conductivity than air was needed, and helium gas was used as that interface medium.

The total thermal resistance of the TCM from chip to coolant along the primary thermal path is 11.2°C/W, of which 9°C/W is "internal resistance" and 2.25°C/W is external resistance of the cold plate. All in all, for a 55°C temperature rise over the local coolant temperature, each chip can dissipate 5 W, or 24 W/cm² based on the chip area.

10.5.2 NEC SX-2

The liquid-cooled module (LCM) used in the NEC SX supercomputer has enhanced thermal conduction paths and a detachable water-cooled cold plate. Shown in Fig. 10.16, the NEC LCM can accommodate 36 chips mounted within individual flipped TAB carriers (FTCs) mounted on a 100 × 100 mm multilayer ceramic substrate. The heat flow path within the LCM from an individual FTC to cooling water is shown in Fig. 10.17. Heat is conducted from the FTC cap to the face of

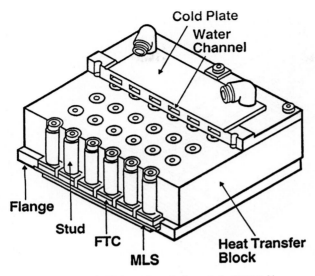

Figure 10.16. NEC liquid-cooled module (LCM).[14]

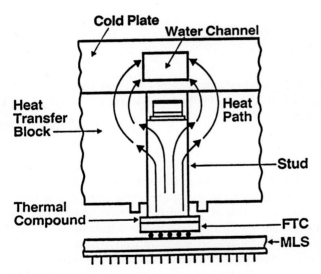

Figure 10.17. Heat flow path in the LCM.[14]

an aluminum stud across a thermal compound and through the stud into the heat transfer block, where it is removed by means of the water-cooled plate which is bolted to the surface of the heat transfer block (HTB).

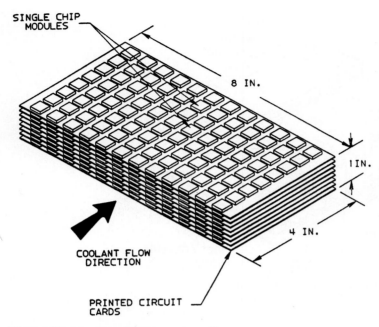

SINGLE CHIP
MODULES

8 IN.

1 IN.

4 IN.

COOLANT FLOW
DIRECTION

PRINTED CIRCUIT
CARDS

Figure 10.18. Cray-2 MCM package.[14]

The maximum power dissipation per chip is 7 W, and the maximum module power dissipation is 250 W. Twelve LCMs are mounted in a 3 × 4 array on a 545 × 465 mm PWB.

10.5.3 Cray-2

Perhaps the most unique MCM package is that used in the Cray-2 computer. Unusual in both package geometry and cooling, it uses total immersion cooling as a method of removing heat. As shown in Fig. 10.18, the MCM used in the Cray-2 is a three-dimensional structure consisting of eight PWBs on which are mounted arrays of single-chip modules. The power dissipation of this module is 600 to 700 W. Although theoretically coolable by air, the large number of MCMs used made air impractical and promoted the use of FC-77 liquid coolant. Fluorocarbon coolants offer a higher density and thermal conductivity than air, properties important in removing and transporting the heat. The FC-77 is distributed vertically between stacks of MCMs and flows horizontally through the modules and over the chip packages at a velocity of 1 in/s. A total flow rate of FC-77 of 200

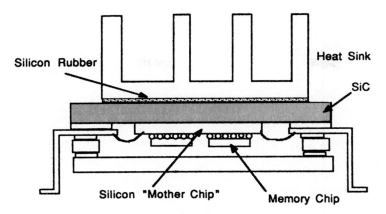

Figure 10.19. Hitachi RAM module.[14]

gal/min is required to cool the 194 kW dissipated in the Cray-2 computer.

10.5.4 Hitachi RAM Module

The Hitachi RAM module provides one of the few examples of through-substrate cooling now used (Fig. 10.19). The Hitachi RAM module is an air-cooled module which interconnects a low number of silicon chips on a "mother" chip or a silicon circuit board. The Hitachi 101 SiC RAM module contains six 1-W ECL chips solder ball attached with 77 solder balls on a silicon substrate. Of the 77 solder balls, 52 serve a primary thermal function. The chips are 0.19 × 0.4 cm. The outer-module dimensions are 2.74 × 2.74 cm by 1.6 cm high when a 0.8-cm² heat sink is attached to the lid. Heat dissipated by the ECL chips is conducted to the heat sink, which is attached to the SiC lid with silicon rubber. For an air velocity of 3 m/s, the total thermal resistance from junction to ambient is about 35°C/W, where about a third is the internal resistance.

10.5.5 Fujitsu FACOM M-780

The multichip packaging technology used on the Fujitsu FACOM M-780 computer is unlike most of the packaging technologies discussed in that it utilizes single-chip modules mounted on a large printed circuit board. Figure 10.20 shows a section of the printed circuit board with single-chip modules sandwiched between two water-cooled cold

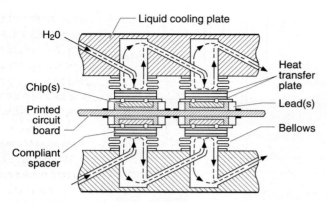

Figure 10.20. Fujitsu FACOM M-780 module.[14]

plate assemblies. These assemblies consist of a liquid-cooled bellows contacting each module. The Fujitsu FACOM M-780 package also utilizes a water-cooled cold plate. The cold plate is attached to the board in the factory and is not separable for field replacement. Thermal resistance from chip to water for each single-chip module is 2.4°C/W. Conduction from the chip to the bellows accounts for 1.5°C/W of this resistance, and most of this resistance takes place at the compliant material across the interfaces. Using the concept of thermal resistance, the Fujitsu package exhibits a value of 18.8°C/W/cm².

References

1. M. A. Zimmermann, K. Azar, and C. D. Mandrone, AT&T Bell Laboratories, "Thermal Performance of High Powered MCMs," *Hybrid Circuit Technology,* July 1991, pp. 51–54.

2. Jim Walcutt, Compix, Inc., "Managing the Thermal Tradeoffs," *Circuits Assembly,* March 1992, pp. 36–41.

3. Gerald Ginsberg, Component Data Associates, *Electronic Equipment Packaging Technology.* New York: Van Nostrand Reinhold, 1992.

4. Thomas Dolbear, Microelectronics and Computer Technology Corporation (MCC), "Thermal Management of Multichip Modules," *Electronic Packaging and Production,* June 1992, pp. 60–63.

5. Alan D. Kraus, Sperry Gyroscope, "Heat Flow Theory," *Electrical Manufacturing,* April 1959, pp. 123–142.

6. Gary B. Kromann, TME Engineering, "Thermal Management for Ceramic Multichip Modules: Experimental Program," TME Engineering.

7. Thomas Dolbear, Microelectronics and Computer Technology Corporation (MCC), "Thermal Management of Multi-Chip Modules," *Proceedings, NEPCON*, 1990, pp, 1186–1207.

8. Howard Markstein, EP&P, "Balancing Heat Transfer and Signal Routing for MCMs," *Electronic Packaging and Production*, November 1991, p. 35.

9. Stephen Heng and Jason Pei, Digital Equipment Corporation, "Cooling MCMs with Pin Fin Heat Sinks," *Electronic Packaging and Production*, October 1991, pp. 54–57.

10. William R. Hamburgen, Digital Equipment Corporation, "Interleaved Fin Thermal Connectors for Multichip Modules," *Proceedings, IEPS*, 1991, pp. 419–426.

11. L. R. Fox, G. Kromann, and R. J. Hannemann, Digital Equipment Corporation, "Multichip Package Cooling with Integral Heat Pipe," *Proceedings, NEPCON*, 1990, pp. 1650–1666.

12. Terry Costlow, "Multichip Modules Are Feeling the Heat," *Electronic Engineering Times*, October 7, 1991, p. 7.

13. Dan Wolff, Mentor Graphics, "Thermal Analysis of Multichip Modules," *Surface Mount Technology*, April 1992, pp. 29–34.

14. R. C. Chu and R. E. Simons, "Review of Thermal Design for Multichip Modules," *Proceedings, NEPCON*, 1990, pp. 1633–1642.

11

Multichip Module Applications

11.1 Introduction[1-3]

Multichip module (MCM) development and use to date have been driven primarily by performance but more accurately by the interrelated requirements of density and performance. In the past decade, there have been amazing gains in speed, density, complexity, and power dissipation in semiconductor devices. Indeed, advances in silicon semiconductor technology have provided a 50:1 reduction in packaging density for modern computers alone.

Future electronics packaging needs will increasingly emphasize the speed and density of interconnections. However, normal printed wiring assemblies and integrated circuit (IC) packages rely heavily on interconnections and dimensions that are considerably larger than those found in the IC chip. Considerable performance is sacrificed in these external paths, but these are not the only causes for loss of performance. The amount of semiconductor substrate area in conventional board-level packaging is as low as 5 percent, causing a substantial effect of relatively large external connections and low active component density.

Much of current packaging technology is motivated by the mechanical requirements of assembling and repairing multiple IC assemblies. Future improvements, therefore, can be made only by adapting this circuit and repair strategy to finer-pitch dense wiring or by abandoning the repairability requirements completely in the interest of speed.

MCMs are attractive primarily for those system applications where interchip delays are critical to performance but also for those applications where a functional unit can be clearly defined.

Applications for MCMs encompass a wide range of industries, including data processing, telecommunications, military electronics, and automotive. These various application areas have their individual reliability and performance requirements, resulting in the development of widely different MCM formats with a myriad of material, process, and packaging designs. MCM applications have found worldwide use. In the past 10 years, organizations in the United States, Europe, and Japan have devoted significant effort to the development of MCM formats. In the early 1980s, IBM, with the introduction of the famous multilayer cofired ceramic thermal conduction module (TCM), showed that high performance could be obtained with high-density MCMs using conventional thick-film cofired technology and flip-chip interconnect.

MCMs have now become commonplace in high-end, high-performance mainframes and supercomputers. NEC first introduced an MCM incorporating thin-film interconnect layers in its SX series supercomputers, followed by use in its ACOS 2000 and 930 mainframes. Hitachi offers cofired mullite MCMs in its high-end systems, and Fujitsu offers a cofired glass-ceramic MCM in its mainframes and supercomputers. DEC has just recently introduced the VAX 9000, which also incorporates thin-film interconnect layers to achieve top performance. Although many MCMs are still of a prototype status in the United States and Europe, several Japanese companies have extensive manufacturing capability.

This chapter is dedicated to providing some case or application studies of various MCM programs. In this chapter, some key companies provide information on their MCM designs. From this information, some knowledge may be gained as to how the crucial decisions to make MCMs may evolve.

11.2   DEC's VAX 9000 Computer[4,5]

Over the past 25 years, the performance of mainframe computers has increased by orders of magnitude. Every performance enhancement due to developments and investment in IC technology has to be countered by an investment in interconnection and packaging. In order to meet the performance requirements of the VAX 9000 and to exploit the growth in IC technology, it was clear to Digital Equipment Corporation that advanced packaging technology was necessary. Although comprehensive studies of other packaging technologies were performed, it was found that the multichip unit (MCU) product technology provided the solution to the challenges of signal, power, and thermal management for the VAX 9000 computer system.

To provide a clearer background for the technologies associated with the high-density signal processor (HDSC) and MCU products, a brief description of HDSC and MCU product design is in order.

The MCU product is made up of several subassemblies, as shown in Fig. 11.1:

- High-density signal carrier (HDSC)
- High-performance ECL integrated circuits with TAB tapes
- Signal and power connector systems
- MCU housing and mechanical hardware
- Pin fin heat sink

One of the driving forces in the selection/development of multichip packaging for the VAX 9000 system was the need to reduce interchip signal transmission delays. The development of the HDSC product, with a signal interconnect density of approximately six times that of a state-of-the-art PWB, has achieved this.

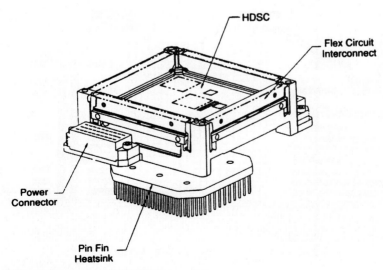

Figure 11.1. The VAX MCU assembly.

The HDSC product provides signal lines for chip interconnect, power-distribution layers providing power to the ICs from the power source, and a metallic base plate for thermal die attachment. The finished HDSC is 4.0 × 4.25 in in size and contains nine layers of interconnect, copper conductors, separated by polyimide insulating layers. Power distribution occupies four metal layers, and the remaining five are used for a variety of purposes. Two are used for reference planes, one for surface pads, and two for signal connections. It is an MCM-D type multichip module (MCM) (see Fig. 11.2). A nominal characteristic impedance of 60 Ω is provided by the controlled-impedance dual structure of the HDSC. A polyimide dielectric material with a dielectric constant of 3.5 is used to optimize signal-transmission speed. Copper conductors provide a line resistivity of less than 1 Ω/cm.

11.2.1 Core Fabrication

The HDSC is composed of two cores, a signal core and a power core. These are fabricated separately and merged together as part of the HDSC fabrication process. The cores are processed on 150-mm

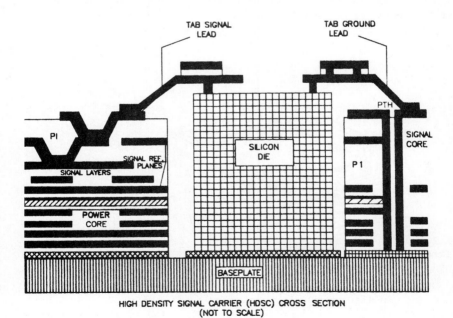

HIGH DENSITY SIGNAL CARRIER (HDSC) CROSS SECTION
(NOT TO SCALE)

Figure 11.2. DEC's MCM for the VAX 9000.

wafers and are copper-polyimide structures with a metallic layer between the copper and the polyimide to promote adhesion. The signal core is a dual-stripline structure consisting of four metal and five dielectric layers. It has a single pair of signal layers between two reference planes. Each signal layer has 18-µm-wide lines on a 75-µm pitch. Polyimide layer thickness is 25 µm, and the reference layers are 4 µm thick. The signal core contains 677 routing layers per square inch.

The power core connects and distributes three different voltage sources to the ECL chips (V_{cc}, V_{ee}, and V_{tt}). Similar to the signal cores, power cores are composed of four copper and five dielectric layers, the copper layers being 18 µm thick and the polyimide in between 10 µm thick.

11.2.2 HDSC Product Fabrication

Merging of the power core and the signal core is accomplished by lamination. The electrical connection between the power core and the signal core is made by a plated-through process similar to that used for printed wiring boards (PWBs). Holes (250 µm) are drilled through the stack, cleaned to remove drill debris and polyimide smear, and plated with electroless and electroplated copper.

Die-site cutouts are produced in the HDSC by means of a laser for bonding of ICs during the HDSC assembly process. The laser cuts are made in the polyimide only, and all the copper in the trench area is selectively removed by masking and etching processes. Following cutting of the die sites, the substrate is laminated to the base plate. A laser is also used to trim the HDSC product to its final form factor of 4×4.25 in.

11.2.3 MCU Assembly

The MCU assembly takes place in two stages. First, the ICs are bonded and connected to the HDSC to comprise the MCU subassembly. The substrate is then transferred to an epoxy dispense station, where a diamond-filled epoxy is injected through a syringe into each die-site cutout area on the substrate base plate. The next step in the process is to perform outer lead bonding of the die on tape. This is done with precision tooling which removes the die from its tape carrier, forms the leads, and automatically drops the die in place, and all four sides of the die on tape are bonded simultaneously to the HDSC's bonding pads using gang-bond blade thermode techniques.

11.3 IBM's Multichip Packaging[6-8]

IBM has been using MCMs since 1964 when it introduced its solid logic technology (SLT) modules based on the use of bare transistor dies. However, the first reference to the term *multichip module* or *MCM* was in 1979, with a circuit module consisting of a 35- or 50-mm^2 ceramic substrate for mounting up to nine large-scale integration (LSI) chips, each with up to 704 logic chips. The substrates had 18 to 23 metallized ceramic layers and contained over 5 m of interconnection wiring.

The 121 C4 (controlled-collapse) chip-to-substrate interconnections were arranged in an 11 × 11 array on 0.25-cm centers. The backside of 50-mm^2 MCM was populated with 361 I/O pins in a 19 × 19 array on 0.25-mm centers; the 35-mm^2 MCM had 196 I/O pins in a 14 × 14 array. These large pin-grid arrays (PGAs) were then mounted and interconnected by multilayer PWBs.

A typical 50-mm^2 MCM contains six LSI chips comprising a total of 4000 circuits. This is equivalent to a circuit count of 18 fully populated PW assemblies in an IBM System/370 Model 148 computer. In this way, in a huge step up from its predecessors, the MCM provided most of the signal and power distribution that was conventionally accomplished on PWBs.

The first generation (1980), which includes both MCMs (with 4 to 64 chips) and TCMs (up to 100 chips), is based on alumina-molybdenum. The second-generation ceramic MCMs were introduced in 1990 and are based on unique glass-ceramic/copper with a dielectric constant of 5.0 compared with 9.4 for alumina and copper metal and a conductivity improvement by a factor of 3 over molybdenum. Additionally, the glass-ceramic/copper substrate has a coefficient of thermal expansion (CTE) exactly matching that of silicon and improvement of seven times in mismatch between the ceramic and the chip.

The third generation of ceramic MCMs now being developed by IBM for use in future PCs and supercomputers includes

- *Large substrates:* up to 166 mm
- *Large numbers of layers:* up to 100
- *Chip I/Os:* approximately 2000
- *Area-array carriers*
- *Surface thin films*

In 1990, IBM introduced the System/390 air-cooled thermal conduction module, which is used in the recently announced IBM Enterprise

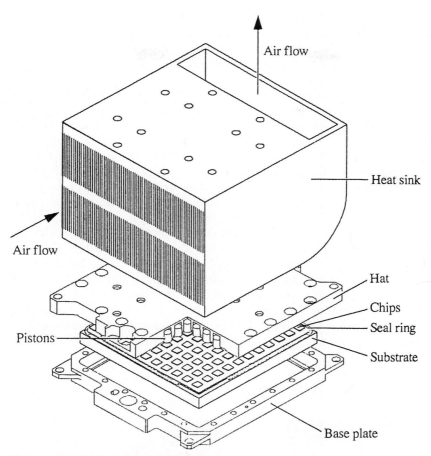

Air flow

Heat sink

Air flow

Hat

Chips

Seal ring

Pistons

Substrate

Base plate

Figure 11.3. IBM S/390 alumina TCM.

System/9000 processor family. The S/390 alumina TCM components are pictured schematically in Fig. 11.3. Assembled, the module measures 166 mm wide by 146 mm deep by 169 mm high; it contains up to 121 logic and array chips with decoupling capacitors, all mounted using controlled-collapse (C4) technology. The S/390 alumina TCM technology utilizes a new MLC substrate, top-film redistribution wiring, and a new air-cooling technology which allows the module to dissipate up to 600 W. It uses 2772 pins to connect with the second-level package.

The 127.5-mm^2 S/390 alumina MLC substrate is composed of 63 metallized alumina layers. Thin-film circuitry is applied directly to the surface of the planarized ceramic, requiring 78,500 vias in the substrate top surface for interconnection among chips, between chips and I/O pins, and between chips and pads for the bonding of engineering change wires. A total of 121 sites are available for chip joining, and 144 locations are provided for the attachment of discrete coupling capacitors to the top surface.

The chips are connected to the substrate with an array of solder balls (flip chip). Surrounding each chip on the surface are rings of engineering change (EC) pads. Each chip I/O is connected to an EC pad through a thin- or thick-film interconnection wire. The EC pads are connected to buried EC wire (BECW) layers in the substrate. The EC wires reroute the chip-to-chip connections printed in the signal distribution layers when changes are required. EC pads also serve as testing probe pads. The ECs are implemented by laser deletes and discrete surface wires. Figure 11.4 illustrates the MCM used in the S/390 mainframe.

The addition of a single-layer top-surface metallization provides the interconnection density required for the ES/9000 application. Detail of the thin-film pattern is shown in Fig. 11.5. Design features for this thin-film interconnect include copper conductors as small as 12 µm, as defined by the lift-off process in the chip interconnection (C4) areas, and as wide as 58 µm, as defined by a wet-etch process in the repair and engineering change (EC) areas. MLC vias are capped with pads nominally 180 µm in diameter. Additional C4 pads, 150 µm in diameter, connect-

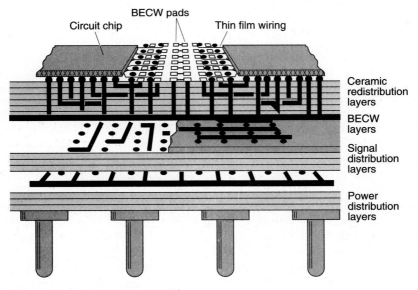

Figure 11.4. IBM S/390 MCM.[9]

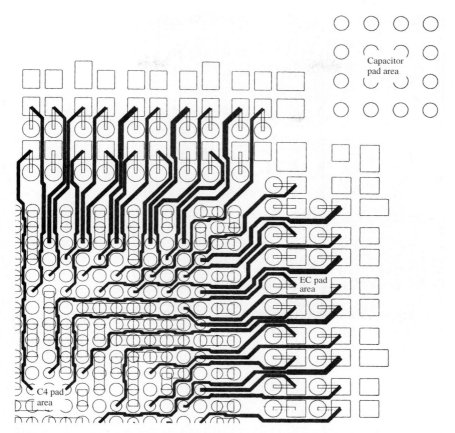

Figure 11.5. Thin-film patterns on the chip-site quadrant.[10]

ed to thin-film lines are deposited on blank ceramic areas rather than on top of an MLC via. Openings to all the C4 pads through the polyimide insulating layer are made by a laser ablation process and are nominally 100 µm in diameter. Through this array of 648 openings on 225-µm centers, the VLSI devices are joined to the MLC substrate. Figure 11.6 shows the glass-ceramic substrate with assembled chips and capacitors.

11.4 The UNISYS A16/A19 Computer[10,11]

The MCMs described herein are used in the UNISYS A16 and A19 systems, which are large, general-purpose, air-cooled commercial main-

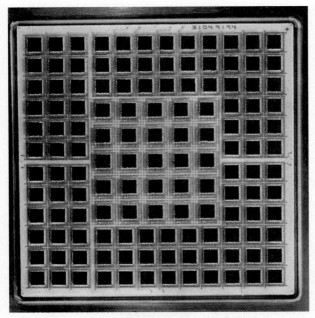

Figure 11.6. IBM S/390 glass-ceramic/copper substrate.

frame computers. The A16 is configured with up to 16 processors for a performance of up to 240 million instructions per second (MIPS), and the smaller A16 is a maximum 2 processor system rated at 54 MIPS. The packaging objectives promulgated for these two programs were based on these requirements:

- IC technology used must be commercially available.
- Thermal management of the system must be compatible with the present air-cooled product line.
- Maximum clock frequency to be 50 MHz.
- The A16 central processor module must be a single-board design, consisting of 375,000 logic gates and 800,000 bits of high-speed static RAM (SRAM).
- The A19 CPM must be a four-board format, consisting of 375,000 logic gates and 800,000 bits of high-speed static RAM (SRAM).

Following a review of the commercially available application-specific IC (ASIC) technologies, a bipolar gate array was chosen, mainly for the quick turnaround time and low tooling charges for this type of logic. An additional attraction of the gate array is the fact the logic dice are all the same size, which minimizes package development costs. Thermal management of the system called for air cooling, and the cooling system modeling resulted in an imposition of a package-level power limit of 20 W.

11.4.1 System Performance Issues

Both single-chip packages (SCPs) and MCMs are used in this computer. Single-chip packages are used for logic gates on the basis that the 20-ns clock cycle time required could be met implementing the logic for the ASIC chip. For the memory array module (MAM), MCMs were used on the basis of reduction in packaging delay.

11.4.2 System Packaging Design

Up to 54 logic packages (50 percent SCPs and 50 percent MCMs) are soldered through hole into an 18 × 20 in PWB (Fig. 11.7). The board is 0.5 cm thick, with a total of 25 conductor layers. The board is made of BT resin.

The single-chip package is a cavity-down alumina-ceramic pin-grid array (PGA), hermetically sealed, with an integral copper-tungsten heat spreader. The goal of the MCM development program was to be completely compatible with the SCP design in materials, assembly, size, manufacturing, and rework processes. The basic package design chosen was an MCM-C, which is the MAM. The package features are as follows:

- Area: 4.6 cm^2
- 15 layers—4 signal, 9 power planes, 2 external layers
- Kovar seal ring
- 155 pins
- Integral copper-tungsten heat spreader to handle 28 W total heat
- Cavity-down design
- One bipolar ASIC 10K gate array and eight bipolar 1K × 4, 5-ns SRAMS

Figure 11.7. A16 central processing module.

The 28 W in an air-cooled environment required a low-resistance heat path to the external heat sink. High-temperature multilayer ceramic (MLC) provided a solution. A copper-tungsten heat spreader was brazed onto the ceramic body to permit direct die attach of the bipolar ASIC to one side and the soldering of a convoluted copper-invar-copper heat sink to the other side. Figure 11.8 shows both sides of a bare package and a package with the heat sink attached. The MCM-C on top is the MAM with the heat sink attached. The modules on the bottom are the front and back views of the 4.6-cm^2 package. The lower left view shows the back of the package with the isolated center copper-tungsten heat spreader. Figure 11.9 shows a cross-sectional view of the module.

A significant portion of the back of the package is metallized to permit the convoluted heat sink to be soldered to the ceramic MCM body. This is important, since the heat flow path through the module is through the ceramic. Small pads noted in the lower left view are test pads to provide access to circuits which are not accessed by pins, permitting the package to be tested before dice are committed to it.

Figure 11.8. A16 multichip module.

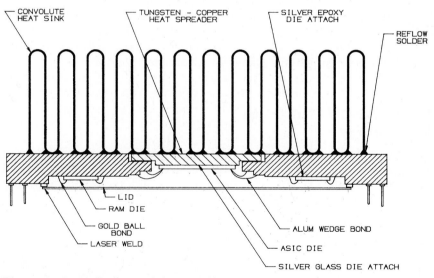

Figure 11.9. Multichip module assembly.

The MAM package achieved a 2:1 reduction in board area as compared with a single-chip implementation. This facilitated a single board instruction processor in the A16 mainframe. In a single-chip module, the packaging delay in a critical circuit would have been 6 ns. The MCM-C package reduced this to 1 ns.

11.4.3 Thermal Packaging Design

Since air cooling was a fixed requirement for this program, every effort was made to accommodate this. In all cases, thermal management of MCMs must consider the mutual heating effect of adjacent dice within a package. In this case, over 30 percent of the device's temperature rise was caused by heating from adjacent chips. System requirements required a maximum power density of 20 W/cm^2 at the die level. It was not possible to meet the junction temperature goal of 65°C with conventional methods due to mutual heating of adjacent chips in the package. A novel method of "impingement cooling" was used to handle this problem, in which a manifold directed cool air to each package individually and in parallel. Figure 11.10 illustrates a cross section of the board with the cooling manifold. Cooling objectives were met with use of the impingement cooling method described and a special custom convolute heat sink attached to the package. Illustrated in Fig. 11.9, this heat sink is made of copper-Invar soldered onto the copper-tungsten package heat spreader.

11.5 NEC's Multichip Technology

Packaging technologies for the NEC computer systems have been developed to achieve the highest class performance, i.e., 1300 megaflops (floating point operations) per second, contrasted with the

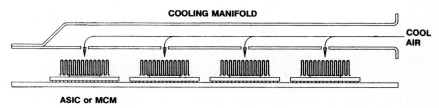

Figure 11.10. Impingement air cooling.

630 megaflops achieved by the Hitachi S-810 array processor. The packaging technology employed by NEC to get these very high data-processing capabilities features three levels: (1) flipped-TAB carriers, (2) microminiature MCMs, and (3) a high-density multilayer printed board assembly interconnection system with ZIF connectors and high-speed coaxial cabling.

The logic flipped-TAB carrier consists of a 1000-gate LSI integrated circuit with 176 TAB (tape automated bonding) leads that is packaged in a 12-mm^2 chip carrier (Fig. 11.11) called the *FTC*. Materials are used that have a low thermal resistance and a low CTE that are well matched with those of the silicon IC chip.

The high-density microminiature MCMs that mount and interconnect the FTCs consist of a multilayer substrate (MLS) that mounts and interconnects with fine lines, higher-speed connections, and a high number of I/O terminals. Figure 11.12 presents a cross-sectional view of the MCP. The basic substrate of the MLS is a 100 mm^2 2.75-mm-thick alumina-ceramic substrate with tungsten-metallized inner layers for power and ground and 2177 I/O pins brazed on its bottom layers on a 2.54-mm staggered grid. Signal layers consist of four polyimide insulating layers and five thin-film conductor layers, including two ground layers with two signal layers sandwiched between them, and a top layer with FTC attachment pads.

Figure 11.11. NEC flipped-TAB carriers (FTCs).

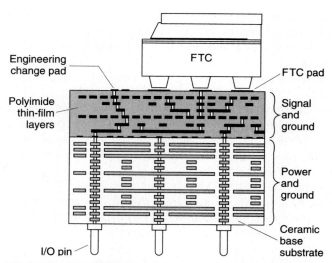

Engineering
change pad

Polyimide
thin-film
layers

FTC

FTC pad

Signal
and
ground

Power
and
ground

I/O pin

Ceramic
base
substrate

Figure 11.12. NEC's microminiature multichip package.

NEC broke new ground in packaging in the use of polyimide insulative layers on the multilayer package substrate in combination with the alumina thick-film ceramic substrate with I/O pins. Using this combination, NEC achieved a multilayer substrate with both high-speed/high-density wiring and high pin counts. The low dielectric constant of the polyimide (3.5) provides a signal delay time that is 60 percent of that of the conventional thick-film ceramic layers, which have a dielectric constant of 9.0. Additionally, the distinctive features of the polyimide, such as smooth surface, fine via-hole formability, and low-temperature curability, facilitate finer signal wiring on the ceramic substrate. Wiring is 25 μm wide on a 75-μm grid with 50-μm^2 via holes. This yields a maximum length of signal lines on the 100-mm^2 MLS of 110 m .

The complete multichip package (MCP) assembly consists of the multilayer substrate (MLS) with a maximum of 36 flipped-TAB carriers (FTCs) and a mounting flange (Fig. 11.13). The 36 FTCs are attached simultaneously on the MLS by tin-lead reflow soldering.

11.6 Cray's Microminiature Packaging Technology

The Cray Research "number crunching" computers have been known for their computing power; the silicon-based Cray-2 was rated at 1200 gigaflops. The use of gallium-arsenide (GaAs) is one of the reasons that

Figure 11.13. Complete 36-FTC multichip module.

Cray's new supercomputer, the Cray-3, is eight times faster than the Cray-2. However, the apparent use of microminiature MCMs is probably the most significant factor in the Cray-3's 10,000 megaflop performance level. This computer employs approximately 50,000 GaAs chips for about 55 percent of its total of 90,000 ICs. The use of GaAs yields at least three times more speed than normal ECL logic parts. The remainder of the circuitry is mainly silicon-based CMOS RAM memories.

The package used in the Cray computer is unique in terms of package geometry and cooling. The Cray packaging consists of chips mounted directly to an eight-layer PWB substrate using a proprietary technology. These microminiature MCMs are then mounted onto a larger printed wiring assembly (Fig. 11.14). There are about 200 of these assemblies, each of which holds up to 1024 (0.8-W average) chips. This packaging approach helps trim the size of the Cray-3 to about half that of the Cray-2, i.e., 32-in octagon by 34-in high versus 53-in octagon by 45-in high. Both computers are liquid cooled by direct immersion, with a system power of approximately 150,000 W.

11.7   Hitachi's Multichip Module

An example of high-density, high-speed surface-mount and multichip packaging technology is that used in the Hitachi Model M-68X com-

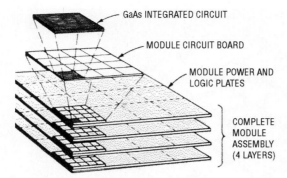

Figure 11.14. Cray-3 packaging hierarchy.

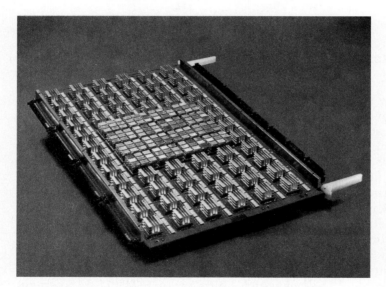

Figure 11.15. Hitachi's M-68X central processing unit.[12]

puter. The logic section of the M-68X consists of a printed wiring
assembly that mounts and interconnects 72 LSI flat packs, either bipolar gate arrays or memory modules (Fig. 11.15). Its 419 × 280 mm
polyimide-glass multilayer board has a total of 20 layers of interconnections: 8 signal layers, 10 power and/or ground layers, and 2 surface layers. Hitachi uses MCMs in its S-810 array processor for large-
scale scientific applications. In this computer, memory chips are packaged in 31 × 29 mm flat packs with a silicon carbide (SiC) ceramic

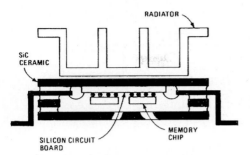

Figure 11.16. Hitachi's microminiature multichip flat pack module.[13]

base. The 16-mm-high RAM MCMs (Fig. 11.16) have 108 I/O gull-wing leads. A relatively large silicon "mother chip" is bonded to the module's SiC base. Then, up to eight 1-W ECL 1.9 × 4.0 mm chips are solder "bump"/flip-chip reflow soldered to the "mother chip" to interconnect the memory circuits.

A silicone gel is used to encapsulate the bare chips within the module to protect them from humidity and alpha particles before a final protective cover is attached. A finned aluminum heat sink is attached to the reverse side of the SiC base with a 50-μm-thick (2 mil) conductive silicone rubber adhesive to complete the modular assembly. In addition, a microminiature multichip pin-grid array (PGA) module has been developed, a 45 × 45 mm module (Fig. 11.17) with 208 I/O pins. This module uses a conventional alumina-ceramic base, with a 20-mm² "mother chip" to interconnect CMOS gate arrays in a silicon on silicon arrangement. Flip-chip reflow soldering and a silicone protective gel are also used.

11.8 Hitachi's M-880 Computer[14]

Figure 11.18 illustrates a cutout view of an M-880 high-density MCM used in the Hitachi M-880 processor. The MCM in this case is called an MCC, for microcarrier for LSI chips. Logic and memory chips are 0.8-μm technology. As noted in Fig. 11.19, the MCC is a combination of thick- and thin-film layers. The ceramic substrate consists of seven mullite-glass/tungsten thick-film layers, and the thin-film portion is composed of five polyimide-aluminum thin-film layers. The chips are bonded to the MCC surface thin-film layer pads. The MCC substrate and its aluminum

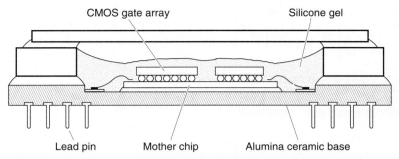

Figure 11.17. Hitachi's microminiature multichip pin-grid array module.[13]

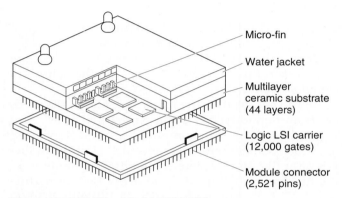

Figure 11.18. Hitachi's M-880 MCM.

nitride cap are hermetically sealed with solder. The I/O pins are attached to the bottom of the module, and it is also hermetically sealed with solder.

11.9 Command-Control-Communications Applications

In the area of command-control-communications (C3), primarily military applications, the success of the mission is of prime importance. In military systems, advanced electronics require increased performance and reliability with reduced size, weight, and cost. Many of these requirements are met by increased developments in semiconductor technology and by innovative packaging and interconnection tech-

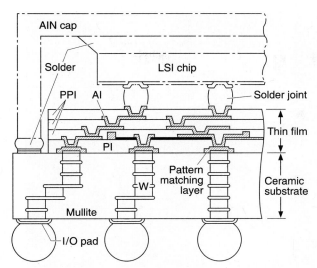

Figure 11.19. Cross-sectional view of the M-880 MCC.

niques. The growth of single-chip packages requiring larger pin counts requires more board space, which not only adds to size and cost but inhibits electrical performance of the system.

Although multichip packaging has been used for a number of years in hybrid microelectronics to provide reduced weight and size, improvements in packaging are required to meet the increased demands for higher performance at lower costs. For this reason, MCMs are being developed. As MCMs continue to be developed in the industry, different types of MCMs are appearing with a variety of conductor types, interconnect substrate types, assembly techniques, and package configurations. The different MCM types provide different interconnect densities and performance levels. The following technology descriptions give some indication of these differences.

11.9.1 IBM's Federal Systems Division Multichip Module

A microminiature 500,000-gate multichip package (MCP) is being offered by IBM for next-generation C3 applications for use with 50-MHz CMOS integrated circuits that have feature sizes as small as 0.5 μm. The 64-mm^2 MCP module, illustrated in Fig. 11.20, has cofired multilayer ceramic substrates accommodating 16 chip sites. Each module

Figure 11.20. IBM's MCP multichip module.

will have 236 signal I/Os. The overall module itself will have 625 I/O pins on 2.54-mm centers, including 498 I/Os for signals. Package hermeticity will be established by using a ceramic cap, which is reflow solder sealed to the substrate. Maximum power for the package is expected to be less than 30 W, with a 3-W maximum power for each chip.

11.9.2 Honeywell Bull's Multichip Module

Honeywell Bull has developed a "silicon on silicon" MCM for both C3 and computer applications. The module (Fig. 11.21) combines flip chips, a silicon substrate, a ceramic package or header, and conventional wire bonding or copper-polyimide beam tape automated bonding between the silicon substrate and the package. Comparatively low-cost packaging can be achieved because the substrate, which is silicon, utilizes conventional IC fabrication materials and processes. Silicon substrate quality is not critical when active devices are not present in the interconnection substrate.

Microminiature multichip packaging of this type also yields high-density interconnects. Using flip-chip technology, the chips can be placed closely together. Another benefit of silicon on silicon packaging is repairability. The solder "bumping" and assembly processes can be

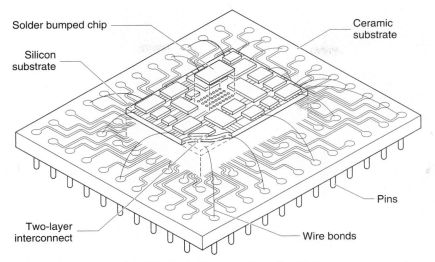

Figure 11.21. Honeywell Bull's "silicon on silicon" module.

repeated if chips have to be repaired or replaced. Also, since the ICs are fabricated independently from the silicon substrate, it is possible to mix chip technology in the same module.

11.9.3 Texas Instruments' Multichip Module[13]

Texas Instruments has developed an MCM (Fig. 11.22) that consists basically of four TAB devices that are interconnected on a thick-film ceramic substrate in a 196-lead package. The four-die module uses multiple-level TAB tape assembled back to back. The etched TAB tape conductive patterns require conductor widths and spaces of 50 μm (0.002 in) in some areas. The thick interconnections are printed on a 50-mm² (2-in²) by 0.9-mm-thick (0.035 in) ceramic substrate. A ceramic substrate was used to prevent possible warpage problems. The final interconnection between the thick-film conductors and the TAB beam leads is done by thermosonic bonding.

11.9.4 Rockwell International's Silicon-Substrate Multichip Module

Studies of various interconnect concepts led the Collins Avionics Division of Rockwell International to the conclusion that MCMs with

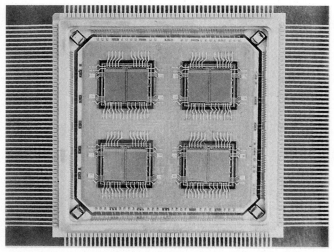

Figure 11.22. Multiple-layer TAB multichip module.
(*Courtesy of TI, Inc.*)

silicon interconnect substrates (SISs) were a viable approach. Their packaging concept provides direct connection of IC dies to a silicon substrate, in this way eliminating one level of packaging and interconnection. The SIS fabrication process starts with an aluminum conductor material which is deposited on silicon wafers using conventional thin-film vacuum deposition techniques. Conductor lines of 25 μm (0.001 in) width and spacing and 2 μm thickness are formed by a subtractive approach, in which a pattern is created by photolithography using standard chrome/glass masks, and unwanted material is removed by wet etching.

Metal layers are separated by 2- to 4-μm-thick polyimide dielectric material. When fully cured, these polyimide films are heat resistant, mechanically tough, and chemically resistant, possess excellent electrical properties, and provide good step coverage by planarizing surface topography. A wet chemical process was developed for forming 75-μm-diameter (3-mil) via holes. Both digital and radiofrequency circuits have been adapted to SIS. Functional testing to prove the validity of the concept was completed on a 32-bit reprogrammable memory module with excellent results.

The principal mechanical design issues are related to providing large 50-mm^2 (2 in^2) silicon substrates with adequate structural support to survive vibration, shock, and thermal cycling environments while also maintaining the SIS advantages of low cost, small size, low weight, and high reliability. Fortunately, although unsupported silicon wafers are quite fragile, bonding to a support plane increases their rigidity. Matched thermal expansion and high thermal conductivity of the support material is of critical importance. Candidate materials are molybdenum, aluminum nitride, silicon carbide, and graphite.

References

1. John W. Balde, Interconnect Decision Consulting, "Overview of Multichip Technology," private correspondence.

2. G. L. Ginsberg, Component Data Associates, Inc., "Multichip Modules for Advanced Applications," *Proceedings, SMART VI Conference,* January 1990, pp. 6–10.

3. G. L. Ginsberg, Component Data Associates, Inc., "Microminiature Multichip Module Packaging," *Proceedings, Institute for Interconnecting and Packaging of Electronic Circuits,* January 1987, pp. 120–126.

4. Mary Wesling Hartnett and E. Jan Vardemen, TechSearch International, Inc., "Worldwide MCM Status and Trends: Materials Choices," *Proceedings, NEPCON West,* 1991, pp. 1111–1120.

5. U. Deshpande, S. Shamouilian, and G. Howell, Digital Equipment Corporation, "High Density Interconnect Technology for the VAX 9000 System," *Proceedings, IEPS,* 1990, pp. 46–55.

6. Louis Palmieri, Digital Equipment Corporation, "Performance Characterization of VAX MCU Flexible Circuit Interconnect," *Proceedings, IEPS,* 1991, pp. 741–749.

7. J. U. Knickerbocker, G. B. Leung, W. R. Miller, S. P. Young, S. A. Sands, and R. F. Indyk, IBM, "IBM System/390 Air-Cooled Alumina Thermal Conduction Module," *IBM Journal of Research and Development,* Vol. 35, No. 3, May 1991, pp. 302–314.

8. Ananda H. Kumar and Rao Tummala, IBM, "State of the Art, Glass-Ceramic/Copper Multilayer Substrate for High Performance Computers," *The International Journal for Hybrid Microelectronics,* Vol. 14, No. 4, December 1991, pp. 137–148.

9. Evan Davidson, IBM, "Designing Multichip Modules," *Electronic Packaging and Production,* October 1992, pp. 16–20.

10. Rao A. Tummala, IBM, "Multichip Packaging in IBM—Past, Present, and Future," *Proceedings, International Conference and Exhibition on Multichip Modules,* 1993, pp. 1–11.

11. John Nelson, Unisys, "Implementing MCM-C Technology," *Electronic Packaging and Production,* October 1992, pp. 26–30.

12. Clayton Jerolmack and Robert Braun, Unisys, "System Design Issues in the Use of MCMs in Unisys A16/A19 Computers," *Proceedings, International Conference and Exhibition on Multichip Modules,* 1993, pp. 271–285.

13. Gerald L. Ginsberg, Component Data Associates, Inc., "Advanced Electronic Packaging and Interconnection Technologies," in Charles A. Harper (ed.), *Electronic Packaging and Interconnection Handbook,* New York: McGraw-Hill, 1991, Chap. 10.

14. Kenji Takeda, Yasunori Naritsuka, and Masahide Harada, Hitachi, Ltd., "High Density Module with Small Packaged LSIs for Mainframe Computers," *Proceedings, International Conference and Exhibition on Multichip Modules,* 1993, pp. 260–265.

Index